William Hickman Smith Aubrey

Stock exchange investments

Their history, practice and results

William Hickman Smith Aubrey

Stock exchange investments

Their history, practice and results

ISBN/EAN: 9783337107802

Printed in Europe, USA, Canada, Australia, Japan

Cover: Foto ©Suzi / pixelio.de

More available books at **www.hansebooks.com**

Stock Exchange Investments:

THEIR HISTORY; PRACTICE; AND RESULTS.

FOURTH EDITION, REVISED AND ENLARGED.

LONDON:
SIMPKIN, MARSHALL, HAMILTON, KENT & Co., LTD.
1897.

(All rights reserved.)

PREFACE TO THE FOURTH EDITION.

THE design of this Work is fully set forth in the Introductory Chapter. Its aim is to be practical, but it also deals fully, and in a manner never before attempted, with the History of Finance. The methods of Stock Exchange Transactions are clearly explained, and valuable information is given such as is likely to be of great service to intending Investors.

Special attention is called to the "Financial Landmarks" and to the Chapters entitled "How Money is Made," "Brokers and Jobbers," "Permanent Investments Utilised for Profits," "Short and Quick Profits," and the "Choice of Stocks." The design is to show how capital may be used to the extent of its money-earning power, and how unprofitable investments, of which millions are held by the public, can be turned to advantage.

Various points suggested by correspondents who have read the preceding large editions have received careful consideration, and have been treated, wherever possible; while the facts and figures are brought down to date.

The Statistical Tables given in the Appendices have been carefully compiled, and are quite unique.

UNIVERSAL STOCK EXCHANGE, LIMITED,
May, 1897.

TITLES OF CHAPTERS.

CHAP.		PAGE
I.	INTRODUCTORY	1
II.	GROWTH OF CAPITAL	7
III.	HOW MONEY IS MADE	27
IV.	SAFE AS THE BANK OF ENGLAND	34
V.	JOINT STOCK AND LIMITED LIABILITY	42
VI.	GOVERNMENT SECURITIES	59
VII.	BANKS	65
VIII.	INDIAN SECURITIES	74
IX.	BRITISH COLONIES	80
X.	RAILWAYS AND TRAMWAYS	91
XI.	MINES	96
XII.	CORPORATION STOCKS	101
XIII.	COMMERCIAL COMPANIES	111
XIV.	AMERICAN VENTURES	115
XV.	FOREIGN STOCKS	119
XVI.	TRANSFER OF STOCKS AND SHARES	122
XVII.	BROKERS AND JOBBERS	128
XVIII.	EIGHT MILLIONS WASTED YEARLY	137
XIX.	INEVITABLE FLUCTUATIONS	146
XX.	BOOMS AND PANICS	151
XXI.	PERMANENT AND TEMPORARY INVESTMENTS	158
XXII.	HOW AND WHERE TO SECURE BEST RESULTS	167
XXIII.	HOW TO START AN ACCOUNT	175
XXIV.	THREE-MONTHLY SETTLEMENT SYSTEM	180
XXV.	PERMANENT INVESTMENTS UTILISED FOR IMMEDIATE PROFITS	186
XXVI.	UNPROFITABLE INVESTMENTS	191
XXVII.	SHORT AND QUICK PROFITS	195
XXVIII.	CHOICE OF STOCKS	201
XXIX.	CONSOLS, AND WHY THEY SHOULD BE BOUGHT	205
XXX.	THE LAW OF AVERAGES	210
XXXI.	HIDDEN PITFALLS	216

ANALYTICAL TABLE OF CONTENTS

	PAGE
BIBLIOGRAPHICAL LIST	xvii
FINANCIAL LANDMARKS OF THE NINETEENTH CENTURY	xxi–xxiv

CHAPTER I.—INTRODUCTORY.

	PAGE		PAGE
Growth of Stock Exchange Investments	2	Dogmatic Ignorance	4
Interest in the Subject ...	2	Newspaper Money Articles	4
Aggregate of Business... ...	2	General Laws apply	4
Bankers' Clearing House Returns	2	Prices and Values	4
		Money and Credit	5
		Supply and Demand	6
Financial Literature	3	Meaning of "Securities"...	6

CHAPTER II.—THE GROWTH OF CAPITAL.

	PAGE		PAGE
Sir R. Giffen's Estimate ...	7	The Colonial Empire	10
Amazing Progress	7	Mercantile and Social Conditions	11
The National Income... ...	7		
Growth of Manufactures ...	8	Gold Discoveries in California and Australia ...	12
The Cotton Industry	8		
The Improvement in Machinery	8	Accumulations of Property...	12
		Increase of Capital 1871-80	12
Pottery : Cutlery...	9	Investments in Railways ...	13
Application of Steam Power	9	House Building	13
James Watt	9	Mines and Iron Works ..	13
Money and Commerce at the beginning of Queen Victoria's reign	10	Continuous Growth	14
		Capital seeking Investment...	14

CONTENTS.

	PAGE		PAGE
Amounts at different periods	15	And that of Mr. Leone Levi	20
Present Estimates	15	Sir Robert Giffen's	20
Mr. John Bright, M.P., on Wages and Prices	16	Growth of Population...	21
Sources of Wealth	17	Estimates for Income and Property Tax	22
Nominal and Real Values	17	The Yield at Various Periods	22
Distribution of Wealth	18	The Imperial Revenue and Local Taxation	22
Production and Cheapness...	18	Exports and Imports	23
Cost of Living	19	Savings Banks and Building Societies	23
Increasing Public Expenditure	19	Life Assurance and Friendly Societies	24
Mr. Dudley Baxter's Estimate	20		

CHAPTER III.—How Money is Made.

Wealth and Earnings	27	Money does not grow...	30
Position of England	27	Hoarding	30
Foreign Competition	27	Reproductive Capital	31
Warnings of Cassandra	28	Two Methods of Obtaining a Return	31
Causes of Trade Disturbances	29	The Course of Exchange	32
Lancashire Cotton Famine...	29	Bankers and Bill Brokers	32
Bank Panics and Failures	29	Financial Facilities	32
The Irish Famine and Emigration	30	Bankers' Deposits	32
		The Circulating Medium	33

CHAPTER IV.—"Safe as the Bank of England."

Safety a Relative Term	34	Bagehot's Dictum	37
Suspensions of the Bank Act of 1844	34	Country Bankers' usage	38
Notes and the Gold Reserve	35	The Baring Collapse of 1890	38
John Stuart Mill's opinion	35	Other Catastrophes	38
Crisis of 1847	36	The Bank intervenes	39
How the Act of 1844 operates	37	Possible Dangers	39
The Bank of England and Mercantile Credit	37	No Interest without Risk	40
		A Sinking Fund	40
		Reserves	41

CONTENTS.

CHAPTER V.—JOINT STOCK AND LIMITED LIABILITY.

	PAGE		PAGE
John Law and the Mississippi Scheme	42	Company Epidemics	51
Macaulay on Projects	42	Transient Virtue	51
Universal Speculation	43	Bacon and Carlyle on Human Folly	52
Preposterous Companies	43	The 38th Section and Contracts revealed	52
The South Sea Bubble	44		
Inflated Prices	45	Methods commonly pursued	52
A Mania for Projects	46	Number of Limited Companies formed	53
A Universal Craze	47		
The Collapse and the Crash	48	Those Registered during 1896	53
Board of Trade Report of 1846	48	Advantages and Drawbacks	54
		Need for discrimination	56
Groups of Schemes	49	Glowing Prospectuses	56
Unlimited Liability	49	Who bears the loss?	56
The Limited Liability Act	49	Inflated Prices	57
Different Kinds of Shares	50	Fluctuating values	58
Joint-Stock Banks	50	How Premiums are forced	58

CHAPTER VI.—GOVERNMENT SECURITIES.

Origin of National Debt	59	Mr. Goschen's Scheme	62
Founding of the Bank of England	59	Specie Payments suspended, 1797 to 1819	62
Growth of the Debt	60	Present National Indebtedness	63
The Great French War	60		
Stringent Terms	61	Gradual Reduction	63
MacCulloch's Opinion	62	Enhanced Price of Consols	64

CHAPTER VII.—BANKS.

Bank Charter Act of 1844	65	Security for Note Issues	66
The Two Departments of Business	66	Drain of Gold	66
		The Act of 1892	67

CONTENTS.

	PAGE		PAGE
Profits made by the Bank of England	67	Leeman's Act	70
Its Private Business	68	Amount of Deposits and of Capital	70
Bank Stock	68	Notes of Country Banks	71
Origin of Joint Stock Banks	69	Comparison of Specie Reserve	72
Growth of Deposits	69	Relative Position of the Bank of England	72
The London and Westminster and other Banks	69	Opinions of Experts	73

CHAPTER VIII.—INDIAN SECURITIES.

	PAGE		PAGE
Vast Extent of the Empire	74	The East India Company	76
Area and Population	74	Gross Indian Revenue	76
The Boundaries Traced	74	State Railways	77
Early Struggles with the French, Dutch, and Portuguese	75	Safe as Investments	78
		Indian Exports and Imports	78
Determined by England's Sea Power	76	Internal Developments	79
		Tea and Coffee Growth	79

CHAPTER IX.—BRITISH COLONIES.

	PAGE		PAGE
Initial Mistakes	80	Nature of Colonial Securities	85
Bacon on "Plantations"	80		
Extent of the Territory	81	Excessive Borrowing	85
Contest with the French for Canada	82	The Grand Trunk Railroad	86
		The Canadian Pacific	87
Capture of Quebec	83	Scattered Population	87
A Great Question Determined	83	South African Colonies	88
		The Dark Continent Opened Up	88
The Dominion of Canada	83		
Australia explored	84	Recent Partitions	88
Successive Settlements	84	English Settlements	89
Gold Discovery in 1851	84	Cape Colony Acquired	89

CONTENTS.

CHAPTER X.—RAILWAYS AND TRAMWAYS.

	PAGE		PAGE
Early Engineering Enterprise	91	Manias of 1836 and 1846	92
		A Financial Panic	93
Macadam and Roads	91	The Present Mileage and Traffic	94
James Brindley and Canals	91		
Beginnings of the Railway System	91	Working Expenses	94
		Favourite Investments	94
Stockton and Darlington Line	92	Tramway Lines	95
		Excessive Loading	95

CHAPTER XI.—MINES.

Spaniards in South America	96	Other Metals	97
Excitement in Queen Elizabeth's time	96	Coal and Iron Companies	98
		Land and Exploration	98
Beginnings of the Iron Manufacture	96	Kimberley Diamond Fields	98
		Richmond Mine	98
Present Production	97	West Australia	99

CHAPTER XII.—CORPORATION STOCKS.

Municipal Loans	101	Post Office Savings Bank	105
The Principal Stocks	101	Telegraphs and Telephones	106
Local Government Debts	101	Money Orders	107
The Public Works' Loan Board	102	Complaints of Private Banks	108
Competition with Private Investors	103	Excessive Interest	109
		Cost of Working	109
Treasury Interference	104	Terms to Friendly Societies	110

CHAPTER XIII.—COMMERCIAL COMPANIES.

A Wide Range for Choice	111	Submarine Cables	113
British Shipping	111	English Waterworks	113
Perils of Trading Companies	112	Conversion of Business Enterprises	114
Gas Undertakings	112	Risks to be Avoided	114
The Electric Scare	113	Further Liability	114

CHAPTER XIV.—American Ventures.

	PAGE		PAGE
Railways in the United States	115	Many Millions Hopelessly Lost	117
Powers of Presidents	115	"Watering the Stock"	117
Repudiations and Reconstructions	116	Political Derangements	118
		Venezuela Case	118
First Mortgage Bonds	117	Possible Developments	118

CHAPTER XV.—Foreign Stocks

Largely Speculative	119	Dishonourable Methods	120
South American States	119	Knowledge and Care Required in Dealing	121
Mr. Lowe's Select Committee	120	Special Case of Egypt	121
Its Severe Censures	120	Foreign Relations	121

CHAPTER XVI.—The Transfer of Stocks and Shares.

Different Kinds of Stocks	122	Fees on Transfers	125
Inscribed Stocks at Bankers	122	Transfer of Colonial Stocks	125
Personally, or by Power of Attorney	123	Stocks transferred by Deed	125
		Ten Days Allowed	126
The Object to insure Accuracy	123	American Shares	126
		Special Arrangements	126
List of Inscribed Stocks	123	Bonds and Shares to Bearer	127
Prices *Ex div.*, or *x.d.*	124	The Issue of Coupons	127
Dividend Warrants	124	Care in the Preservation	127

CHAPTER XVII.—Brokers and Jobbers.

Mercantile Exchanges	128	Vast Increase of business	130
The Stock Exchange	128	New Methods and New Facilities	130
The Members form a close Corporation	129	The Need for Caution	131

CONTENTS.

	PAGE		PAGE
Difference between Brokers and Jobbers	131	Rates of Commission	133
		Written Contracts	135
Modes of Transacting Business	132	Days of Settlement	136
		Carrying Over: Contangoes	136
"Turn of the Market"	133	The Heavy Cost	136

CHAPTER XVIII.—EIGHT MILLIONS WASTED YEARLY.

	PAGE		PAGE
Need for Accuracy	137	The Objection that Charges are small	144
Two Kinds of Contracts	137		
Settling Day Accounts	138	How they Accumulate	144
Excessive Charges	139	Advantages of Direct Dealing	145
An Illustration	139		
Cause of discrepancy	140	Mutual Confidence	145
Position of the Jobber	142	Essential Conditions	145
A Needless and Costly Luxury	143	Customers' Interests Paramount	145

CHAPTER XIX.—INEVITABLE FLUCTUATIONS.

	PAGE		PAGE
Their Frequency	146	Relation to the Prices of Commodities	148
Changes foreseen	146		
Their Periodicity	147	Common Mistakes	149
Vacillations of Prices	147	Not Luck or Chance	149
Epochs and Cycles	147	The use of available Means	149
Sensitiveness of the Money Market	147	Carefully selected Stocks	150
		No Invariable Rule	150
How Securities are affected	148	Safeguards	150

CHAPTER XX.—BOOMS AND PANICS.

	PAGE		PAGE
Their Common Causes	151	President Cleveland and Venezuela	151
A Scare in the Money Market	151		
		The Effects of his Message	156

CONTENTS. xiii

	PAGE		PAGE
Panic in Wall-street ...	... 152	Opportunities for the wise	
Depreciated Securities	... 152	and judicious... ...	... 155
Effects of Rumours and Apprehensions ...	... 153	Panics in Recent Years	... 155
		Preliminary Inquiries	... 156
How Panics Spread ...	... 153	How a "Boom" is got up	156
Run on the Birkbeck Bank	153	The Objects Sought ...	... 156
Unfounded Alarms ...	... 154	The Public suffer	... 157
Sagacious Action	... 154	A sure Remedy ...	... 157

CHAPTER XXI.—PERMANENT AND TEMPORARY INVESTMENTS.

Business Ventures ...	... 158	"Gilt-edged Securities"	... 162
The Dew-Point ...	... 159	Trust Funds	... 162
Fluctuations ...	... 159	Possible Increased Incomes	... 163
Interest and Profit ...	... 159		
Instances	... 160	Supply and Demand...	... 164
Varying Prices ...	... 161	Dividend-paying Railways	165
Secret of Success	... 161	Some of the Best	... 165

CHAPTER XXII.—HOW AND WHERE TO SECURE THE BEST RESULTS.

Universal Stock Exchange...	168	Ruling Prices	... 171
Capital and Reserve ...	... 168	Telegraphic Orders ...	... 172
Testimonies	... 169	*Weekly Market Report*	... 172
Salient Principles ...	... 170	Selected Securities ...	.. 173
Modes of Business ...	... 171	Lists of Shareholders	... 173

CHAPTER XXIII.—HOW TO START AN ACCOUNT.

Apparent Difficulty removed	175	Part Purchase Money and Interest allowed ...	... 176
Banker's Reference ...	... 175	Correspondence Simplified .	177
Statement of Holdings	... 176	Market Information ...	... 178

CONTENTS.

CHAPTER XXIV.—Three-Monthly Settlements.

	PAGE		PAGE
An Advantageous Plan	180	Brokers Irresponsible	182
The Method Pursued	180	Large Saving of Expenses	183
Time, Trouble, and Money saved	182	The Test of Experience	183
		An Instance	184

CHAPTER XXV.—Permanent Investments Utilised for Immediate Profit.

Twofold Values	186	A Practical Plan	187
Capital used to extent of its Money-making power	186	Specific Illustrations	188
		How they work out	189
Advance in Price, or Increased Dividend	187	Reasonable Probabilities	189
		Increased Incomes	190

CHAPTER XXVI.—Unprofitable Investments.

How to Utilise them	191	Methods of Dealing	193
380,000 Shareholders	191	Profitable Purchase of Home Railways	193
Locked-up Money	192		

CHAPTER XXVII.—Short and Quick Profits.

A Rapid Turn-over in Trade	195	Avoidance of Brokerage	197
The Rule Applies to Stock Dealing	195	An Actual Example	197
		Money needs to Circulate	198
Re-Investments	196	The Nimble Ninepence	198
Conditions of the hour	196	Accumulation of Fractional Profits	199
A careful choice of Stocks	196	Aggregate of Littles	200

CONTENTS. xv

CHAPTER XXVIII.—The Choice of Stocks.

	PAGE		PAGE
Determining Factors ...	... 201	The Reasonable Probabilities	... 203
The Reasons not always known	... 201	When to Buy and to Sell	... 203
Peculiar Preferences ...	... 202	Various Contingencies	... 204
History of a Stock ...	... 203	Aids to the Choice ...	... 204

CHAPTER XXIX.—Consols, and Why they should be Bought.

Suited to Large or Small Capitalists	... 205	Three Years' Fluctuations	206
Safest for Quick Profits	... 205	Examples	... 207
Larger Amounts with Less Risk	... 206	£300 in four months	... 208
Range of Prices... ...	... 206	A possible Return of from 10 to 20 per cent. per annum	... 209

CHAPTER XXX.—The Law of Averages.

No Short Road to Success	210	The General Tendency to be Watched	... 212
The Operation of the Law	210	An Accurate Forecast	... 212
How it Works	... 211	Other Instances... ...	... 213
An Instance	... 211		

CHAPTER XXXI.—Hidden Pitfalls.

Diversities in the Market...	216	Investment an Art ...	... 217
Judgment and Decision ...	216	Favouring Conditions	... 218
"The Elegant Simplicity of the Three per Cents"	217	No Absolute System ...	... 218
"High Interest and Low Security"	... 217	Two Maxims of Vital Importance	... 218
Limits of the Maxims	... 217	Safe Rules	.. 219
		Design of the Work ...	... 219

CONTENTS.

APPENDICES.

A.—Definitions of Stock Exchange Terms and Phrases 223

B.—Classified List of the Principal English Investments 233

C.—Price of Consols, their Mean Yield, the Bank Rates of Discount and of Dividend, and the Mean Price of Wheat, 1850-96 235

D.—The National Debt and the National Expenditure at Periods of Five Years, and the Rate of Income Tax, with the Debts and the Taxation of other Countries.. ... 237

E.—The Principal Joint-Stock Banks, with their Capital, the Nominal Share Values, and the last Dividends 239

F.—Highest and Lowest Prices of Stocks and Shares, 1881-96 242

G.—Highest and Lowest Prices of the Principal Mines, 1891-96 262

H.—Dividends on Leading Stocks, 1890-96 266

I.—Dividends on Principal Mines, 1890-96 272

K.—Table for Computing Dividends 274

BIBLIOGRAPHICAL LIST.

Reference may be made to the following books for additional information on the various subjects treated in this Volume.

Acworth (W. M.), The Railways of England. 1889.
Aubrey (W. H. S.), Rise and Growth of the English Nation. 1896.
Bagehot (Walter), Lombard Street. Eighth edition, 1882: Economic Studies. 1895.
Bankers' Magazine. (Monthly.)
Bannister (S.), Wm. Paterson: His Life and Trials. 1858.
Bastiat (F.), Essays in Political Economy. 1881.
Baxter (Dudley), National Income of the United Kingdom. 1868: The Taxation of the United Kingdom. 1869.
Beeman (G. B.), Australian Mining Manual; a Handy Guide to the West Australian Market. 1896.
Bradshaw's Railway Shareholder's Manual. 1896.
Brassey (Lord), Foreign Work and English Wages. 1879.
British India Statistical Abstract. 1884 to 1895.
British South Africa Annual Report.
Buckley (H. B.), Law and Practice under the Companies Acts. 1887.
Burdett (Henry C.), Official Intelligence. 1897.
Canada Statistical Year Book. 1896.
Cape of Good Hope Statistical Register. 1896.
Castelli (A.), Traité des Opérations de Bourse à Primes. 1882.
Cobb (A. S.), Banks' Cash Reserves. 1891.
Coghlan (T. A.), Statistical Account of the Seven Colonies of Australasia. 1895-96.
Colonial Possessions Statistical Abstract. 1880-94.

Cordingley (W. G.), Stock Exchange Guide. 1893.
Crump (Arthur), The Theory of Stock Exchange Speculation. 1875 : Key to the London Money Market. 1877 : Banking, Currency, and the Exchanges. 1866 : English Manual of Banking. 1878.
Cunningham (W.), The Growth of English Industries and Commerce during the Early and Middle Ages and in Modern Times. 1890-2.
Customs Commissioners' Reports.
Dilke (Sir C. W.), Greater Britain. 1889.
Dowell (Stephen), The History of Taxation and Taxes in England. 1888.
Economist, The Banking Supplements, May and October, Annually.
Evans (D. Morier), The Commercial Crisis of 1857-8, and the Stock Exchange Panic of 1859 : Facts, Failures, and Frauds. 1859 : Speculative Notes. 1864.
Fenn's Compendium of the English and Foreign Funds ; by R. L. Nash. 1893.
Finance Accounts of the United Kingdom.
Francis (John), History of the Bank of England. 1848 : Chronicles and Characters of the Stock Exchange. 1855.
Gabbott (E. R.), How to Invest Money. 1895.
George (E. Monson), Railways in India. 1894 : The Silver and Indian Currency Questions. 1894.
Giffen (Sir Robert), Stock Exchange Securities : An Essay on the General Causes of Fluctuations in their Price. 1879 : Essays in Finance, First and Second Series. 1887 : The Growth of Capital. 1889.
Gilbart (Joseph), History, Principles, and Practice of Banking. 1882.
Goldmann (C. S.), South African Mining and Finance. 1895-6.
Goschen (G. J.), Theory of the Foreign Exchanges. 1886.
Greville (Edward), Year Book of Australia. 1895.
Hayter (H. H.), Handbook to the Colony of Victoria.
Higgins (L. H.), The Put-and-Call. 1896.
Hunt (Robert), British Mining. 1884.
Hunter (Sir W. W.), Indian Empire. 1893.

Inland Revenue Commissioners' Reports.
Jenks (E.), Australasian Colonies from their Foundation. 1895.
Jevons (W. Stanley), Investigations in Currency and Finance. 1884.
Joplin (T.), Principles and Practice of Banking. 1826.
Journal of the Institute of Bankers. (Monthly.)
Keltie (J. Scott), The Partition of Africa. 1895.
Kerr (Andrew W.), History of Banking in Scotland. 1884.
Kindell (A.), African Market Manual. 1896.
Kinnear (George), Banks and Exchange Companies. 1847.
Kinnear (John G.), The Crisis and the Currency. 1847.
Levi (Leone), History of British Commerce. 1880: Wages and Earnings of the Working Classes. 1885.
Local Taxation Returns (England).
Macleod (H. D.), Theory and Practice of Banking. 1883-6: History of Economics. 1896.
Mathieson's Highest and Lowest Prices and Dividends paid during the past six years. 1896: Investor's Vade Mecum. 1890: Railway Traffic Tables. (Monthly): American Traffic Tables. (Monthly): Investor's Handbook of Railway Statistics. 1896: Indian Railway Companies. 1896.
Melsheimer (Rudolph E.), The Law and Customs of the Stock Exchange. 1891.
Merchant Shipping, Annual Tables showing Progress of.
Mill (John Stuart), Principles of Political Economy. 1888.
Mineral Statistics of Great Britain and Ireland.
Mitchell (Wm.), Our Scotch Banks. 1879.
Morgan (Henry J.), Canada Dominion Annual Register and Review. 1894.
Mulhall (Michael E.), History of Prices since the year 1850. 1885: Dictionary of Statistics. 1892: Industries and Wealth of Nations. 1896.
Nash (R. L.), Inquiry into the Profitable Natuie of our Investments. 1881.
National Debt Annual Accounts.
New South Wales Statistical Register. 1895.
New Zealand Official Year Book. 1895.

Ormerod (J. J.), Municipal Taxation at Home and Abroad. 1894.
Palmer (F. B.), Company Precedents subject to the Acts. 1891.
Pattinson (J. P.), British Railways. 1893.
Playford (W. M.), Hints for Investors. 1882.
Poor's Manual of American Railroads, &c. 1896.
Post-Office, Annual Reports of the Postmaster-General.
Price (Bonamy), Currency and Banking. 1876.
Queensland Statistical Register and Year Book. 1895.
Railway Returns. (Annual).
Reid (John), Manual of Scotch Stocks and British Funds. 1841.
Report of Royal Commission of 1877.
Rogers (J. E. Thorold), Industrial and Commercial History of England. 1892.
Royle (Wm.), The Laws relating to English and Foreign Funds, Shares and Securities. 1875.
Shaw (W. A.), Writers on English Monetary History, 1626-1760. 1896: History of Currency. 1252-1894.
Skinner (T.), Stock Exchange Year Book. 1897: The Mining Manual. 1897.
Somers (Robert), The Scotch Banks and System of Issue. 1873.
South Australian Annual Statistical Register and Blue Book.
Statesman's Year Book.
Statistical Abstract for the United Kingdom, 1881-95.
Statistical Society's Journal.
Stutfield (G. H.) & Cantley (H. S.), Stock Exchange Rules and Usages. 1893.
Tasmania Annual Statistical Register and Blue Book.
Van Oss (S. F.), Stock Exchange Values; a Decade of Finance. 1895.
Victoria Annual Statistical Register and Blue Book.
Walker (J. N.), Investor's and Shareholder's Guide. 1894.
Wilson (A. J.), A Glossary of Colloquial, Slang, and Technical Terms in use on the Stock Exchange and in the Money Market. 1895: The Investor's Review. (Monthly): Handbooks for Investors. 1893.

FINANCIAL LANDMARKS OF THE NINETEENTH CENTURY.

1801. First iron railway, Croydon to Wandsworth.
Five per cent. Property Tax.
1803. Bank of France established.
Bimetallic Currency in France.
1805. Consols 58¾.
1806. Property Tax 10 per cent.
1807. Resignation of Abraham Newland, cashier of Bank 50 years.
1810. Commercial crisis.
Report of Francis Horner's Bullion Committee.
1811. Bank issues silver tokens for 3s. and 1s. 6d.
1814. Cape Colony ceded by the Dutch.
1816. Savings Banks brought under Parliamentary control.
Legal tender of silver limited to 40s.
1821. Cash payments resumed. (Suspended since 1797.)
1825. Stockton and Darlington Railway.
Colony of Van Diemen's Land, or Tasmania.
1825-6. Commercial Panic; 770 banks stopped.
1826. Joint-stock Bank Act for the provinces.
English and Irish currency assimilated.
1827. Bank of England opens country branches.
1828. Savings Banks Amendment Act.
1829. Colony of West Australia.
1830. Fauntleroy's forgeries cost the Bank £360,000.
Liverpool and Manchester Railway.
1833. Bank Act : Quarterly statements of its affairs.
1834. South Australia colony formed.
Joint-stock banks established in London ; the London and Westminster being the first.
1835. Railway mania.
Savings Banks Act extended to Scotland.
1836. London Joint-Stock Bank, and London and County Bank.

xxii FINANCIAL LANDMARKS OF NINETEENTH CENTURY.

1838. London and Birmingham Railway.
1839. Union Bank of London established.
1840. Penny Postage inaugurated.
1841. Colony of New Zealand.—Census of United Kingdom, 27,057,923.
1842. Peel's Income Tax Act.
1843. Colony of Natal.
1844. Bank Charter Act.
Board of Trade empowered to examine railway schemes.
1845. Peel's new Tariff.
Irish and Scotch Banking Acts.
1845-6. Railway mania; 272 Acts passed.
1846. Corn-Laws repealed.
Numerous bubble companies.
1847. Commercial panic through railway mania.
Discount rate 8 per cent.
Gold discovered in California.
1849. Silver florin issued.—Navigation Laws repealed.
1850. Railway Clearing House.
1851. Australian gold discovered.—Colony of Victoria.
Census, 27,595,388.
1853. Income Tax extended to Ireland.—Succession Duty imposed.
First Indian Railway opened, from Bombay to Tannah.
Australian Mints established.
1854. Crimean War; Income Tax 1s. 4d. and 11½d.
Usury Laws repealed.
1855. Strahan, Paul, and Bates' bank failed.
Limited Liability introduced.
1856. Grand Trunk Railway of Canada opened.
Royal British Bank failure.
1857. Commercial panic through American failures.
Bank Charter Act suspended.—Bank Reserve £1,462,000.
Discount rate 9 per cent.—Many Banks fail. (Nov. 5.)
1858. India transferred to the Crown.—First Atlantic Cable.
1859. Colony of Queensland.
Commercial panic, through fear of European war.
1859-66. Period of contractors' railways.
1860. Commercial Treaty with France. (Jan. 23.)
Great failures in the leather trade. (July.)
Bronze coinage issued. (Dec. 1.)
1861. Census, 29,321,288.
Cash payments suspended in America.
1862. Cotton famine in Lancashire, owing to the American Civil War.
Companies Act amended.
1863. Savings Banks Acts consolidated.—Underground Railway opened.
Confederate States Loan for £3,000,000.
1865. Commercial Treaty with Austria.
250 Railway Bills passed.—Indo-European telegraph.

FINANCIAL LANDMARKS OF NINETEENTH CENTURY. xxiii

1866. Commercial panic, through over-speculation in companies.
"Black Friday," May 10. Overend, Gurney and Co.'s failure.
London, Chatham, and Dover Railway stopped payment.
Second Atlantic Cable laid.
Mansion House Indian Famine Relief Fund of £493,000.
1867. Companies Act further amended.—Leeman's Bank Act.
Dominion of Canada formed.
1869. Albert Assurance Co. failed for £8,000,000.
Telegraphs acquired by the Post Office.
Suez Canal opened. (Commenced in 1858.)
1870. Commercial panic.
Coinage Act. (April 4.)
1871. European Assurance Society failed.
Census, 31,845,379.
1871-3. Payment of Franco-Prussian War Indemnity of £200,000,000.
1872. First Railway in Japan. (June 19.)
Depressed Trade and numerous Strikes.
1873. Regulation of Railways Act.
1874. Fiji annexed.
1875. Railway Jubilee at Darlington.
1876. Imperial Bank of Germany opened. (Jan. 1.)
Demonetization of silver in Germany.—Suez Canal Shares bought.
1877. Mr. Goschen's scheme of Egyptian finance.
1878. City of Glasgow Bank stopped payment.
Gold at par in the United States for the first time since 1862.
Bland Silver Coinage Bill. (Feb. 16.)
Royal Commission on the Stock Exchange.
1880. Canadian Pacific Railway sanctioned.
1881. Census, 35,269,483.
1883. Bankruptcy Act and Board of Trade control.
Parcels Post established. (Aug. 1.)
Northern Pacific Railway opened. (Sept. 8.)
1884. Conversion of Three per Cents. into 2¾ by Mr. Childers.
Metropolitan Inner Circle Railway completed.
1885. Egyptian Financial Scheme for reduction of Interest and loan of £9,000,000.
Canadian Pacific Railway opened.
Glyn, Mills, Currie & Co. formed into a Joint Stock Company.
1886. Royal Niger Co. incorporated.—Witwatersrand Gold Fields.
1887. Johannesburg founded.
Double florin, &c., issued. (June 20.)
1888. Bimetallic League.
Conversion of Three per Cents. by Mr. Goschen.
1889. British South Africa Co. incorporated.
Numerous strikes and labour disputes.
1890. Winding-up Amendment Act for Companies.
Bank of England authorised to increase note issue by £250,000.

1890. The Baring collapse.
1891. Census, 37,732,922.
1892. Railway and Canal Traffic Amendment Act.
Silver coined in Victoria, Australia.
Utah (U.S.A.) Gold Fields.
Bank Act.—Coutts' Bank formed into a Company.
1892. Failure of Liberator Group of Companies. (Sept.)
Department of Trade and Commerce created in Canada.
Sir Julard Danvers retires after fifty years' service as Government Director of Indian Railways.
Value of Indian rupee 1s. 3d.
Committee appointed to consider Australian Federation.
1893. India Currency Committee Report.
Silver Purchase Repeal Bill passed by United States Congress.
Imperial and Intercolonial Conference at Ottawa.
Twelve Australian Banks stopped payment. (May.)
New Coinage Act. (March 28.)
East India Loan Bill of £10,000,000. (Dec. 21.)
1894. India Stock converted from 4 to 3½ per cent.
Manchester Ship Canal opened. (Jan. 1.)
New Zealand Loan and Mercantile Agency Co. reconstructed.
Loss to Bank of England of £250,000 on unsecured advances.
Coolgardie Gold Fields.
1895. Financial Crisis, Newfoundland. (Jan.)
Australian Federation Enabling Act. (Feb. 6.)
Treaty of Peace between China and Japan, the former paying an indemnity of £20,000,000. (April 16.)
President Cleveland's Message to Congress respecting Venezuela and England. (Dec.)
1896. Consols reached 113⅞. (June 1.)
Budget estimates for year 1896-7: Expenditure, £100,047,000, and Revenue, £101,755,000.
Capital of New Limited Companies formed Jan. 1 to June 30, £97,000,000.
Bank Rate of Discount raised to 2½ from 2, at which it had stood since February, 1894. (Sept. 10.)
Bank Rate again raised to 3 (Sept. 24), and to 4 (Oct. 22).
1897. Bank Rate reduced to 3½ (Jan. 21), and to 3 (Feb. 4).

CHAPTER I.

INTRODUCTORY.

ONE of the most remarkable developments of modern times is the rapid growth of Stock Exchange investments. Every year an increasing number of persons take a deep interest in the fluctuations of the Money Market. Probably no portion of the newspaper is perused with more attention and interest than the columns devoted to this subject. Many weekly papers are entirely occupied with it, and several daily papers, conducted with signal ability and enterprise, are wholly engaged in the discussion of financial topics, and in recording financial information gathered from a wide area. Nor is this surprising, considering the enormous monetary interests involved.

As is shown in a subsequent Chapter, the wealth and the savings of the country are rapidly increasing, and scope must be found for profitable employment. It is natural, therefore, for investors to make themselves conversant with a subject that concerns them so intimately, and they are to be commended for their intelligent study and for their watchfulness over the laws and the events that so vitally affect their prosperity. They manifest a growing desire to become acquainted with the business in which their fortunes are embarked, and with the many circumstances, direct or remote, that tend to cause fluctuations in value. To help to satisfy such laudable thirst for information is the design of the present work.

Upward and downward movements in the prices of securities, if genuine, and not caused by "rings" and "corners," indicate the political and commercial positions of States and corporate bodies whose stocks are quoted. On a moderate estimate £5,237,000,000, representing the national savings,[1] are largely dependent for their value and yield upon the quotations current on the Stock Exchange. Its aggregate of business is enormous, as shown by the cheques passed through the Bankers' Clearing House on settling days, which occur every fortnight, all the year round, besides special settlements. According to the returns, the total for 1896 was £7,574,853,000, or £18,033,000 less than in 1895. The amount in 1868 was £3,425,185,000. The average on ordinary days during the past year was £21,633,000, which increased by two millions and a

[1] See Appendix B.

half on the fourth of each month, and by ten millions on Consols settling days; while on those of the Stock Exchange the average rose to £48,452,700. The whole of the very large amount is promptly settled day by day, without trouble or inconvenience, merely by receiving or paying the difference by a single cheque on the Bank of England. The Provincial Clearing Houses of Birmingham, Leeds, Leicester, Liverpool, Manchester, and Newcastle-on-Tyne transact an average annual business of £400,000,000.

Many books have been written upon the subject, like Burdett's *Official Intelligence*, Skinner's *Stock Exchange Year Book*, Francis' *Chronicles of the Stock Exchange*, John Stuart Mill's *Political Economy*, Giffen's *Essays in Finance*, Fenn *On the Funds*, Poor's *Manual*, &c., but their size, intricacy, and technicalities repel ordinary readers. Numerous smaller manuals and *vade mecums* have appeared from time to time, such as those mentioned in the prefixed Bibliographical List. Occasionally a writer appears of the "I am Sir Oracle" temper, or of the Doctor Slop type, with no special knowledge of the subject, or like the proverbial literary hack of the Grub-street order, ridiculed in Pope's *Dunciad*, who, having egregiously failed himself, sets up as a conceited censor of others.

Nothing is easier than for the arm-chair critic of

politics, war, literature, or finance, to pronounce an absolute and a dogmatic opinion on subjects of which he is profoundly ignorant. The value of his opinion is in exact proportion to the extent of his information, which may be represented by x, the unknown quantity. The prisoner for debt, in Hogarth's famous picture, being wholly impecunious, writes a pamphlet to show how the National Debt may be paid off quite easily. He advises others in making the fortune which he has dismally failed to make for himself. It is a safe aphorism that by no financial legerdemain can lead be transmuted into gold.

Most of the works mentioned above pre-suppose an amount of information on the part of the reader as to the usages of the Stock Exchange. The daily newspapers, both metropolitan and provincial, usually devote much space to a Money Article, and give elaborate tabular lists with cabalistic or arbitrary signs. Yet the necessity exists for a plain, clear, elementary, authentic elucidation of the subject. Stock transactions are regulated by general laws similar to those which govern commerce, trade, industry, wages, and prices. It is mathematically demonstrable that an increase of securities or commodities, like a diminution in the quantity of money, will cause a general fall in prices, and that a diminution in articles, like an addition to the quantity of money, will cause a general rise. A high average yield on capital is a bounty on savings. A low yield tends to check savings, or causes investments to be made elsewhere.

An increase of consumable commodities, where the rate of yield on capital is not at the minimum, will lead to a rise in the price of securities, or, in other words, to a fall in the yield. The tendency of capital is to flow to trades in which the profits are high, and to leave those of low profits, with a consequence that some kind of equilibrium is produced, regard being had to other circumstances. Money lying idle, or at a nominal interest, in the hands of bankers, is instantly attracted towards a trade that is unusually profitable. There is always a large speculative fund ready to be embarked in anything likely to yield high profits.

The amount of money in circulation, and the state of credit, are important elements in fixing the price of securities. The conditions of business depend also upon political and public events; upon harvests and trade; upon the glut or the scarcity of money; and upon the number and the necessities of intending dealers. Dull and disagreeable weather, as a rule, affects the Stock Market, more or less. Other conditions being equal, the first half of the year is more active than the second, when the moneyed classes scatter for the holidays, and the activity of general business is lessened. But prices always regulate themselves, in the end, by the inexorable laws of supply and demand.

In the language of the Money Market, "security" means almost any kind of property which can be given in pledge for an advance ; with the special characteristic that the article can be divided into such parts as can be exactly defined, and then submitted to the speculative manipulation of the market. Lands, houses, mortgages, bills of exchange, bills of lading, dock-warrants, and other things have an interest-bearing power in common with shares of joint-stock or of limited companies, or the debts of States. There are also articles capable of easy definition, but without interest-bearing power, such as raw materials in bulk and manufactured goods, which can be dealt with in Produce Markets. But the combination of interest-bearing power with facility of handling in a light and compact form, renders Stock Exchange securities easy and safe.

CHAPTER II.

THE GROWTH OF CAPITAL.

IN a paper read before the Statistical Society, December 17, 1889,[1] Sir R. Giffen estimated the increase in total capital at from £6,113,000,000 in 1865 to £8,548,000,000 in 1875, or 40 per cent.; and at £10,037,000,000 in 1885, or $17\frac{1}{2}$ per cent. By way of contrast, it may be stated that Sir William Petty and Sir William Davenant, who were among the earliest to study political arithmetic, writing at the end of the seventeenth century, and with the imperfect data at their disposal, estimated the property of England at from 250 to 320 millions, at a time when its population was only five millions and a half. The growth during two hundred years is amazing. It was then, taking a mean between the amounts, only £52 per head. Now it is £270.

A century ago the national income could be estimated at not more than £200,000,000. It is

[1] *Journal*, March, 1890.

upwards of seven times that amount at the present day. In other words, there has been an increase from £16 to £35 per head. Similar increases have occurred in Germany and France, and to a less extent in other Continental countries. A wonderful impetus was given during the latter part of the eighteenth century to every branch of manufacturing industry. Old, tedious, and expensive methods of production were superseded. Marvellous ingenuity and enterprise were displayed in the improvement of machinery.

The first marked increase in the cotton manufactures of Great Britain had taken place about 1751. The cotton imported annually was £976,610. Twenty years later it had doubled; in 1780 it had risen to £6,767,613; and in 1895 the value was £30,429,428, in addition to £3,360,330 of yarn and goods. Inventive genius had long been engaged in devising improvements on the domestic spinning wheel, which could spin only one thread at a time, and that of an inferior description. The practical difficulties were at length overcome, mainly by the genius and perseverance of Sir Richard Arkwright, of James Hargreaves, of Samuel Crompton, and of Dr. Cartwright. Arkwright invented the spinning loom; Hargreaves the carding machine and the spinning jenny; Crompton the mule jenny, and Cartwright the power loom.

THE GROWTH OF CAPITAL.

By these means the productive capacity was enormously increased. Great improvements were also made in other textile manufactures, such as linen, cambric, silk, lace, and the allied industries of dyeing, bleaching, and calico printing ; and the cheapening of the supply led to a corresponding increase in the demand. Josiah Wedgwood founded the great pottery works in Staffordshire about 1760, at the same time that Matthew Boulton commenced his great hardware works in Birmingham. Sheffield also about the same period became distinguished for its cutlery.

The above important inventions were crowned, and, indeed, were rendered practicable, by the application of steam power. Ever since the time of the Marquis of Worcester, in 1655, and of Savery and Thomas Newcomen at the end of that century, efforts had been continually made to devise steam machinery. James Watt, about the year 1763, commenced those investigations which ended in his great discoveries and applications. He succeeded in making a steam engine capable of being worked with a comparatively small expenditure of fuel, and of yielding any desired amount of power. Lord Jeffrey remarks of him, " His remarkable contrivance has become a thing stupendous alike in its force and flexibility, for the prodigious power which it can exert, and the ease and precision and dignity with which that power can be distributed and applied."

Just after the commencement of Queen Victoria's gracious reign the wealth of England, though much in excess of other countries, was small when compared with the recent increase. Foreign commerce was only beginning to reveal its latent possibilities. Money advanced for great exploring, manufacturing, engineering, and mercantile enterprises, at home and abroad, large in amount as it appeared to financiers and economists in those days, fell far short of the "potentiality of wealth beyond the dreams of avarice" of which Dr. Johnson spoke in sonorous phrase. The great Empire of India was a vision of the poets, who sung of golden sands, and spicy breezes, and pearls and gems. Not a third of the territory and of the people now comprised within that vast Oriental sovereignty then recognised, even indirectly and remotely, the British sway. Only a thin and broken fringe of the Australian continent was settled. Cape Colony and Natal were small and insignificant, and the Africa beyond was unexplored and unknown. Canada was a scattered and half rebellious province, of which England knew little and cared less. Its thousands of square miles in the Far West, given over to a few hunters and trappers who returned once a year to the borders of civilization, were as shadowy as the fabled land of Prester John in the Middle Ages.

Nor were the home resources comparable to existing accumulated and available capital. England had gone through a long and difficult crisis since the Great French War, at the close of which the National Debt was £885,186,323; or one-third of the estimated wealth of the country. With continual trade struggles; prices ever falling; enormous expenses of government; a plague of pauperism that seemed incurable; the rapid growth of a surplus population which agriculture was insufficient to employ and to which the manufacturing system was imperfectly adapted, the country, just emerging from the prolonged Corn-Law strife, was hardly able to make ends meet. Of twenty-five millions of people, one-third were in Ireland in a state of semi-starvation through disastrous failures of the potato crop. In England and Scotland the great modern army of well-to-do artisans and factory operatives had not been formed, and there was no miscellaneous manufacturing industry to mitigate the sufferings of particular classes, like hand-loom weavers, whose primitive machinery was being rendered obsolete. Railways and steam-shipping were in their rudimentary stages; as were the thousand and one ingenious inventions since devised for utility and comfort.

The commencement of the second half of the nineteenth century witnessed the gold discoveries in California and Australia ; a wide extension of the railway system, on the Continent as well as in England ; and improvements in every branch of manufacture. Home trade and foreign commerce received a mighty impetus. The national wealth increased by leaps and bounds. Accumulated property compelled fresh outlets for its profitable investment, in shipping, in expanded trade, in telegraphy, in the iron, coal, and textile industries, in great public works, and in numerous useful inventions and processes. Compared with what was the case under a purely agricultural system, England is not only far richer absolutely under an improved manufacturing and commercial *régime*, but the extremes between good and bad years, owing to occasional failures in crops, are fewer and less irksome ; and even the most untoward events have diminished in intensity, because of almost boundless supplies that can be drawn from other countries.

The decade 1871-80 was especially remarkable for an abundance of capital. No less a sum than £2,000,000,000—the greater portion being from England—was devoted to the construction of railways in different parts of the world, besides £800,000,000 in loans to various nations. Many new factories, equipped with improved machinery, were built at enormous cost in Lancashire, Yorkshire, and elsewhere, to meet growing demands for textile fabrics. Fresh shafts were sunk to open prolific beds of coal and ore, and gigantic engineering establishments began to work. The vast sum of 967 millions, as compared with two millions in 1850, is now invested in Railways; besides enormous amounts in the Funds, in Municipal and Foreign Stocks, and in American, Indian and Colonial enterprises of various kinds. The total value is estimated at £7,276,031,441 according to a table given by Burdett.[1]

Fifty years ago, the foreign investments held in this country can scarcely be said to have existed. Judged by recent facts and figures there is an annual increase of capital, that is, of savings, to the extent of more than £200,000,000, for which, of course, profitable employment must be found. Besides the incessant expenditure on railways, agriculture, notwithstanding long depression, shows a constant outlay. House-building has gone on at an increasing rate in London and in all large towns. Mines and ironworks, it is true, show a diminution, after the busy and somewhat inflated period a decade and more ago. Machinery in the textile trades has been virtually superseded within living

[1] *Official Intelligence*, 1897 ed., p. 2086, and Appendix B.

memory by new appliances, and gigantic structural works have been reared at enormous cost. From the nature of the case, every other species of accumulation continues as before, but on a larger scale. The truth is that, owing to a wide division of labour, there must be a vast disorganization of industry, not a mere falling off from a former inflation, before accumulation can be suspended. Then, and only then, would the building trades, railway construction, ship-building, and numerous other industries, exhibit a widespread stoppage of work. There would be masses of unemployed labourers, far exceeding anything witnessed even in the terrible times of depression that were frequent before the free-trade period, when industry was deranged, and pauperism assumed threatening dimensions.

In the absence of such effects, it may reasonably be assumed that the causes are not present, and that there is no stoppage of accumulation. On the contrary, it goes on at an average annual rate; steadily increasing every decade. A considerable portion of it, beyond what is employed in the productive works or solid investments above named, may be described as floating capital, employed in what are known as liquid investments easily realisable. They have a great influence upon the Money Market and the Stock Exchange. Some of the millions thus used are in steady, if not in fixed, securities; but a varying surplus, always large in amount, is ever available, and the changes in this surplus indicate the general state of trade. Whatever the amount, it is constantly accruing, and must find some suitable investment. Sir Robert Giffen estimates the annual average of what he terms "free saving," for investment purposes, at about £80,000,000.[1]

Mr. G. R. Porter[2] estimated the personal property of the nation in 1814 at £1,200,000,000, and at £2,200,000,000 in 1845. Thirty years later it had risen, according to Sir R. Giffen, to close upon five thousand millions, and real property was £6,643,000,000. The same writer, in his work on *The Growth of Capital*, estimated the total income of the country in 1885 at £1,200,000,000, and its capital value, ranging from four to thirty years' purchase, at £10,037,436,000. This is more than a two-fold increase since 1850, when, from somewhat imperfect data, it was estimated at £4,050,000,000, or a growth from £150 to £270 per head of the population. The present annual income is probably £1,500,000,000. Withal, no rise has occurred in prices, except in house rent in large cities, but rather the reverse; while there has been a marvellous diffusion of comfort.

[1] *Growth of Wealth*, p. 153.   [2] *Progress of the Nation*, p. 600.

Mr. John Bright, in a letter to a correspondent, and published in *The Times*, November 18, 1884, after referring to the great reductions in the prices of wheat, tea, sugar, and other commodities since the introduction of free trade, went on to say, " As to wages in Lancashire and Yorkshire, the weekly income of the thousands of workers in factories is nearly, if not quite, double that paid before the time when free trade was established. The wages of domestic servants in the county from which I come are, in most cases, doubled since that time. A working brick-setter told me lately that his wages are now 7s. 6d. per day; formerly he worked at the rate of 4s. per day. Some weeks ago I asked an eminent upholsterer in a great town in Scotland what had been the change in wages in his trade? He said that thirty to forty years ago he paid a cabinet-maker 12s. per week; he now pays him 28s. per week. If you inquire as to wages of farm labourers, you will find them doubled or nearly doubled in some counties, and generally over the whole country advanced more than 50 per cent., or one-half, while the price of food and the hours of labour have diminished. It may be said that milk and butter and meat are dear, which is true, but these are dear because our people by thousands of families eat meat who formerly rarely tasted it, and because our imports of these articles are not sufficient to keep prices at a more moderate rate."

These observations are not weakened after the lapse of twelve years, and it is gratifying to know that cheapness and comfort are so widely diffused. Other considerations, however, must be kept in view. As Mr. Bagehot points out,[1] popular writers and speakers, ignorant of Political Economy, but eager for a cheap popularity, are prone to flatter the working classes by telling them that they create the wealth of the country. As well might it be said that the compositors produce *The Times* newspaper day by day. The craftsmen are necessary, but there must be inspiring, directing, controlling minds, who have the sagacity to perceive what is required, and the enterprise and the capital to adopt proper means and to open up new markets.

It must be remembered, however, that nominal values are not everything, nor are they the surest test. The range of prices for most commodities is far lower than it was formerly, so that the average real income per head must have more than doubled. The facts are exactly known as regards wheat and other staple articles, while it is equally well known, as regards articles of manufacturing industry such as coal, iron, and the textile trades, that the cost of production has enormously diminished. The uniform testimony of statisticians of the highest order, in England, on the Continent, and in America,

[1] *Economic Studies*, p. 69.

shows that there has been a general rise of money wages within the period; in few cases of less than 50 per cent, and in many of 100 per cent.

This tends to refute a misapprehension, not infrequently entertained, as to the distribution of the increased wealth of the country. It is sometimes said, for example, that the labourers, so called, produce the whole of the £1,500,000,000 of annual income, which, it is alleged, is largely consumed by a small minority. The difficulty, however, lies in determining what is really labour and what is really production. An inventor, a great merchant, or a distinguished artist is as much a producer as the man who labours with his hands for daily wages. Those who contribute under Schedule D of the income tax, which embraces trades and professions, are most certainly to a very large extent producers, as is the case with the farming class, who return their income under Schedule B.

The unskilled labourer cannot work machines, which are essential to modern production. Left to himself, he would be unable to carry on the work. It is his misfortune, if not his fault, that he is so poorly equipped as to be able to produce so little. Not only has there been a large increase in money wages, but the hours of labour have materially diminished, probably to the extent of nearly 20 per cent. There has been at least this reduction in the textile, engineering, and house-building trades. Thus the skilled workman receives from 50 per cent. to 100 per cent. more money for 20 per cent. less work, in addition to which the purchasing power of money, perhaps with the sole exception of house rent, has been enormously increased, and the style of living is an immense advance upon that which prevailed one or two generations ago. Moreover, while the cost of government has been greatly diminished to the artisan, he receives more from the public expenditure than was the case formerly. Many indirect taxes upon the necessaries of life have been wholly abolished, and the rest have been reduced to an extremely small amount.

Few people seem to be aware how, simultaneously, there has been an increase of expenditure out of the taxes and rates for miscellaneous public purposes, of the benefit of which the working classes receive their full share, and, as some allege, considerably more than their share. Stating the case broadly, it may be said that nearly £20,000,000 of the public expenditure for education, for the Post Office, for inspection of factories, and for other purposes, is entirely new, as compared with fifty years ago. It is the same with local government; the total of which has trebled in the same period, mainly from improved systems of poor relief and from the enormous outlay for sanitary purposes.

Mr. Dudley Baxter, in his estimate of the national income in 1867, arrived at the general conclusion that there were in the United Kingdom 13,720,000 persons having incomes or wages, out of about 30,000,000 of the then population. He further estimated that 1,162,000 were assessed for income tax; that 1,497,000 belonged to the middle and upper classes, with incomes of less than £100 a year; and that 10,961,000 belonged to the manual labour class: by no means to be identified or confused with the working classes in the economic sense of the word. Their incomes were estimated at £325,000,000, and the total income of all classes at £814,000,000. Mr. Leone Levi, by a different process, arrived substantially at the same conclusion, which of course must be regarded only as approximate. Making comparison, so far as means exist, with fifty years ago, the total income of the country then was only about £500,000,000; two-fifths of which were derived from agriculture.

Sir R. Giffen [1] gives a table showing how, in his judgment, the income of the capitalist class has increased only 110 per cent. in 50 years, whereas the income of the working class appears to have

[1] *Essays in Finance*, Second Series, p. 404.

increased 160 per cent. At the same time the former class has greatly increased in number, so that the amount of capital possessed among them per head has only increased 15 per cent., notwithstanding the great increase in the capital itself. In his opinion the richer become more numerous, but not richer individually, while the poorer are, to some smaller extent, fewer, and those who remain poor are individually twice as well off, on an average, as they were fifty years ago ; so that he thinks they have enjoyed almost all the benefit.

Not to burden these pages with statistics, full particulars of which may be found in the works already mentioned, the following items of information are interesting. They will give point and emphasis to subsequent Chapters which deal with the judicious use and profitable investment of accumulated wealth. No one is likely to expose himself to the reproach which Shakspere puts in the mouth of Shylock, " Tell not me of money. This is the fool that lent out money gratis." [1]

According to the census of 1851, the population of the United Kingdom was 27,595,388. In the middle of 1896, according to the Registrar-General's estimate, it was 39,465,720. Owing to migration, the growth has been chiefly in London and in

[1] *Merchant of Venice*, iii. 3.

the large centres. Property and income tax returns show steady progress. The gross assessments fifty years ago were £251,000,000 for Great Britain and thirty-two millions for Ireland. The last returns for the whole of the United Kingdom give £690,251,675. The largest items under Schedules A and D were for houses, £151,645,646; for land, £55,769,961; for railways, £34,354,852; and for mines, £13,744,712. Of the total annual value of the property and profits assessed for income tax, the increase per head of the population is from £9 14s. 3d. to £18 0s. 10d. The increase in the assessments for houses is almost five-fold in the half-century. The following table sets forth the growth of the income tax, a penny of which yielded £770,773 in 1843, whereas now the yield for each penny is £2,012,500. The assessments and the yield were as follows at different periods :—

Year.	Assessments.	Rate.	Yield.
1813	£140,000,000	2s.	£14,978,557
1843	283,000,000	7d.	5,350,000
1853	308,000,000	7d.	5,509,637
1865	395,000,000	4d.	7,958,000
1875	571,000,000	2d.	4,315,132
1895	706,130,875	8d.	16,100,000

During the same period the Imperial revenue has swollen from £60,000,000 to £101,974,000; nearly one-half of which comes from Customs and Excise. Reductions in taxation have taken place

THE GROWTH OF CAPITAL. 23

to the extent of twenty-five millions over new taxes imposed. The National Debt has been diminished from £820,000,000 to £619,998,590, and the annual charges of all kinds from £28,100,000 to £25,068,092. Against these reductions, however, must be placed the rapid growth of local expenditure, from about fourteen millions to £82,129,425, including expenditure of every kind for local purposes; though the ability to meet this has increased with the increase of wealth, excepting as regards persons with fixed incomes, and the very large number of struggling tradesmen. The amount allocated to local purposes from beer and spirit duties, licenses, and probate and estate duty was £7,366,117 for the year that ended March 31, 1896, in addition to which the contributions to local purposes for Government property were £3,316,881.

According to the last returns of the Board of Trade, the total declared value of the year's exports was £285,832,407, and that of the imports £418,689,658. The capital employed in banking is £188,802,775, and the aggregate deposits exceed £700,000,000. The number of depositors in Post Office Savings Banks is 6,454,763, and those in Trustees' 1,521,583; the amount standing to their credit being £107,830,000 in the former and £46,188,000 in the latter. There are 2390 building societies making returns to the Registrar, with a total capital of £51,538,691.

In addition, there are 1677 industrial and provident societies registered under the Acts, with a membership of 1,284,662 and a total capital of £18,579,024. Ordinary life assurance companies have a paid-up capital of £11,120,920, accumulated life and annuity funds £190,918,237, and reserve funds £4,070,823. Fire and marine funds of companies transacting life business amount, in addition, to £10,389,422. The above and other modes of insurance, as guarantee, accident, hailstorm, and plate-glass, are carried on by proprietary companies, and are of interest to investors, but the shares are not dealt in extensively. They may be bought to yield from 4 to 5 per cent. The business has been reduced almost to an exact science, and is conducted within a narrow area. There are also industrial assurance companies with a paid-up capital of £1,106,085, and life and annuity funds £12,473,373; and numerous friendly societies, headed by the Oddfellows and Foresters, with a membership of upwards of four millions, and property valued at £22,000,000, in addition to many unregistered societies. These figures serve to indicate the enormous growth of capital in recent years, and it must be repeated that suitable outlets have to be found for its profitable employment.

Personal enterprise, energy, courage, and skill, becoming a mighty aggregate in the mass, have achieved incalculable benefits in the past, and will accomplish yet more in the future, with free and fair scope. Every man must judge and act for himself. The world of investment is before him where to choose. If he succeeds, he has himself to thank. If he fails, the blame is his own. By following the directions in these pages, it ought not to be difficult to avoid the latter and to ensure the former. The rules laid down and the hints given have stood the severe test of experience, and can be confidently recommended for adoption. It is certain that much latent wealth in the country might be brought to light, and made to increase and grow with perfect safety, at a far more rapid rate than at present.

The world was amazed, at the close of the Franco-Prussian war, when the enormous indemnity of five milliards of francs, or £200,000,000 sterling, was raised with comparative ease, mainly out of the unsuspected hoards of French peasants and shopkeepers. When the loan was opened they subscribed in a few days more than twice the required amount, so that Bismarck is reported to have expressed regret and vexation at not having exacted a larger indemnity. The case of France is typical and instructive. In every civilized country there are to be found many hundreds of people whose aggregate savings represent a large total. This is especially true of England. Notwithstanding all complaints of badness of trade, and of failures in crops, it is indisputable that the accumulated and surplus capital is steadily growing. Any who can tap this vast reserve, so as to employ it in sound and paying investments, will increase the income of thousands of persons, will add to the volume of trade, will set money in profitable circulation, and will extend the wealth of the country.

CHAPTER III.

HOW MONEY IS MADE.

INDUSTRIES, values, and prices depend in a large measure on the wealth and earnings of a country. Rich nations are always the largest consumers. Their supplies of necessaries and luxuries are drawn from every part of the world. Great Britain has the most extensive import trade, while Spain and Russia have the smallest. The real estate of the English people consists in their superior industrial qualities; in their skill and enterprise; in their vast and varied foreign commerce; in being the sea-carriers of the world; in their acquired capital; in their established credit; in their large investments at home and abroad; in ample stores of coal and iron; in great manufacturing resources; and in the ability to import boundless stores of food and of raw materials.

It is not forgotten that other nations are advancing along similar lines; but, if England is true to herself, she will hold her own. No amount of foreign competition can really injure an industrious, enterprising, thrifty, and vigorous community with a far-reaching and long-established trade. If danger exists, it is from the same direction as that which enfeebled and at length overthrew the pride and pomp of ancient Rome. Luxury, supineness, self-indulgence, an aversion to hard and honest work, an excessive craving after mere amusement and excitement, constitute the bane and entail the ruin of any nation.

Without yielding to mere pessimism, it may be conceded that enough truth lies in the warnings of some modern Cassandras to justify an appeal to all who occupy responsible positions, and who wield influence over others, to warn them against the indolence and the shirking of disagreeables which are apt to appear with the swift possession of assured wealth. Shorter hours, frequent holidays, and extravagant living can only be justified by increased energy and skill in work. Production must continue, in spite of artificial rules to limit and regulate it, if wealth is not to be lost. The maximum of pay with a minimum of labour is not the end of existence, or the means of securing individual and collective prosperity. The great object with many seems to be to extort the highest possible wages for the fewest hours of perfunctory work, with as many holidays as possible, and a gratuitous pension in old age, provided at the expense of others, like self-respecting, industrious, and thrifty artisans, who must not be identified with the clamorous and incompetent assertors of pretended " rights."

Such events as the gold discoveries in California and Australia disturb the normal course of trade by causing an immense migration and temporary colonization, and by the commercial demands which are suddenly created. The Lancashire cotton famine, also, itself one of the secondary consequences of the American Civil War of 1861, disturbed the trade of the civilized world. For nearly fifteen years it stimulated the growth of cotton in India, Egypt, and Brazil, leading to a great export of capital to those countries for their further development, and induced a great movement of the precious metals, which in turn stimulated trade in various ways, and finally contributed to such incidents as the City of Glasgow Bank failure in 1878, due to the excessive investment of capital in the Eastern trade during the cotton famine.

The payment of the German indemnity in 1871-3 was another disturbing event which swelled for a time the export trade of France, and the countries which lent money to France. Besides such notable events, the history of the last fifty years comprises the Irish famine, and the exodus to America which followed; the Crimean, the Franco-Austrian, and the Franco-Prussian wars; the demonetization of silver in Germany; the resumption of specie payment of gold in the United States; and cycles of bad seasons of agriculture in England.

Money does not increase of itself. To use Lord Bacon's expressive phrase, " Money is like muck: no good except it be spread."[1] The fable of Aladdin, in the *Arabian Nights*, has no counterpart in real life. The ancient plan, still largely practised in the East, was to hoard gold and jewels, or to bury them in the earth for safety. Some people in England are not much wiser. During the last financial panic a man drew £5000 from a bank that was perfectly solvent; preferring to have the sovereigns tied up in bags in his house, where he kept them, in constant apprehension of fire and burglars, until his decease some years later. Not only did he run the risk of fire and thieves, but the money yielded him absolutely nothing. Even at 2 per cent. he lost £500 in five years, to say nothing of his constant anxiety over his treasure.

If an extreme instance, in degree, the above is far from being solitary in kind. It is wanton and wicked waste to destroy the necessaries of life, or

[1] *Essays*, No. 16.

to burn valuable pictures and books. It is surely culpable for ignorance or indolence to lock up money in unproductive investments, or to be content with a paltry return when the bulk of the capital might be judiciously and safely increased, and its actual money-earning power extended. Every one should seek to obtain the most he can for his money; but in the eager desire for high dividends the principal is not seldom lost. In preference to locking up the money in unprofitable investments, of which mention is made later on, advantage should be taken of the fluctuations of the market to buy and sell opportunely, so as to earn a percentage far beyond the usual rates of dividends.

Possessing capital, even to a moderate extent, conjoined with common sense, it is easy enough to earn money. There are two ways of obtaining a return for capital; either in the form of dividend, or by an increase in the value of stocks or shares on realization or redemption. Hence there may be but a small dividend declared, or none at all, and yet a good profit may result from enhanced value. The difference in price, added to the accrued interest, if any, represents the percentage gained during the holding. Care must be taken in the selection, and none chosen without full investigation as to their history, or without reasonable probability of success in some form, either in the way of dividend, or, better still, by selling to advantage and then re-investing, and so on, *da capo*.

In our complex commercial and industrial system the use of actual cash is economised in many ways. Bills of Exchange are at once certificates of debt and substitutes for cash. By their means remittances between different countries become possible. Debts owing by various persons in distant places are exchanged and balanced by bankers and bill discounters, and the actual use of cash is economised. Bank notes are also certificates of debt and substitutes for cash, of which only a part is kept for the total of the nominal value issued by banks, thus saving usually two-thirds or more of the amount. Besides, paper circulates more easily than gold or silver, and the same nominal amount is more serviceable in settling transactions.

The introduction of banking deposits and of cheques still more economises cash and increases its potency. In this way capital is kept in constant circulation. The amount as represented by loans from banks, and by deposits with them, may vary from day to day, but the adjustment is easy and instantaneous. Facilities are now so great, that any one possessing fixed capital can command circulating capital at any moment, either by borrowing on his securities or selling them. The final result is that enormous payments are made, and extensive operations are carried out daily, for which the cash actually available would be a mere bagatelle. A given, but very small, quantity of the precious metals is thus made to do infinitely more work by means of the banker than it could do otherwise.

The steady increase in the use of cheques and other negotiable instruments in carrying on the growing volume of trade with all parts of the world, shows that the small percentage of $2\frac{1}{2}$ of coin and notes, as against $97\frac{1}{2}$ of credit instruments, the recognised proportion some twenty years ago, is probably still smaller at the present day.

Vast commercial transactions between one country and another, made up of an aggregate of individual transactions, are adjusted, not by actual payments in cash, but by an interchange of commodities, the value of which is represented by paper remittances between bankers, bill-brokers, and other financial agents, who have to collect and to receive money, or money's worth, from their customers.

CHAPTER IV.

"SAFE AS THE BANK OF ENGLAND."

THE phrase at the head of this Chapter is " familiar in our mouths as household words." It is supposed to indicate absolute and unimpeachable security. Strictly speaking, there is no such thing. This is a disagreeable doctrine, but it is true. The Old Lady of Threadneedle-street herself has gone through a number of serious financial crises. The gravest during the last fifty years were in 1847, 1857, 1859, 1866, and 1870, when the Bank reserve was reduced from the average of ten millions to less than two, and when universal panic and terror prevailed. The immediate remedy resorted to was the suspension of the Bank Act of 1844, under authority of the Government, which had to be condoned by the Legislature at its next meeting. That Act provides for the separation of the business of the Bank of England into two departments, having entirely distinct accounts; the one for the issue of notes, and the other for ordinary banking transactions. The design was to prevent

"SAFE AS THE BANK OF ENGLAND." 35

a note-issue beyond a certain amount, unless against an equal amount of gold held, so that the mixed currency of notes and coin might expand or contract with circumstances.

Experience has shown, however, when a foreign drain of gold occurs, that the quantity exported is chiefly taken from the Bank's reserves; being the withdrawal of deposits or loans. The amount of notes in the hands of the public has not been affected by the Act of 1844. In practice, when there are signs of a foreign drain, and the reserve is diminishing, the Bank counteracts the tendency by raising the discount rate, and thus restricting advances. The purchasing power of the public is thereby limited, and prices are kept down. At the same time gold is attracted to this country for investment, and the circulation is not really interfered with.

Some economists doubted at the time whether the unquestionable advantages obtained by the Bank Act of 1844 might not be too dearly purchased. Since the stringent test to which it was subjected in 1847, writers of high authority have expressed unfavourable opinions. Mill points out that the extension of credit by bankers is a great benefit in seasons of collapse, and the aid formerly yielded by the Bank, at whatever cost, was salvation in a crisis like that of 1825-26; that the notes thus issued in aid do not circulate, but go where they are wanted, or lie by, or come back again immediately as deposits; that the new law does not allow expansion till gold comes for it, when the worst of the crisis is over; and that, as banks must be the source of aids in crises, such an Act as that of 1844 must, in such times, be either repealed or suspended.

The experience of 1847 suggests a yet worse objection. There are many causes of high prices besides that of undue expansion of credit. Prices may rise by war expenditure; by foreign investments; by the failure in supplies in raw material from abroad; or by extraordinary importations of food owing to bad harvests at home. In these cases the gold would not be withdrawn from circulation, but from hoards and bank reserves; but the arrangement of the Act for securing convertibility is aimed at a state of high prices from undue expansion of credit, and from no other cause. The result is that the paper currency is contracted on occasion of every drain, from any cause whatever, and not merely when the gold is withdrawn from circulation; and thus a crisis is occasioned by every derangement of the exchange, or, at least, whenever there is pressure in the money markets.

Before the crisis of 1847 there had been no

speculation which could account for such a terrible collapse. The railway mania raised the rate of interest, but it could not affect the exchange. The drain of gold was caused chiefly by the failure of the potato crop at home and by the partial failure of the cotton crop abroad. The Act of 1844 could not operate beneficially here; but, on the contrary, it wrought injuriously, by compelling all who wanted gold for exportation to withdraw it from the deposits at the very time that interest was highest and the loanable capital of the country most deficient. If the Bank might then, before there was any collapse of credit, have lent its notes, there would have been no crisis: only a season of pressure. As it was, it was necessary to suspend the Act of 1844; and Mill's conclusion concerning the measure is that the disadvantages greatly preponderate.

Bagehot remarks, "All our credit system depends on the Bank of England for its security. On the wisdom of the directors of that one joint-stock company it depends whether England shall be solvent or insolvent. This may seem too strong; but it is not. All banks depend on the Bank of England, and all merchants depend on some banker."[1] He also says, "All country bankers keep their reserve in London. They only retain in each country town the minimum of cash necessary to the transac-

[1] *Lombard Street*, p. 35.

tion of the current business of that country town. They send the money to London; invest a part of it in securities; and keep the rest with the London bankers and the bill brokers. The habit of Scotch and Irish bankers is much the same, and therefore the reserve of the banking department of the Bank of England is also the banking reserve of all London, England, Ireland, and Scotland too."[1]

Who could have foreseen, unless familiar with the inner arcana, the overthrow of the great House of Baring, in 1890, for liabilities exceeding £21,000,000, with all its presumed wealth and its long-continued financial prestige; or such failures in 1857 as the Liverpool Borough Bank, the Royal British Bank, and the London and Eastern Banking Corporation; or the collapse of Overend, Gurney & Co., for eleven millions, on Black Friday, May 10, 1866; or the stoppage of the City of Glasgow Bank, for twelve millions and a half, in October, 1878; or that of the West of England Bank; or of the Oriental Bank Corporation? To be wise after the event, and to say that such catastrophes were only to be expected, is easy enough; but with regard to most of the above, few, if any, persons were really apprehensive. Even those "in the know" on financial matters were staggered by the rude awakening to unexpected disasters.

[1] *Lombard Street*, pp. 30, 31.

A crisis was averted at the time of the Baring collapse in 1890, by the Bank of England and other great banks boldly standing in the breach, and taking over the assets and guaranteeing the liabilities. If in this case the usual course of liquidation had been followed, one result must have been a heavy fall in prices, and that not only in the securities directly affected, but in every class of investment. Finance is like a galvanic battery. A shock applied to any portion of the chain, however remote, is instantly felt throughout the entire circuit. Persons affected indirectly by the cataclysm of the Baring stoppage would have been forced to sell good securities at a low price, so as to meet losses upon others of a less solid character, and there would have been varying but universal depreciation, ending in " confusion worse confounded."

It will be seen, therefore, that the phrase, " Safe as the Bank of England," is of restricted application. A danger exists of a partial loss of capital in any investment, apart from the question of unsoundness of the security. Prices are constantly fluctuating, as is shown in subsequent chapters, owing to the state of the Money Market. Though there are natural limits to the fluctuations, and they operate under general laws which only the few comprehend, the many who do not may lose by this incessant movement. Buying at a high price, and being compelled to sell at a low price, necessarily diminishes capital; but it is so common as to cease to awaken surprise.

Hence the term "Safe as the Bank," is true only in an accommodated sense and in a limited degree. It is the same in other things. There are risks in all securities. It is a truism to say that where no risk obtains there can be no interest accruing. Even "gilt-edged" stocks have possible danger attaching to them, either from the risk of diminished income or from falling off in the capital value. This is the case with all things mundane and human. Storms, earthquakes, floods, drought, pestilence, war, catastrophes, accidents, and other unforeseen events may occur at any time to destroy valuable property, to stop productiveness, and to spread ruin and desolation over a wide area.

Prudence suggests that, no matter how solid the security may be, or how trustworthy the income, a portion should always be set aside as a sinking fund to guard against danger from inevitable losses. Large investors virtually do so by spreading their risks over a variety of investments, as Shakspere makes Antonio say—

> " My ventures are not in one bottom trusted,
> Nor to one place : nor is my whole estate
> Upon the fortune of this present year." [1]

---

[1] *Merchant of Venice*, i. 1.

"SAFE AS THE BANK OF ENGLAND." 41

As occasional realisations are unavoidable, there is always a risk of losing some nominal capital. Well-managed banks and other institutions adopt the precaution of having a reserve fund in solid and easily realisable securities, and writing off every year a part of the cost of purchase. It is not possible to avoid all risk, and those most concerned must make the best of it, even if they cannot, in a financial sense, carry out Lady Macbeth's advice, to " make assurance doubly sure."

" Find me an investment to yield me a regular four per cent., without risk or fluctuation," is a common remark. To do so is not always practicable, owing to the constantly accumulating wealth seeking profitable outlets, and to the amount of trust money and of other funds for which a permanent investment must be found. But it is possible, by watching the fluctuations of numerous perfectly sound dividend-paying stocks, to buy when they are low, and to sell when they improve ; repeating the process continually as occasion serves, and in this way obtaining returns, in the shape of enhanced values, far beyond the usual rates of dividends. Some security should be selected at a price below its normal rate, as shown by its recent history, but with a reasonable probability that it will rise again ere long.

CHAPTER V.

JOINT STOCK AND LIMITED LIABILITY.

JOINT-STOCK enterprise is of ancient date. John Law's Mississippi Scheme in 1716, and the South Sea Bubble of 1720, are commonly regarded as its congeners, excepting a few earlier incorporated trading bodies, like the East India Company, the demand for the stock of which was greater than the supply. Macaulay has pointed out that in the interval between the Restoration of 1660 and the Revolution of 1688 wealth had rapidly increased. The difficulty of finding safe and profitable investments led to much hoarding of gold and silver. " The natural effect of this state of things was that a crowd of projectors, ingenious and absurd, honest and knavish, occupied themselves in devising new schemes for the employment of redundant capital. It was about the year 1688 that the word 'stock-jobber' was first heard in London. In the short space of four years a crowd of companies, every one of which confidently held out to subscribers the hope of immense gains, sprang into existence : the Insurance Company, the Paper Company, the Lutestring Company, the Pearl Fishery Company, the Glass Bottle Company, the Alum Company, the Blythe Coal Company, the Sword-blade Company.

" There was a Tapestry Company, which would soon furnish pretty hangings for all the parlours of the middle class, and for all the bedchambers of the higher. There was a Copper Company, which proposed to explore the mines of England, and held out a hope that they would prove not less valuable than those of Potosi. There was a Diving Company, which undertook to bring up precious effects from shipwrecked vessels, and which announced that it had laid in a stock of wonderful machines resembling complete suits of armour. There was a Greenland Fishing Company, which could not fail to drive the Dutch whalers and herring busses out of the Northern Ocean. There was a Tanning Company, which promised to furnish leather superior to the best that was brought from Turkey or Russia. There was a society which undertook the office of giving gentlemen a liberal education on low terms, and which assumed the sounding name of the Royal Academies Company.

" In a pompous advertisement in was announced that the directors had engaged the best masters in every branch of knowledge, and were about to issue twenty thousand tickets at twenty shillings each. There was to be a lottery. Two thousand prizes were to be drawn, and the fortunate holders of the prizes were to be taught, at the charge of the company, Latin, Greek, Hebrew, French, Spanish, conic sections, trigonometry, heraldry, japanning, fortification, book-keeping, and the art of playing the theorbo."[1] Jonathan's coffee-house and Garraway's were in a ferment with buyers and sellers, with brokers and agents. Time bargains came into fashion. Preposterous tales were circulated, so as to raise or depress share prices. Every day some new bubble was blown; only to burst the next day or the next week. The result, as might have been expected, was widespread disaster, and, to many, irretrievable ruin.

The South Sea Bubble of 1720 was accompanied by a mania just as absurd. Dean Swift satirized it in his sketch of Balnibarbi, a region in his fabled Island of Laputa, colonized by chimerical projectors and schemers. Hogarth made it the theme of one of his most pungent caricatures. Daniel Defoe's *Essay on Projects*, many of which, being practical, have since been carried into effect, was probably suggested by the outbreak of the speculative spirit. It was a time when characters flourished like those

[1] Macaulay's *History of England*, iv. 320.

embodied recently in Charles Mathews' favourite impersonation in *The Game of Speculation*, or in that of Jeremy Diddler in Kenny's farce of *Raising the Wind*.

The origin of the craze was a proposal made by the South Sea Company to purchase the irredeemable annuities granted in the two preceding reigns, and to amalgamate all the public funds into one stock, so as to become the sole public creditor. The Bank of England made a rival proposition, and the two great corporations continued to outbid each other until an offer was accepted on the part of the South Sea Company to provide a sum of seven millions and a half. In a few weeks the £100 shares of the South Sea Company sold for £1000. The directors opened supplementary subscriptions, all of which were eagerly taken up; and they asserted that a dividend of 50 per cent. would be realised. Some of the holders of stock sold out when the price was at the highest; thereby realising immense fortunes. During the short time that it lasted, the excess to which the general intoxication proceeded is almost incredible.

Anderson, in his *Deduction of Trade and Commerce*, published in 1762, has given a curious table of the crowd of new projects, and an interesting description of the general scene of competition and clamour among the dealers and purchasers of the various stocks. The East India Company £100 shares rose to £445; those of the Bank of England to £260; and the Royal African Company's £23 shares rose to £200. There was a vast number of what Anderson describes as "projects or bubbles, having neither charter nor Act of Parliament to authorize them : none of which were under one million, and some went as far as ten millions; very many whereof are distinctly remembered by the author of this work, how ridiculous and improbable soever they may now seem to many not acquainted with the infatuation of that year."

Among them are enumerated eleven fishing projects ; four salt companies ; ten insurance companies ; four water companies ; two for the remittance of money ; two sugar companies ; eleven for settlements in or trading to America ; two building and thirteen land companies ; six oil companies; four harbour and river companies ; four for supplying London with coal, cattle, and hay, and for paving the streets ; six hemp, flax, and linen companies ; five for carrying on the manufacture of silks and cottons ; fifteen mining companies ; and a miscellaneous rabble, sixty in all, among which were projects for the building of hospitals for bastard children ; for importing a number of large jackasses from Spain, in order to propagate a larger kind of mules in England ; for trading in human hair ; for the fattening of hogs ; for a grand dispensary ; for a wheel for perpetual motion ; for furnishing funerals ; for insuring and increasing children's fortunes ; for trading in and improving commodities of this kingdom. The most absurd of these schemes seem not to have wanted dupes.

No one thought of inquiring if the projects were practical or not. One was announced, and its shares bought, which was merely advertized as " for an undertaking which shall in due time be revealed." Within two or three days after they were subscribed for, the shares in these different companies sold for amazing prices. " From morning till evening," says Anderson, " the dealers therein, as well as in South Sea stock, appeared in continual crowds all over Exchange Alley, so as to choke up the passage through it." The utmost that appears to have been paid even on those projects that " had one or more persons of known credit to midwife them into the alley " was ten shillings per cent.

About Midsummer it was calculated that the value of the stock of all the different companies and projects at the current prices exceeded five hundred millions sterling ; probably five times as much as the current cash of all Europe, and more than twice the worth of the fee-simple of all the land in the kingdom. It is impossible to conjecture how much higher the prices of shares in the most absurd of these bubbles would have risen, if the mania had not received a sudden check and collapse. There was a painful awakening to the absurdity and danger of the mania. Within a month, South Sea stock fell from 850 to 175. By this time all faith in the possibility of its being kept up at a price above its original cost and real value was irretrievably gone. The bubble had burst; the delusion was over; the drunkenness had passed away, and only exhaustion, aching ruin, and repentance were left. But the hurricane which so greatly disturbed the air probably made it purer and healthier for a long time to come. The calamitous effects of the mania were individual and immediate, not general or permanent. The national credit was not impaired, nor was there an actual loss of property, but the ordinary course of business was for a time deranged, and the skilful piloting of Sir Robert Walpole was required to escape from the financial panic.

A report issued early in 1846 by the Board of Trade demonstrated a fertility of invention on the part of promoters of joint-stock companies which rivals that of any former period. Among the nondescript projects included in the return were a Biographical Dictionary Company; the Tehuantepec

JOINT STOCK AND LIMITED LIABILITY. 49

Colonization and Canal Company; the New Protecting Society; the Norfolk Ramoneur Association; the Patent Cork-cutting Company; the Great British Advertising Company; the General Canal Steam Haulage Company; the Patriot Association; the Miniature World, or Grand National Association for the Profitable Employment of Capital, Skill, and Labour in Trade, Commerce, and Agriculture, with companies for concentrated tea, patent fuel, baths, spinning, mining, drainage, discount, insurance, glue, sugar, glass, timber, cotton, water, sewage, gas, cemeteries, hops, newspapers. The recital could be extended by a reference to the manias and projects of more recent years.

Under the old joint-stock law every shareholder was liable to his uttermost farthing for the debts of a company, even though he had no direct control over and no acquaintance with its business affairs. He could seek relief only by the costly process of an action against his fellow-shareholders. Instances have occurred, like the City of Glasgow Bank, where shareholders have seen their all swept away to meet gigantic claims, or they had to take refuge in bankruptcy. To prevent the recurrence of such a catastrophe, the Limited Liability Act was introduced in 1855 by Mr. Robert Lowe, afterwards Viscount Sherbrooke. It was an adaptation of a French plan, which had also been carried out in the

United States. It provided that each shareholder should be responsible for no more than the nominal value of the shares allotted to him. For the protection of the public in doing work or in supplying goods, the word "Limited" has to be appended to the name of the company, and to appear on all documents. Various Amending and Consolidating Acts have since been passed, but there is still a keen struggle between the law, on the one side, and promoters on the other,

Shares in Limited Companies are usually divided into Ordinary, Guaranteed, Preference, and Deferred. To the first are accorded, *pro rata*, such profits as may be made. The second and the third agree to accept a smaller but fixed dividend, while the fourth usually receive a moiety of the remaining profits after the others' claims are met. Companies also usually take powers to borrow money on mortgage by the issue of Debentures, constituting a prior charge on the assets. All these kinds of holdings are negotiable, with more or less facility, on the Stock Exchange. The price secured represents the market value of the property, which necessarily fluctuates. The large joint-stock banks have availed themselves of a recent statute (42 & 43 Vict. c. 76) whereby the liability of their shareholders is restricted. The nominal amount of capital may be increased, without rendering it liable to be called unless in the event of winding up, or a portion of the existing uncalled capital may be set aside by resolution for such a contingency. Liability for notes remains unlimited.

With a kind of periodicity an epidemic of company-promoting breaks out. Transient or apparent success induces a crowd of imitators. During the last decade or two there have been several hot mining fits, located in England or Wales, in the United States, in India, in Australia, and in Africa. Electricity, shipping, co-operative stores, hotels, asphalt, tramways, skating-rinks, coffee-palaces, foreign loans and mines, Continental mineral springs, entertainments, tea plantations, nitrates, and trusts of all descriptions have had their little day, usually followed by a long and dark night for those who were so verdant as to find the money. Then there is an indignant outbreak, which ought rather to be directed to their own folly and credulity.

If there were no dupes, knaves could not thrive. Demands are heard for condign punishment. Legislation is forced through in a hurry. Officialism displays spasmodic energy. A great parade is made of inquiries and examinations, and much talk is heard of prosecutions; which usually end in smoke. After a brief lull, the company epidemic breaks out in some new form; to be followed by the old and miserable round of blind acceptance, foolish trust, and untold disaster. Bacon says "There is in human nature generally more of the fool than of the wise, and therefore those faculties by which the foolish part of men's minds is taken are most potent." This remark anticipates Carlyle's severe and cynical dictum, in *Latter-Day Pamphlets*, "The population of Britain consists of twenty-seven millions of people—mostly fools."

Probably no Statute can be framed for the protection of fools who are tempted, like gudgeons, by an alluring bait. There is no Act of Parliament through which legal ingenuity will not contrive, as Daniel O'Connell said, to drive a coach and four. The 38th section of the Companies Act, 1867, was thought to be a sure remedy against secret and fictitious contracts; but it is openly violated every day by a clause in most prospectuses requiring applicants to waive it. "More is meant than meets the ear." One company is formed to take over another, or to produce a brood of subsidiary companies, as "flat, stale, and unprofitable" as itself. This was notoriously the case with "Father Brush" and a swarm of electric companies, and with the Date Coffee swindle of a few years since. The Founders'-Share dodge is nearly played out, happily for investors. But human credulity is still largely appealed to, with success, by a long parade of Press

JOINT STOCK AND LIMITED LIABILITY. 53

Notices, of the authenticity of which there is no proof, and which in many cases are supplied to a certain class of unscrupulous black-mail newspapers as one of the conditions for a large and costly advertisement.

Many persons are frightened to invest their money, because others have been overwhelmed by disaster through carelessly placing money in things they knew nothing about. Investments, especially in the shoal of new companies, is beset with risk and uncertainty, as many of these ventures are proverbially short-lived. Since the Limited Liability Act was first passed, no fewer than 49,607 companies were registered, but nearly three-fifths—28,384 out of the whole—are believed to be extinct, and only one-fifth are more than ten years old.

No fewer than 4276 companies were registered during 1896, with a nominal capital of £263,423,167; being more than thrice as much as in 1893. The nominal capital of mining companies, the largest in the group, was £94,419,194; followed by manufacturing and trading, £18,139,000. Breweries and distilleries stood for £18,162,200; Home, Indian, Colonial, and Foreign railways, £17,816,300; British, Colonial, and Foreign Corporation stocks, £13,490,100; cycles and appliances, £17,187,100.

The last-named is a curious illustration of the way in which fashion reacts upon commerce and investments. In the United Kingdom, of the 21,223 companies actually existing the capital is £1,145,402,993, which exceeds by £300,000,000 the amount invested in French and German companies.

Thus during forty years there has grown up the present vast system of joint-stock enterprise in association with the principle of limited liability. One great object has been realised to an extent far beyond all expectation, viz., to call into the direct service of industry and of all orders of production and commercial enterprise whatever available money resources were possessed by the community. These resources, without such an easy and effective outlet, safeguarded by limited liability, might have continued to be hoarded, unproductively consumed, or merely put out at interest. Under the company system, with limited liability, the amount of capital embarked in various operations and enterprises is enormous, and, notwithstanding defects and abuses, it demonstrates the value of the machinery which has called forth such a capital for the expansion of productive industry and of profitable trade. Having regard to the resources, the energy, and the enterprise comprised within the system, it may be justly described as colossal, and it occupies a place of constantly increasing importance in the industrial and commercial life of England and of other nations. Gigantic manufacturing and trading concerns, when properly managed, can undertake business to an extent which no private firm dare attempt, and with highly satisfactory results to the shareholders.

On the other hand, many an enterprise which has been successful when conducted by one or two persons, has signally failed as a limited company for lack of competent supervision and personal responsibility. In other cases the loading has been excessive and crushing, and promoters and intermediaries have created a fictitious capital on which it was impossible to pay a dividend. It not infrequently happens, also, that companies are floated merely for purposes of allotment, so as to secure for vendors and promoters as much ready cash as possible, and then the duped shareholders are left to face a winding-up order. Investors should be cautious about embarking in such ventures, because, in round numbers, fourteen shillings out of every twenty actually subscribed are irrecoverably lost.

The outside public, forming the major part of the investors in new companies, are made to pay through the nose by promoters and their associates. The market is rigged with vendors' shares, always a glut as to number, and never worth anything like the face value which they bear. To force these off at par is a supreme object, and it is aided by the foolish eagerness of many to get in at the outset for what they have been told by interested parties is a good thing. Ere long, and perhaps within a week, they wake up to the unpleasant discovery that any number of the shares may be had at a discount. If they had waited, instead of swallowing the first alluring bait, they might have obtained ten or twelve shares for the price of nine.

The application of this caution is especially needed in the case of the numerous trading and manufacturing companies formed during recent years to acquire private businesses. A comparison of the price of similar ventures already on the market should furnish a clue to the actual value of the dazzling schemes that appeal every week to the investing public. The old saying, " Fools build houses, but wise men buy them," is true of most of the commercial enterprises that have been launched as limited companies. The wise investor reads between the lines of a glowing prospectus. He compares and judges as to the chances, by reference to similar undertakings. By waiting a short time, and watching his opportunity, he obtains such a holding as he desires, at a price that enables him to realise a fair profit when he sells again ; as he will assuredly wish to do ere long.

It is not intended by the above criticism to depreciate mercantile limited companies, or to suggest that all new ventures are to be avoided as undesirable or dangerous. But it is well to allow the first flutter of excitement to pass, and to wait until the business is fairly on its feet under the new arrangements. The commercial value can better be judged from actual trading than from promoters' and accountants' estimates. Many original holders of the shares are sure to wish to dispose of them, at prices that are worth considering. Anyway, it is a safe rule that a new company without a history furnishes no means for determining the actual value of its shares, which should therefore be avoided until some accurate and reliable *data* are known. Their original price is fixed by vendors and promoters, " snappers-up of unconsidered trifles," as well as of lump sums, whose interest it is to obtain just as much as credulous and confiding members of the public can be induced to pay.

A wise man, therefore, will not apply for such shares prior to allotment, unless he has good reason to believe that they will at once go to a premium. By this is meant a genuine premium, not a bogus one got up for selling purposes, and unattainable by an outsider. As a rule, it is safer to wait until there is an actual market when the real price is known. It will probably be from two to ten or more points under the price of emission. Then, if the business is sound and progressing, the discount may tempt an investor to purchase for a brief holding. Should they return to par, or rise to a premium that may be really secured, the purchaser will know that value has been obtained for his money. It is a safe maxim not to join any company without being prepared to pay up the whole of the liability, and to lose it, if the emergency arises. Far greater caution would then be exercised ; and less would be heard of disasters caused by misplaced confidence in tricksters and their newspaper touts. There are not a few feeble prints, hanging on to the outer skirts of the noble profession of journalism, the sole reason of whose fitful existence is to extort money, as the price of silence, or of turgid puffs and sickening laudation.

CHAPTER VI.

GOVERNMENT SECURITIES.

GOVERNMENT securities represent the debt of the nation, secured upon the public credit, with a Parliamentary title and the guarantee of the Exchequer. They rank highest as financial investments, and are probably unequalled in the world. Dating back to the year 1689, the National Debt has furnished for two centuries a convenient means for securing moderate interest at regular intervals. With the founding of the Bank of England the system of public credit was established on a plan first mooted in 1658 by Samuel Lamb, a sagacious and enterprising London merchant. He published a pamphlet, in the form of a letter to Cromwell, urging the formation of a bank in London, similar to the successful one at Amsterdam, and giving reasons to explain the vast superiority of Holland as a commercial nation.

William Paterson (1658–1719), a Scotchman, has the credit of the actual formation of the Bank, which received its charter as a joint-stock association July 27, 1694, with a capital of £1,200,000; being the amount lent to the Government, at 8 per cent. to relieve existing embarrassments. This character of financial agent has been maintained ever since by successive renewals of the Charter. Certain privileges and immunities were granted in return, in the issue of notes; in managing the Public Debt and paying the dividends; in holding the State deposits and making temporary advances; and in aiding in the collection of the revenue.

In this way the National Debt was created; the money being lent on condition that the principal could not be demanded, although power was reserved to pay it off. At the end of the reign of William III. the amount was sixteen millions. Not until the great French War, from 1793 to 1815, did the Debt assume gigantic proportions. The principal additions prior to that time had been during the reign of George II. and the earlier part of that of George III., arising chiefly from the American War of Independence. The amount was enormously increased by the French Revolutionary War; to the extent of £601,500,000.

The burden of the war was largely transmitted to posterity. On January 5, 1816, the National

Debt, including liabilities of every kind, was £885,186,323, or nearly four times the amount at which it stood at the close of the American War of Independence; and seven times more than in 1760. The taxes from 1793 to 1816, irrespective of loans, amounted to £1,129,000,000, an average of nearly fifty millions per annum; whereas the total expenditure in 1792 was under twenty. This is exclusive of the cost of collection, which, under the system then in vogue, was deducted from the sums paid into the Exchequer.

Most of the loans were raised on stringent and wasteful terms for the nation—as is shown in Fenn's treatise on the Funds—while highly lucrative to money-jobbers, speculators, and fundholders. In 1797, for instance, a loan of £14,500,000 was obtained by giving, for each £100 actually paid, £175 of Three per Cent. Consols, with twenty of Four per Cent., and an annuity of six shillings for sixty-three years. Another loan was raised by an issue of £219 Three per Cents. for each hundred. In the following year £17,000,000 were obtained for exactly double the sum in Consols, with an annuity of 4s. 11d. for sixty-two years. Other large sums were borrowed from time to time on conditions more or less onerous and costly.

Of £480,000,000 actually paid into the Exchequer from 1801 to 1815, stock was issued for £572,000,000 at 3 per cent. for £37,000,000 at 4 per cent., and for £99,000,000 at 5 per cent., besides annuities for £316,529, terminable in 1860. Taking the whole period of the war, the average issue was £169 of debt for each £100 actually borrowed. MacCulloch affirms that, owing to the method of funding, the country has been paying ever since for interest from six to seven millions annually more than was just or needful. A partial adjustment, but at the expense of existing bondholders, was made in 1888, when Mr. G. J. Goschen was Chancellor of the Exchequer; the rate of interest being reduced from 3 to $2\frac{3}{4}$ per cent., until 1903, with the option of redemption by the Government in 1923. Other Three per Cents. had been reduced to $2\frac{3}{4}$ in 1884 by Mr. Childers, redeemable in 1905.

A further difficulty arose during the Great War. Owing to the continuous exports of bullion the Bank of England was in great straits, and an Order in Council authorized a compulsory suspension of specie payments, and was confirmed by an Act of Parliament. The suspension continued from 1797 until 1819, by which time the market price of gold was 42 per cent. above the Mint price, and the pound notes sunk in value by one-third. The evil was aggravated by a sudden return to specie payments. Those who had lent money when the currency was at par, and the owners of house property and the public creditors, had been receiving only two-thirds of the nominal values; but, on resumption, all who had borrowed money during the depreciation had to repay in full. Thus trade and commerce were deranged.

From 1793 to 1801 the average price of £100 Three per Cents. was £57 17s. 6d., and from 1803 to 1815 it was £60 17s. 6d. The present gross indebtedness is as follows; but the net amount, after allowing for the present value of Suez Canal shares, Exchequer balances, &c., is £619,998,590. Comparative figures are given in Appendix D.

Funded Debt	£589,146,878
Unfunded Debt	9,975,800
Estimated Capital Value of Terminable Annuities	49,351,465
Other Capital Liabilities	4,066,002
Total	£652,540,145

Strictly speaking, the obligation is confined to the payment of a quarterly annuity. The principal cannot be demanded, although the Government can repay it on certain notice. If the holder wishes to realise, all that he can do is to sell to another, and then execute a form of transfer. Being readily marketable, great facilities are furnished to investors. But the gradual reduction of the National Debt, and the holdings by various Government departments, to the extent of £198,701,782, and by banks, insurance companies, trustees, and others, with the state of the Money Market, have tended to enhance the price of Consols. The average from 1851 to 1880, during which the fluctuations were slight, was $90\frac{3}{8}$. Then they reached par, but again sunk when the interest was reduced in 1887. For some time they ranged at 105-107, but on February 27, 1896, they rose to $109\frac{7}{8}$ as the actual selling price, and on June 1 to $113\frac{7}{8}$. The price is affected by the state of home and foreign politics, by the harvest, by commerce, and manufactures. It also serves as a barometer of the degree of national prosperity, and of confidence in the Government of the day. The prices and the mean yield during the last forty-seven years are given in Appendix C.

CHAPTER VII.

BANKS.

THE Bank of England, as stated in the last Chapter, was incorporated in 1694. A charter was granted for eleven years, and it has been renewed fifteen times, under varying conditions. The last was in 1844. Exclusive privileges were conceded, and no other joint-stock bank was allowed in the country until 1826, and then only beyond a radius of sixty-five miles from London. Even now the Bank has the sole right to issue notes in London. Any country bank possessing the privilege forfeits it on opening an office in the metropolis.

In May, 1844, Sir Robert Peel introduced a measure into the House of Commons for the better regulation of the affairs of the Bank of England, and of banking business generally. In doing so he propounded his famous financial conundrum, " What is the signification of that word 'pound,' with which we are all familiar?" He entered at considerable length into an examination of various theories as to the standard of value, and avowed himself in favour of retaining the existing gold standard. He proposed, and the Legislature agreed, that in future the business of the Bank should be separated into two distinct departments—one for the issue of notes, and the other for ordinary banking transactions. The former was to be based on the possession of a definite amount of public securities, and on bullion; notes not being allowed to be issued on deposits and on discounted bills. The fixed amount of securities was to be £14,000,000; while of the remainder the note circulation was to be exclusively on the bullion in stock. The periodical publication of accounts was ordered.

The design of the Act of 1844 was to prevent the issue of notes beyond a certain amount, unless against an equal amount of gold held by the issuing bank, so that the mixed currency of notes and coin might automatically expand or contract. Experience has shown, however, that when a foreign drain of gold occurs the quantity exported is taken chiefly from reserves in the Bank of England, and that the amount of the notes in the hands of the public has not been seriously affected by the Act of 1844. Practically, when there are signs of a foreign drain, and the reserve is diminishing, the Bank counteracts the danger by raising the rate of discount and by restricting its loans. The purchasing power of the public is thereby limited, prices are kept down, and at the same time gold is attracted to this country for investments. The currency in circulation is not really interfered with.

The annual sum payable by the Bank for its exclusive privileges is now £180,000. All profit from the increase in the issue of notes beyond £14,000,000 is directed to go into the Exchequer. By the Act of 1892 the remuneration payable to the Bank for the management of the National Debt is a yearly sum at the rate of £325 per million of the debt, up to five hundred, and of £100 for every million beyond. The arrangement holds until the year 1912, and thereafter as Parliament shall direct; but the total amount is not to be less than £160,000. A sum of £100 per million is paid for the management of Exchequer Bonds and Bills, and £200 per million for Treasury Bills, on the amount outstanding on the last day of the preceding financial year.

The profit derived by the Bank upon its issue department is the interest of 3 per cent. on the £14,000,000 of Government debt and securities, less £120,000 paid for its exclusive privileges, and £60,000 in lieu of stamp duties. The net yearly profit is about half a million, and in addition there is a profit of £30,000 to £40,000 upon bullion, which the Bank is bound to purchase whenever offered at £3 17s. 9d. per ounce. For the management of the National Debt the Government pays nearly a quarter of a million annually, and the remaining profits of the establishment are derived from the use of the Bank capital, and of deposits by customers, on which no interest is given.

The Bank also transacts private business, but this department has to be kept distinct, and its interests are somewhat antagonistic to those of the other branch. The Bank Stock, belonging to the proprietors, is now £14,553,000, and the "Rest," or surplus funds, necessarily varying from week to week, about £3,500,000. Its stock is regarded as one of the best investments. The earnings correspond with the rates of discount, which are regulated by the state of trade and of the Money Market. It is natural that the proprietors should desire even a better return, as they cast longing eyes upon the much larger dividends of other banks. In 1844 the dividend was 7 per cent., and the price of Bank Stock was 212. It is now—March, 1897—from 329 to 332, and the rate in 1896 was $8\frac{1}{2}$ per cent. Details are given in Appendix C.

In the same period London and Westminster

Bank shares, in spite of a doubling of the capital have risen from 27 to 51, while the dividend has increased from 6 to 10 per cent. One explanation is that whereas this bank has only 13 per cent. of its liabilities lying idle, the Bank of England has over 40 per cent. The creation of joint-stock banks in London arose from a discovery that the Bank Charter Act did not really prohibit such institutions being formed to carry on business on the lines adopted by private banks. The only exclusive privilege was the issue of notes payable on demand, but there was no monopoly granted for receiving deposits. In the olden time, when the Charter was first framed, banking referred exclusively to the issue of notes. Deposits were scarcely known. Goldsmiths had acted as bankers, and they were accustomed to deposit surplus coin and bullion in the Exchequer, the arbitrary closing of which by the Government in 1673 caused wide-spread ruin, and deranged trade and credit for many years.

The Bank Act of 1833 contained a new clause, permitting joint-stock banks—which had existed in the provinces since 1826—to be formed in London, provided they did not issue notes; but for some years legal technicalities arose as to the acceptance of bills, the power to sue for debts, and similar questions, which constantly embarrassed the operations. The London and Westminster was the first joint-stock bank founded in London, in 1834. Its great success speedily led to the formation of the London Joint-Stock Bank, the Union Bank of London, the London and County, the National Provincial, and others. The dividends of the best range from 10 to 20 per cent., but then the market price of the shares, even with the unpaid capital involved, is proportionately high (see Appendix E).

Bank securities are naturally regarded as being among the best. Since the passing of Leeman's Act every seller of bank shares must supply the numbers of those he is disposing of. Reckless advances, fraud, and misappropriation, as in the notorious case of the Royal British Bank in 1856, or that of Strahan, Paul, and Bates, in 1855, are the chief dangers of banking. Sudden crises in finance and trade have to be guarded against by means of a judicious reserve, securely invested and easy of realisation. Few persons possess the philosophy of the man who, being asked on the failure of his bank, "Were you not upset?" replied, "No! I only lost my balance."

The liabilities on deposits and on current accounts are shown in the following instances, taken from the reports of 1896; the aggregate deposits in banks that publish accounts being upwards of £770,000,000 :—

BANKS. 71

National Provincial Bank	£45,889,744
London and County	38,202,824
London and Westminster	24,306,081
Lloyds	32,644,925
London Joint Stock	16,760,060
Union of London	15,633,056
Capital and Counties...	14,567,805

The total capital held by the banks in the country which publish accounts may be stated in round figures as follows :—

	CAPITAL.	RESERVE.
Bank of England ...	£14,553,000	£3,000,000
English Banks ...	54,520,000	27,336,000
Scotch Banks... ...	9,302,000	5,927,000
Irish Banks	7,109,000	3,177,300
	£85,484,000	£39,440,300
Total	£124,924,300	

Allowing for the banks which do not publish accounts, the estimated total capital is brought up to £188,802,775, of which the capital actually paid, according to Burdett, is £58,712,600. The main increase, about forty millions, during the last twenty years has been in England and Wales. The increase in Scotland, amounting to about a million and a half, has been confined to the Reserve Funds. The Bank of England has about £26,000,000 of notes in circulation, country joint-stock and private banks about one and a half millions. and the Scotch and Irish banks together fourteen and a half millions. Since the Act of 1844 158 private banks and 37 joint-stock banks in England and Wales have ceased to issue notes, to the amount of £5,119,780.

The position of the Bank of England with respect to specie reserve, though somewhat improved when contrasted with 1876, is not nearly so strong as compared with other countries, where similar institutions have made greater advances. This will appear from the following statement:—

BANK OF ENGLAND.

Reserve of Notes and Coin.

1876 ... ... £19,200,000 | 1896 ... ... £25,400,000

BANK OF FRANCE.

1876 ... .. £85,600,000 | 1896 (Gold) £79,200,000
,, (Silver) £49,200,000

Total £128,400,000

IMPERIAL BANK OF GERMANY.

1876 (*Coin and Bullion*)... £24,500,000 | 1896 ... ... £41,600,000

NEW YORK ASSOCIATED BANKS.

1876.		1896.	
Specie...............	£3,600,000	Specie...............	£12,700,000
Legal Tenders ...	8,500,000	Legal Tenders ...	12,100,000
Total ...£12,100,000		Total ...£24,800,000	

The above increase shows that the Bank of England is a little stronger, but that while banks in other countries have felt the necessity of improving their position, it has not done so in the same proportion. It cannot be denied that an adequate specie reserve, which is the first requirement of business security, is not maintained, or that in proportion to the banking liabilities of the country the reserve is smaller now than it was twenty years ago.

As Bagehot points out, and as Sir R. Giffen confirms, the cash reserve of a banker is the condition of his solvency. If all depositors and holders of notes demanded their cash at once, they could not be paid. A banker has to keep enough in hand for current demands, and also a reserve for emergencies. Practically, however, the ultimate resource is in the Bank of England, which dominates not only other banks, but has many foreign connections. The latter, and provincial banks generally, have London agencies, usually the leading joint stock and private banks, which in their turn keep deposits with the discount houses, the bill brokers, and the Bank of England. Thus one bank leans on another, and the final result, as was shown in the sixth and the seventeenth Chapters, is that the main reserve is kept by the Bank of England only. Its proportion of reserve to liabilities at the end of 1896 was 54 per cent.

CHAPTER VIII.

INDIAN SECURITIES.

FEW persons have any idea of the extent, the area, and the population of British India, and of the native States under British protection. According to the Census of 1891 the area in square miles was 1,560,160. The number of towns and villages was 717,549. Houses occupied, including, of course, large numbers of frail constructions, were 52,932,102. The total population was given at 287,223,431 ; being 184 to the square mile.

The British Empire in India extends over a territory larger than the Continent of Europe, excluding Russia. In addition, there are vast tracts on the North-Western and North-Eastern frontiers which are under the political influence, though not under the administrative rule, of the Indian Government. Its actual barrier extends from Persia along the Russian territory as far as the Oxus ; thence by the Panjah branch to Victoria Lake, and up to the line of Chinese territory as defined in 1895; from which it passes along the crest of the Himalayas to Siam, and half way down to the Malay Peninsula.

Continental India, including Baluchistan, reaches from the 8th to the 87th degree of North Latitude, and from the 61st to the 100th degree of Longitude. In addition, the great province of Burmah was annexed to the Asiatic dominions in 1886. The whole comprise a territory compared with which the ancient Mogul Empire fades away into insignificance. Most of this has been acquired within the present century. Since the Indian Mutiny, in 1857, the supreme control of affairs is invested in the Secretary of State for India in Council, who is always a member of the English Government.

For upwards of a century prior to 1750 the English and French, the Dutch and Portuguese had been carrying on, with varying but slight success, a trade with India. There were mutual jealousies and rivalries and frequent collisions with native rulers. The English had been barely tolerated in 1640 in founding a settlement in Madras. By the middle of the next century they became formidable. Clive, Warren Hastings, and other capable and daring men had the courage to undertake responsibilities from which weaker men would have shrunk.

In the dispute with the French, which was brought to a crisis by the great game of political chess played between Clive and Dupleix, the determining factor was England's supremacy on the sea, which rendered her ultimate conquest of India not only possible but certain. In this way was determined the question whether France or England was to rule India. Possibilities were opened up, such as not even the most adventurous and far-seeing could have anticipated, of a sovereignty or a protectorate embracing within about a century more than one-fourth of the human race.

The great trading corporation, so long known as the East India Company, was established in 1702 by an amalgamation of two existing chartered bodies dating back to the time of Queen Elizabeth. Ere long it wielded sovereign authority. It set up and dethroned princes; made peace and war; levied vast taxes, and exercised a commercial monopoly which no private persons could break down. Successive charters were granted, conferring additional powers; always in return for valuable consideration, and reserving a control to the English Government.

The gross revenue in India during the year 1895-6, the last for which the returns are available, was £97,877,900, chiefly derived from the land, from taxes on opium and salt, and receipts from railways. These comprise 19,677 miles, three-fourths of which are State lines owned by the Government. There are also four guaranteed companies, like the Great Indian Peninsula, with a mileage of 2587, and a small number of assisted companies. The native States, which retain a certain amount of independence, have also 1560 miles. The grand total of passengers conveyed on all the systems during the year was 153,081,477, and the quantity of goods and minerals 33,628,030 tons. 5789 miles of railway were also sanctioned.

The aggregate receipts from all sources were £26,236,906; the working expenses being 46·15 per cent. The total capital raised by the railway companies to the end of the year 1895 was £114,701,259. The companies pay into the Treasury the net receipts, and if these do not suffice the amount required is made up from the public revenue. Any profits in excess are paid to the stock-holders, after refunding any advances made in previous years by the Government, which has six months' option of purchase on the expiration of a lease, on the average price of the stock for three years. No competing lines are allowed, and those constructed are under rigid supervision, both in building and in working. They are essential for the rapid transit of troops and materials of war, and this was the principal reason for the State guarantee in such a vast territory, where 287 millions of people are governed by a mere handful of English administrators.

Indian railways are safe investments, and pay a fair rate of interest. The general prospects are good. Rich and productive districts have been opened up for the cultivation of grain, tea, coffee, chincona, jute, cotton, silk, and other valuable products. China used to supply us with tea. In 1872, the imports thence were 122,000,000 lbs. In 1895, they were only 31,500,000 lbs. India now grows fourfold the quantity. Its annual exports exceed 133,000,000 lbs. A few years ago but little corn was raised in India for export, but a large portion of the staple supply of food now comes to England from her Eastern possessions. The abundant supply of cheap labour, and the prolific tropical growth, have largely supplanted Russia and the United States as the sources of England's supply of cereals.

India is now our principal market. The imports from England of such articles as manufactured textile goods, metals, machinery, salt, beer, &c., amounted, by the last returns, to £58,322,906, and the exports to £40,578,469; one-third being cotton, jute, and seeds. The India Public Debt, now amounting to £233,186,886, and largely held in this country, has been incurred partly for war expenses, but chiefly by the large outlay on public works, such as roads and water supply and storage. Irrigation works alone have cost £30,343,404. The country has been greatly benefited, and the money is reproductive. The interest is charged upon revenue. Indian Government securities are deemed as safe as Consols, and they yield a better return. The debt is managed and the dividends are paid by the Bank of England. Of a widely different order are the numerous tea and coffee plantations in India and Ceylon that have been brought forward of late years under the guise of limited companies. To those who are thinking of investing in the great majority of such ventures may be applied the immortal advice given by *Punch* to persons about to marry—" Don't."

CHAPTER IX.

BRITISH COLONIES.

OUR Colonies have experienced great and rapid alternations. Of late, disaster has been more marked than prosperity. Fatal mistakes in the methods of settlement, in the convict system, in land and labour troubles, in sending unsuitable emigrants, and in reckless trading and borrowing, have borne their certain fruit. If Lord Bacon's sage advice, given at the time when "Plantations," as they were called, began to be formed across the Atlantic, had been followed, much subsequent trouble and disaster might have been avoided. He wrote: " It is a shameful and unblessed thing to take the scum of people, and wicked, condemned men, to be the people with whom you plant. Not only so, but it spoileth the Plantation, for they will ever live like rogues, and not fall to work, but be lazy, and do mischief, and spend victuals, and be quickly weary; and then certify over to their country to the discredit of the Plantation. The people wherewith you plant ought to be gardeners, ploughmen, labourers, smiths, carpenters, miners, fishermen, fowlers; with some few apothecaries, surgeons, cooks, and bakers."[1]

This wise counsel was disregarded. Even so late as the settlement of Australia the things were done from which Bacon dissuaded; and hence the calamities occurred which he foretold. He added, "Let there be freedom from Customs, till the Plantation be of strength; and freedom to carry their commodities where they may make the best of them, except there be some special cause of caution. Cram not in people by sending in too fast company after company; but rather hearken how they waste, and send supplies proportionably, but so as the number may live well, and not by surcharge be in penury. When the Plantation grows to strength, then it is time to plant with women as well as with men, that it may spread into generations, and not be ever pieced from without."[2]

Australasia, that is Australia, or Southern Asia, comprises the great island continent of that name, with New Zealand and Tasmania, and a vast number of smaller islands in the Southern hemisphere, together with a portion of New Guinea. The whole of the British possessions in this scattered area are estimated to contain $3\frac{1}{4}$ millions of square

[1] *Essay*, No. 34.   [2] *Essay*, No. 34.

miles. Portions of the coast on the north-west and south of the main continent were sighted by the Dutch, the Spaniards, and the English at different times, but no attempt was made to explore or settle it. Practically it was made known to the world by Captain James Cook in 1770.

The first British settlement was formed in 1788 at Port Jackson, now called Sydney. William Dampier, in the course of his voyage round the world, from 1684 to 1690, visited Australia and New Guinea, and gave his name to the Dampier Archipelago and Strait. The only use to which the continent was put by England for many years was as a penal settlement, with which the name of Botany Bay will always be dismally associated, Captain George Vancouver afterwards discovered the island that bears his name; and this led to the eventual acquisition of the vast territory of British Columbia. The Spanish monopoly of the Pacific was finally broken, after an existence, almost unchallenged, of nearly three centuries.

Across the Atlantic the French occupation of Canada for a century and a half had been more in the nature of a military post than of a colonial and commercial dependency. The French movements in Canada were always viewed with dislike by the English settlers in New England and in Virginia the feeling was intensified when the French aimed to establish a connection between the basins of the St. Lawrence and the Mississippi, by the great intermediate lakes and waters lying to the west of the British possessions. Local collisions had frequently occurred long before Sir James Wolfe was sent in 1759 to lay siege to Quebec, where "he fell upon the lap of smiling Victory." His achievement led to the surrender of the whole territory to England by the Treaty of Paris, February 10, 1763.

In this way England took a leading place among European people. She had already given birth to two nations, in America and in India, destined to become mighty empires such as the world had never seen, not even in the palmy days of Egypt or Persia, of Greece or Rome. She was also destined, ere long, to call into being other settlements in Africa and in Australia, constituting, with older and later dependencies, the Greater Britain on which the sun never sets.

The Dominion of Canada includes the various provinces of North America, formerly known as Upper and Lower Canada, New Brunswick, Nova Scotia, Prince Edward Island, British Columbia, Manitoba, and the North-West Territories. Newfoundland and Labrador alone remain outside. This territory, nearly as large as Europe, stretches from the Atlantic to the Pacific, and contains a total area of nearly 3½ millions of square miles, exclusive of the great lakes and rivers. Canada and Newfoundland have a population of 5,031,073. The gross revenue is £7,816,138, of which Customs yielded £4,257,189. The total value of imports is £26,864,217, and the exports £25,359,622. The public debt is £62,258,461.

The interior of the vast continent of Australia had been heroically explored since 1813 by men like Wentworth, Mitchell, Lander, and Burke. A thin and scattered fringe of settlements was formed around the coast; imaginary and arbitrary lines dividing what are now known as the separate colonies. New South Wales was the generic name given by Cook to the whole of the vast continent. South Australia was established in 1834; Victoria, formerly called Port Phillip, in 1851; and Queensland in 1859. Van Diemen's Land, or Tasmania, was settled by Englishmen in 1825, and New Zealand in 1841. The island of Fiji was annexed in 1874.

Within a decade after the discovery of gold in Australia, in 1851, quantities of no less value than £960,000,000 reached England from New South Wales and Victoria. Seventeen years later a similar excitement attended the discovery of diamonds in

Cape Colony. In course of time things found their natural level. Trade and industry reaped the chief share of the benefit, and the community found the advantage in a diffusion of wealth that assisted the development of the colonies.

The population of the Australian Colonies at the end of 1894 was given at 4,149,084, and their gross public revenue at £27,969,108; of which Customs yielded £7,822,208. The value of imports for the year was £48,817,685, and of the exports £62,900,055. The public debt exceeded £200,000,000. In addition, there were Treasury and Deficiency balances outstanding to the amount of nearly £10,000,000.

For a time Colonial Securities were in great request, and some of them are still deservedly popular. But it cannot be denied that certain colonies have borrowed recklessly, far beyond their financial strength. In a natural desire to construct railways, harbours, and docks; to lay out towns and cities; to provide drainage, lighting, and water supply; and to open up the resources of the interior, they have attempted too much within the time, and have undertaken extensive works that ought to have been spread over a lengthened period. These remarks apply not only to the obligations of particular colonies, as a whole, but to certain cities and towns which have incurred heavy debts. So long as English investors were willing to provide the money, so long was there a disposition to borrow; and it is to be feared that sufficient heed was not given to the inevitable day of reckoning.

This applies especially to New Zealand and to the two great railways that traverse the Dominion of Canada. Both the Grand Trunk and the Canadian Pacific must be regarded as speculative lines. What they may become in the future cannot be predicted. The original shareholders in the former have long since lost the whole of their money, and the line, which was essentially a contractor's line, has had to be reconstructed from time to time, so badly was it built and equipped. No less a sum than £32,000,000, chiefly of English capital, has been embarked, and for the most part hopelessly sunk, in the Grand Trunk and its associated lines, which are comparable, as a bottomless pit, to the Erie and the Philadelphia and Reading roads.

The proposal to construct a line of nearly 3000 miles, mainly through a desolate and unprofitable region, with the scandalous political jobbery connected with the transaction, involved the downfall of the Macdonald Ministry in 1873. The public memory is proverbially short, and, seven years later, the project was revived by the restored Cabinet, and glowing pictures were drawn of the vast wealth which the line was expected to develop and of the commercial and political future that awaited the country. The measure was forced through, in the face of strenuous opposition, and by means, as was alleged, of unscrupulous bribery and of lavish promises.

As finally settled, the terms on which the Canadian Pacific was constructed were onerous for the Dominion; but everything is there done on a reckless scale, for political reasons and ends. The Company received a free gift of £500,000, of 713 miles of completed road, and of 25,000,000 acres of land, free of taxation for twenty years. All materials were admitted duty-free. The Company had absolute control in fixing rates and charges until a 10 per cent. dividend was paid, and no competitive line was to be sanctioned for twenty years. The results have been unsatisfactory from an investing point of view, whatever gains may sometimes have accrued to the promoters and to professional politicians.

Perhaps one through railway is more than Canada requires, or is likely to require for a long time to come. Its entire population is not five millions, scattered over an area extending 3300 miles from the Atlantic to the Pacific, and numbers of emigrants—perhaps a majority—continually cross the border into the United States. Omitting Montreal, Toronto, Hamilton, London, and a few other cities, and a dwindling place like Quebec, there are none of any size or importance, and the agricultural and mineral resources are checked by six months of severe winter.

South Africa was colonized after the middle of the present century to a much greater extent than formerly. Cape Town had been ceded to England by the Dutch in 1814, and new settlements were established at Natal and elsewhere in 1843. The centre of the vast continent was supposed for ages to be a trackless desert. Many intrepid explorers were foiled in attempts to penetrate into the interior, until, in 1849, David Livingstone opened up a way into the Dark Unknown, revealing populous regions teeming with natural resources. Later discoverers have completed the task which Livingstone set himself to accomplish, and there has been in recent years a scramble among the English, French, Belgians, Germans, Italians, and Portuguese for the apportionment of the coast line, giving access to the hitherto unsuspected wealth of Central Africa with such of the interior as can be seized and held.

The two leading groups of British colonies in

Africa consist of those on the west coast near the Equator, and those in the southern extremity, which alone are adapted for European settlement. The latter comprise Cape Colony, Natal, Bechuanaland, Basutoland, and Zululand. These partially surround the two Dutch-speaking republics, the Transvaal and the Orange Free State, with certain dependent native territories, and the South African protectorates of Germany and Portugal. Besides the above-named colonies large portions of territory are under British protection, such as those of the Royal Niger Company, the British South Africa Company and others. The total area of these colonies, excluding the protected territories, is more than 300,000 square miles, and the white population is about 330,000.

Considering that four hundred years have elapsed since Bartholomew Diaz and Vasco da Gama first doubled the Cape of Good Hope, it is somewhat surprising that the European Settlements along the South African coast have not much more rapidly increased. The African Colonies, including the West Coast Settlements, had a population in 1894 of 3,871,721. Their united public revenue was £4,909,032, of which £1,979,364 were derived from Customs. The imports amounted to £16,245,691, and the exports to £17,887,130. The Public Debt, so far as it can be given—returns from some smaller settlements, like the Gold Coast and St. Helena, being missing—was £36,000,000.

Other colonial settlements, like the West Indies, the Windward and Leeward Islands, British Guiana, &c., have a population of 1,635,472, with a gross public expenditure of £232,309, about one-half of which was derived from Customs. The total imports were £9,851,156, and the exports £9,353,570. The Public Debt stood at a little more than £4,000,000.

CHAPTER X.

RAILWAYS AND TRAMWAYS.

ENGINEERS like Telford and Rennie did much at the beginning of this century to open up communications and to facilitate traffic by the great roads which they constructed. From 1760 to 1773 no fewer than 452 Acts of Parliament authorized the making or the improvement of roads, which led to an amount of travelling hitherto unknown. The name of Macadam is associated with a later method of using broken granite, pressed so as to cohere. James Brindley, aided by the far-seeing Duke of Bridgewater, developed the system of navigable canals. Other great works of public utility were constructed in the closing decades of the last century. New Titanic forces, undreamed of years before, were employed to assist the growing manufacturing industries which made England for generations the workshop of the world.

The first Act of Parliament for the construction of a railway was that of the Surrey Iron Railway

Company in 1801, for a line of six miles from Croydon to Wandsworth, so as to make connection for goods with the river Thames. The development of the iron trade in the North of England, and inventions by William Symington, William Murdoch, James Watt, Richard Trevethick, Stephenson, and others, in the direction of a workable locomotive, led to the rise of the great railway system in the pioneer Stockton and Darlington line, which was opened September 27, 1825. This was followed by the Liverpool and Manchester line, five years later, and by the one from London to Birmingham in 1838 Then set in the era of railway extension and development, with which every intelligent reader is acquainted.

Until the middle of 1836 few railway undertakings had been projected since 1825, but a host of proposals then appeared for lines to almost every part of the country. The wildest schemes were freely entertained. One projector proposed sails to propel his engine. Another offered to use rockets, and confidently promised a speed of one hundred miles an hour. Railways to carry invalids to bed were advertized. A safety railway out of reach of injury was proposed. With the excitement there was a sudden rise in the shares of existing companies. Scrip in the greater number of the new projects speedily commanded a premium, usually fictitious. The time of reaction soon arrived. Money became scarce. The eyes of the public were opened to their folly, and shares of every description fell.

A panic occurred in the City. The Bank rate of discount was raised to 5 per cent., and interest on Exchequer Bills was from $1\frac{1}{2}$d. to $2\frac{1}{2}$d. per day, yet they fell to 10 per cent. discount. Consols fell to $89\frac{3}{8}$. Merchants of high character, who were known to be more than solvent, could neither sell the goods which crowded their warehouses, nor discount their bills. Many great houses were brought to the brink of ruin, and not a few sank beneath the struggle. Half the cotton mills of the country were closed, and the skilled operatives suffered much distress. Notwithstanding all this, the country was seized with another and a worse mania of the same kind ten years later, and recovered from it only after more aggravated sufferings had been endured. A few keen and clever men made immense fortunes, and more netted thousands by knowing when to sell; but the majority, as was inevitable, were plunged into grievous loss or utter ruin.

Railways hold on land the same relative position as ships on the sea, and exercise a powerful influence on trade and prices. In 1850 the total mileage in Great Britain was only 6621, and in the whole world 24,487. Now, in the former case, the railways opened and at work have a reported mileage of 21,174. The ordinary paid-up capital is £364,037,405, and the guaranteed, preferential, and loan and debenture stock £637,072,816. The number of passengers conveyed, exclusive of season-ticket holders, during the year was 929,770,909. The weight of goods and minerals conveyed was 334,230,991 tons; the gross receipts from them were £44,034,885, and from passenger traffic £37,361,162, or an average from both sources of £3844 per mile of line open. The working expenditure was £47,876,637, or 56 per cent.; the chief part being in the form of wages. Upwards of 350,000 men are directly employed. Adding those employed indirectly, half a million are dependent for a livelihood on railway enterprise. In 1850 the ordinary cost of land-carriage for goods was £3 per ton for 100 miles, or six times the present amount.

Railways are among the soundest investments. The excitement, waste, and recklessness that marked the mania of 1845-6 have long since given place to careful working and judicious management. Profits depend on the prosperity of the country, on the state of trade, on the cost of fuel, on the weather, and on the absence of accidents and of strikes. Weekly traffic reports enable an approximate calculation to be made of actual earnings and of prospective dividends. Some lines come to be regarded as favourites because of prudent management, or economical working, or immunity from accidents. The North-Western attained its present high credit, in part, from a belief, widely diffused, in the rigour of the auditing, whereby numerous items of expense were charged to revenue instead of to capital. A general opinion that any stock is well thought of enhances its reputation and its value.

According to a return issued in January, 1897, the length of 154 tramway lines open is 1009 miles, and the total capital expenditure £15,195,993. Only twenty-seven miles were added during the previous year. The number of passengers conveyed was 759,466,047; the gross receipts were £4,151,016, and the working expenses £3,105,511. The excessive cost and "loading" of some of the earlier tramways, preventing a profitable return upon a fictitious capital, and often ending in bankruptcy, and the smirched character of many of the promoters, have created a strong prejudice. Yet many persons deal in them largely, and with satisfactory results. Care should be exercised in the selection, for it is easy to make fatal mistakes in the choice.

CHAPTER XI.

MINES.

FROM the time of the great discoveries by the Spaniards of gold and silver in South America hope and cupidity have been eager to share in what seemed to be fabulous wealth. The comedy of *Eastward Hoe!* first performed in 1605, and ascribed to the joint authorship of Ben Jonson, George Chapman, and John Marston, expresses the popular opinion then cherished as to the supposed wealth of Virginia, as the vast, unknown region beyond the Atlantic was termed: "Gold is more plentiful there than copper is with us. All their dripping-pans and pots are pure gold . . . and as for rubies and diamonds, they go forth on holidays and gather them by the sea-shore." The covetous hunger after wealth, aroused by such rumours, is also shown in Michael Drayton's spirited *Ode to the Virginian Voyage*, and in Ben Jonson's *Alchemist*.[1]

Iron and steel manufactures rapidly developed

[1] Act ii. scene i.

under new and improved mercantile appliances. The first iron bridge on a large scale was erected in 1776 over the Severn at Coalbrookdale. In 1802, 168 blast furnaces were at work, producing annually 170,000 tons. Steam was also applied to the drainage of mines, and to the raising of their produce to the surface, and this, combined with improved methods of constructing the working galleries, and providing effectual ventilation, gave a great impetus to this important branch of industry. In 1762 only 570,774 chaldrons of coal were brought to London. The quantity increased by 1785 to 675,995. The last return, for 1895, gives 189,661,362 tons raised in the United Kingdom, valued at £57,231,213. The number of persons employed in mining was 739,097, of whom 589,689 worked underground; 559,824 being engaged in coal mines. The quantity of salt raised was 2,236,000 tons, valued at £763,629.

Metals were produced from British ores during the year in the following quantities: pig iron, 7,703,459 tons; fine copper, 579 tons; metallic lead, 29,687 tons; white tin, 6290 tons; zinc, 6654 tons; and silver from lead, 280,434 ounces. The estimated value of the whole at the places of production was £76,601,257. Home coal and iron, though representing a large industry and an enormous capital, make an unsatisfactory show when judged by results, owing to competition, strikes, royalties, and heavy fixed expenses. Risks and speculations abound. Successful coal and iron companies are few, and failures are numerous and serious.

Land and exploration companies, especially in South Africa, look for valuable results from selling or leasing some of their extensive mineral properties. The prospects are good; remembering the great wealth of the Transvaal and other districts. The Kimberley Diamond Fields have become famous for their riches, but this branch of mining is fickle, owing to the caprices of fashion, and the constant risk of outbreaks from local jealousies and rivalries, and is highly speculative. Moreover, the enormous "loading" of some of the concessions has created a fictitious paper capital, that is perpetually being thrown on the market.

Mining shares therefore require caution, as the notorious and disgraceful case of the Emma Mine demonstrates; but, with good judgment, large profits can be made, notwithstanding Bacon's caution, "Moil not too much underground, for the hope of mines is very uncertain."[1] Indeed, they offer greater opportunities than any other kind of investment. The Richmond Mine produced in

[1] *Essay on Plantations.*

twenty years 83,183 tons of lead, 15 tons of gold, and 460 tons of silver ; the total worth exceeding five millions, and £915,502 was paid in dividends. £5 shares sold at £16. Other mines have done as well, or better. Many that pay no dividends are yet in a sound and hopeful state, though not sufficiently developed to yield present returns. Shares are bought and held for a time, with a view to probable value, or in order to watch the market for a rise, which is certain to occur as soon as there is a prospect of dividends. Values are then often doubled or quadrupled.

West and South Australia present possibilities on which even a sober forecast would be thought by some to be extravagant. The aggregate nominal capital of companies formed in connection with mining, financing, and a few subsidiary concerns, is a little over forty-six millions within two years. A growing interest is being taken in this market, which bids fair to become a leading market for speculators. It is impossible at present to say how many of the swarm of new undertakings will prove to be successful, until something more definite is known of the actual returns. In certain cases rich results have been indicated, and undoubtedly some will prove to be large prizes. The output of gold is growing. In 1895, according to official returns, it reached 231,512 oz., valued at £880,000.

The number of persons interested as investors in mines is very large. Our register embraces nearly 100,000, compiled from the shareholders' lists at Somerset House. Circumstances have arisen, especially in the Transvaal, to depress values, but, judging from experience, this is only temporary. A revival of business in this department may be confidently expected. With the opening of new districts, with improved methods of extracting the ore, and with favourable and authenticated reports of crushings, an impetus will be given to the mining market, and investors may anticipate gratifying results. Among mines and exploration companies we believe in the future of the following, among others: the Associated Groups in West Australia, the British Dominions Exploration, the Mount Catherine Gold Mine in the Coolgardie district, the Talunga Gold Fields Development Company, near Adelaide, Aladdin's Lamp, Great Boulder, Hannan's Brownhill and Mount Lyell, in Australia, and, among South African, City and Suburban, Crown Reef, Durban Roodepoort, Ferreira, Henry Nourse, Meyer and Charlton, and Worcester mines. As an instance of valuable information being placed at the disposal of our customers, we were in a position in 1895 to advise the purchase of shares in the Associated Gold Mines of Western Australia, about 29,000 of which we were able to place at the par price of £1. They subsequently reached $3\frac{1}{2}$ in the market.

CHAPTER XII.

CORPORATION STOCKS.

LOANS for municipal purposes are extensively dealt in. Raised for such objects as paving, drainage, lighting, and water supply, the payment of principal and interest is secured on the rates, and is usually deemed safe. The amount of such debts in the United Kingdom is £106,141,632. The chief stocks are those of the City Corporation, of the London County Council, and of places like Manchester, Liverpool, Birmingham, Glasgow, &c. Most of them, at existing prices, yield only about $2\frac{1}{2}$-$\frac{3}{4}$ per cent., and the fluctuations in price are inconsiderable. In buying, notice should be taken of the time of redemption, lest the purchaser loses any premium he may have paid. So far as the imperfect data exist, down to the year 1893, and not including the whole indebtedness of the kind in Scotland and Ireland, for which there are not complete returns, a sum of £240,000,000 has been borrowed by Municipalities and by Local Boards of

Health, Boards of Guardians, School Boards, and other authorities, for various purposes.

The Public Works Loan Commissioners issued a circular in December, 1895, to various local bodies who made application to be allowed to repay loans before the time agreed upon. The London School Board, for instance, asked for leave to repay about three millions, and a like amount was offered by various local authorities. The Treasury department intervened to forbid the arrangement, although heretofore it has been the practice to accept repayment without question. The reason assigned for the refusal was that, although the practice worked well enough when the amounts were comparatively small, it could not be allowed to an extent of six millions at one time. It was apprehended that other local authorities might apply to repay the loans which they have obtained from the Treasury, amounting in all to nearly twenty-two millions. It was said that such a contingency would destroy the solvency of the Public Works Loan Board, and would impose a heavy and unjust burden upon the taxpayers.

There is, however, another side to the whole question. From the point of view of the borrower, the application was natural and reasonable. With a glut of money, Local Boards, School Boards,

Sanitary Authorities, and others, can go into the open market and borrow money more cheaply than they can from the Commissioners. It would be possible, therefore, to pay off their indebtedness to the Government, and at the same time to diminish the annual charge for the benefit of the ratepayers. But they are also taxpayers for Imperial purposes, and in that capacity it is said by the Treasury that their interests must be studied.

The Local Loans Stock, amounting to £38,856,034, by means of which money has been raised and advanced to local authorities, bears interest at the rate of 3 per cent. It was created under the National Debt and Local Loans Act, 1887, at a time when high-class securities were much lower in price. The stock is now quoted at the large premium of nearly 11 per cent., and is not repayable until 1912. It was urged therefore by the Treasury that large repayments on account of loans could not be employed in cancelling the stock, except on terms which would involve the ultimate insolvency of the capital account; for every million received in repayment would cancel only £900,000, because of the above premium.

The only other way of investing the money would be in Consols, which at their present price yield about $\frac{1}{2}$ per cent. less than the average interest earned by loans to local authorities. The Treasury therefore decided that, in future, applications to repay local loans in advance shall be complied with on three conditions: firstly, that three months' notice be given; secondly, that the applicants agree to repay at such times and in such instalments as the Treasury require, after consulting with the National Debt Commissioners; and thirdly, that for every £100 outstanding on the loan account, such sum shall be repaid as may be certified to be equivalent to the price at which £100 of Local Loans Stock can be purchased.

Of course, looking at the matter from the departmental point of view, nothing can be said against the substantial justice of the decision, but there is a much wider question. Why should the Government enter into competition with the great body of the investing public? The leading municipal corporations of the country experience no difficulty in raising loans at a reasonable rate of interest. Usually the amount required is subscribed several times over. Thousands of persons are always to be found ready to invest their money in perfectly safe securities of this kind that are easily negotiable. A recent illustration is furnished by the issue, in March, 1896, of £71,854 Ipswich Corporation Three per Cent. Redeemable Stock. The tenders for it amounted to £933,966, and applicants at

£110 6s. 6d. only received about 4 per cent. of what they applied for. Allotments in full were not made below £111 10s., and £10,000 was subscribed as high as £112 11s. 6d.

The Treasury can only enter into competition by means of money raised in a similar way ; but there is no necessity for a great Government department to become an intermediary between the local authorities and the investing public. The latter are quite competent to manage their own affairs, and the former are precluded from borrowing in excess of their rateable security. In all matters of finance, commerce, and industry, the less there is of Government interference the better. Affairs of this kind can be far more easily and advantageously carried on in the open market, and the prices of emission will always be regulated by the current value of money.

A cognate objection arises in connection with the Post Office Savings Bank. The Post Office does for the nation what no individual could possibly do for himself in the transmission and delivery of letters and papers. It has added other functions, and undertaken other duties, professedly in the public interest, but chiefly with an eye to larger profits, so as to hand over a greater surplus to the Exchequer by means of indirect and unnoticed taxation. The gross receipts from the Post Office and the Telegraphs, according to the last returns, were £14,639,000, out of which a profit of £3,632,000 was paid into the Exchequer.

The action of the Post Office with regard to the telephones was characterized by what would be styled sharp practice if perpetrated by private individuals. In 1869 the telegraphs were acquired on extravagant terms, at a cost exceeding ten millions. At that time the telephone was not invented or dreamed of, but a general clause was inserted in the Act, which the Courts held, when the question was raised in 1880, to constitute an absolute monopoly for the Post Office, not only of methods existing at the time of the passing of the Act, but of any others since devised, or to be devised, in connection with telegraphy by means of electric wires, including all such inventions as the phonograph, the telephone, and the photophone. The case was decided on a mere technicality, and on a stringent verbal construction of a comprehensive clause in the Act.

The Telephone Companies were driven into an arrangement to pay a royalty to the Post Office, and the cost was thereby greatly enhanced. Whether it will lessen through the Post Office taking over the trunk lines, April 4, 1896, remains to be seen. What has been for many years a necessity in America, used at reasonable rates, is a costly luxury in England, owing to the toll levied by the Post Office. Many more business houses, and probably ten times the number of dwelling-houses, are supplied with telephone communication in the United States, because of the greater facilities and the lower cost. The Telephone Companies there work in alliance with the Post Office, while both are distinct. From every country telegraph station a telephone wire branches out to most of the gentlemen's houses in the district, as well as to commercial premises, so that orders can be transmitted, and inquiries made, and much time and labour saved by being able to communicate direct, at slight cost.

With the enormous growth of the remunerative Money Order business there has been little, if any, alteration in the methods devised forty years ago, when the scheme was in its infancy. It would appear as if the design was to cause the public as much trouble and irritation as possible in cashing the Orders. Literal traditions are kept up, while their essential spirit is violated by the functionaries themselves in their rigid adherence to red-tape. Pedantry pervades the Department, and the Quarterly Postal Guide is crowded with petty and vexatious rules. The primary object of the Post Office is to raise the largest possible revenue. A subordinate and incidental object is to convey the letters of thirty-nine millions of people, who are fined in ingenious petty ways as a penalty for not observing hundreds of trivial regulations and exceptions, which life is not long enough to master, and which only irritate by their microscopic character.

How far some departments of Post Office business interfere with trade in the open market is a question on which much controversy wages. Bankers, for instance, complain that they are handicapped by the way in which Money Orders are issued and deposits are received and paid in the Savings Bank branch. Insurance companies also allege that they are unfairly treated through the operation of the Annuity and Insurance department. It is said that the machinery and the staff of the Post Office are used in a way that places private undertakings at an unfair disadvantage.

The arguments advanced in connection with banking demand consideration. The amount standing to the credit of depositors in the Post Office Savings Bank in the middle of November, 1896, was £107,830,000, being an increase during the year of £10,480,000. It is also stated that 35,874 persons deposited the maximum annual limit of £50 in one sum, or an aggregate of £1,793,700. Under the new rules deposits are also received for investment in Government stock up to £200 in one year, and to £500 in all, instead of £100 and £300 respectively, as used to be the case.

The increase is not surprising when it is remembered that the rate of interest allowed, $2\frac{1}{2}$ per cent., is more than can be obtained elsewhere with existing values, and on the highest possible security. The amount credited for interest during the year was no less than £2,015,903. But at the recent and present price of money it cannot be earned, so that the business is really carried on at a loss. Owing, moreover, to the intricate checks devised, so as to guard against mistakes and defalcations, it is said that every transaction, both of deposit and withdrawal, costs on an average nearly sevenpence. The actual cost cannot be determined, because much of the work in receiving houses and local offices is done by general members of the staff in the midst of other duties.

Besides all this, bankers naturally complain that depositors are allowed to transmit money free, or at nominal charges, and to nominate persons to receive the amount on death, if under £100—although the official difficulties interposed, and the pedantry of red-tape, render the latter practically inoperative—thus unfairly competing with ordinary banks. Even manifest public advantages ought not to be conceded unjustly or at the expense of other great sections of the community. It is further stated that the National Debt Commissioners are offering exceptional terms of £3 0s. 10d. per cent. to friendly societies which now place their funds in trustee savings banks, though it is difficult to perceive how such an amount can possibly be paid except at a loss to the Exchequer.

CHAPTER XIII.

COMMERCIAL COMPANIES.

THESE include a large and miscellaneous class, such as manufacturing concerns and gigantic shops and stores which have been turned into limited companies; hotels, breweries and distilleries; shipping, canals, docks, and harbours; tramways, omnibuses, and cabs; telegraphs and telephones; and the supply of gas and water. British shipping registered under the Merchant Shipping Acts amounts in number to 21,206, and in tonnage to 8,956,181. Of steam vessels the number is 8263, and the tonnage 5,969,020. Lloyd's *Register of British and Foreign Shipping* shows that during 1896, 579 vessels, of 841,447 tons, were launched in the United Kingdom. Only one-fourteenth of the number and the tonnage were sailing vessels. The war ships built in Government and private dockyards amounted to 59, of 148,111 tons. The total output was less than in 1895 by 109,520 tons. The proportion to steamships was much higher. Of the entire number, 16,547, or about three-fourths, are engaged in the home and foreign trade, and they employ 240,458 persons.

Trading companies are always attended with a measure of risk. Even if they pay large dividends for a time, the capital is by no means secure, or an adequate amount is not written off for depreciation of plant and stock. The business is never so carefully and economically administered as when it belonged to an individual or to a firm. Moreover, there are risks arising from keen competition, from caprices of fashion, from the launching of other companies with more seductive baits, from overtrading, from careless purchases, from waste and speculation, and from similar causes. If 10 per cent, or even 5 per cent., be paid—probably out of capital—for a time, and the holder then has to dispose of his shares for one-fourth of their cost, he is manifestly a heavy loser. Not a few such instances occur annually. They have proved to be mere castles in the air, with lofty battlements, long corridors, and spacious apartments ; all of which, being unsubstantial and shadowy, are tenantless.

Gas companies are fairly sound investments. Occasionally a scare arises that a new and cheaper illuminant may be invented. Electricity is the most formidable rival, but for domestic purposes coal-gas is likely to continue in great demand. Profits are large, and the shares are for the most part well held. The last Parliamentary return relating to all authorized gas undertakings in the United Kingdom, other than those of local authorities, gives the receipts of the Metropolitan companies at £5,402,197, leaving a gross profit of £1,756,443. Outside London the total receipts were £7,604,022, and the gross profit £2,139,291. Measured by cubic feet of gas the receipts for London represent 3s. 10d. per thousand, and in the provinces 4s. A similar return for gas undertakings belonging to local authorities gives the total receipts at £6,402,046, and the gross profits, after allowing for certain cases in which the expenditure exceeds the receipts, at £1,721,011; these receipts represent an average of 3s. 4d. per thousand cubic feet of gas, or 6d. per thousand less than the average for London, and 8d. per thousand less than in the provinces, as stated above.

With improved and economical methods in generating and storing electricity, and in applying it to a variety of purposes, an impetus will be given to the shares of electric lighting companies. Those formed for laying and working submarine cables—now extended to every quarter of the globe—have hitherto been manipulated by a "ring." The expense of working and of repairs is great, as is the risk of fracture, and the transmission of messages is largely affected by the state of commerce. English waterworks furnish a steady form of investment, and are likely to extend with the increase of local self-government.

As regards manufacturing and trading companies, it is essential to allow for casualties, for contingent liabilities to pay up the capital, and for commercial fluctuations. As a rule, small ventures should be declined, and those liable to severe competition; with such as spring up in new and untried countries. Especially should further liability be avoided, as in the case of banks and insurance companies which treat the uncalled capital as a reserve fund. It may never be required, and will not be, so long as business is prosperous and large gains are secured. Yet, in the event of commercial depression or of financial panic, it may be found needful to call up the working capital, to the great inconvenience, or loss, or ruin of many persons.

It is needless to enter into details regarding investments in other things, each group or member of which has its own market and its own special sources of information. There are personal and local reasons, and what may appear to be accidental circumstances, that largely determine their selection.

CHAPTER XIV.

AMERICAN VENTURES.

THE great and rapid development of railways in America has brought many securities on the English market. Some are very good, others are extremely bad. The whole system of management in the United States differs from the one in vogue in this country. "Pools," and "deals," and "cut rates," exert a disturbing influence. Returns of traffic are not always reliable. The powers exercised by "presidents," with enormous salaries and with opportunities for making money out of contracts and by rigging the share market, are perilous to the interests of shareholders. Political influence is largely exerted, and politics form a lucrative trade with unprincipled adventurers in America.

Hence, although many lines, such as the New York Central, the Pennsylvania, the Illinois Central, and others are ably managed, and are comparable for construction and equipment to the London and North Western, the Midland, the Great Northern, and similar English roads, the confidence of investors has been so rudely shaken by repeated repudiations, bankruptcies, reconstructions, and assessments of notorious roads like the Erie, the Philadelphia and Reading, the Wabash, the Union Pacific, and many others, that ordinary stock is, not unnaturally, viewed with suspicion and dislike. With regard to the second of the above lines, the question is often asked whether there is a reasonable hope of recuperation? English investors have provided during the last twenty-five years at least eighteen millions sterling in its shares and bonds. If to this enormous sum be added unpaid interest and dividends, the aggregate becomes still more serious.

It is a pitiable story. All concerned know too much about suspended coupons, and first, second and third mortgages, and deferred income bonds, and voluntary assessments. They have been made to run up and down the gamut of hope and fear. Plausible statements have been made, and estimates without end, all more or less roseate, have been issued, but their realisation is a thing yet to be desired. Of voluble talk, by successive presidents, managers, and receivers, there has been more than enough. Brilliant but empty promises have been as thick as blackberries. Solid pudding, in the shape of actual dividend, has been conspicuous by its absence. It is not surprising, therefore, that many English investors in American railroads will only accept First Mortgage Bonds—that are really bonds, and not illusory—or Gold Bonds payable in London. Even then there is a haunting fear of possible repudiation, or of an utter derangement in the market value by some political panic. Yet, by exercising due precaution, numerous good temporary investments are to be found in American railroads.

The marvellous development of the Western and Southern States calls for increasing facilities of communication; but, in the absence of personal knowledge of the country, it will be well to seek advice from reliable experts in order to estimate the value of new and prospective roads. Through lack of this many millions have been hopelessly sunk in American lines. They have been over-capitalized by reckless "watering" of the stock. The origin of the expressive phrase is attributed to a plutocrat who began life by purchasing cattle along the Hudson River Valley for sale in New York. He gave the animals salt, and then as much water as they could imbibe, because they were sold by weight. Fictitious capital has been created by a mere stroke of the pen, without any actual increase of property.

Considerable money has been made by judicious investment in American stocks, as is shown later in the chapter on Temporary Investments, and there is every facility for making more by watching the markets and knowing when to buy and when to sell. The panic caused in the closing days of December, 1895, in connection with President Cleveland's message to Congress on the affairs of Venezuela, as already mentioned, caused an enormous number of shares to be flung upon the market by timid English holders. The result was that prices rapidly deteriorated. The depression was sure to be only temporary. Those who had the discernment and the courage to purchase were rewarded within three weeks by the gradual recovery, and they were able to realise to great advantage. It was not to be supposed that the great trunk lines of America, with their perfect equipment, their volume of traffic, and an established reputation, could be permanently affected by what, after all, was a false move on the political chessboard, made for ulterior purposes of the game.

American Railway Stocks are quoted in dollars; most of them being in $100 shares, excepting those in the State of Pennsylvania, which are fixed by law at $50. Five dollars may be taken as equal to a sovereign, so that fifty American Railway Bonds or Shares of $100 each are equivalent to £1,000 English Stock, nominal value.

CHAPTER XV.

FOREIGN STOCKS.

FOREIGN stocks are not regarded with much favour; being largely speculative. Some of them are more or less rotten, like those of Chili, Bolivia, Paraguay, Peru, Argentine, and other South American countries, which are badly governed, or are liable to constant revolutions, or have the vicious and dishonest habit of repudiating their obligations. Debts were contracted under the pretence that the money would be applied to works of public utility and to mineral and commercial development; whereas it was squandered on luxurious living by political adventurers, on military and naval display, and on similar wasteful expenditure, or it was openly stolen and misappropriated, or was illegally spent in paying interest on other and dubious claims; a modern version of *A New Way to Pay Old Debts*. This condition of things explains the periodical panic in foreign stocks, which are handled only by daring speculators, who have freely to discount the extreme risk.

A Select Committee of the House of Commons, under the presidency of Mr. Robert Lowe, afterwards Viscount Sherbrooke, made a searching inquiry into the circumstances attending the making of contracts for foreign loans, and into the causes which led to the non-payment of principal and interest. The inquiry was not directed to the old defaulting States of Greece, Spain, and Turkey, but to the four South American Republics of Honduras, Costa Rica, San Domingo and Paraguay, whose recent default was peculiarly aggravated and deceitful. By a series of clever but unscrupulous operations on the Stock Exchange, the loans were forced up to artificial prices. Important information was suppressed, and false statements were made.

The Committee reported that certain persons, whose names were given, had been "regardless of the financial resources of the borrowing States ; had violated undertakings that the proceeds were to be spent on works calculated to develop the industrial resources of the different countries ; had resorted to means which in their nature were flagrantly deceptive," with a view of inducing the public to lend money upon a totally insufficient security ; and, by trading upon credulity, had obtained money and then betrayed the interests of the lenders. One beneficial result of the inquiry was that the investing public became more wary with regard to foreign loans.

States that are well-governed, and have established a reputation for prompt payments, are viewed more favourably. They yield a higher return than English funds, but knowledge and care are needed to deal in them with confidence and success. The hypothecation of special sources of revenue for the payment of interest is a guarantee in little more than in name, for no means exist of enforcing it in case of default.

Egypt is an exceptional instance. England and France hold such a gigantic stake in that country, and occupy such a position, that terms were effectually dictated in the interests of foreign bondholders. But Egyptian stocks are not what they were in the palmy days of Ismail Pasha, when he was Khedive, and freely expended the money so readily furnished, on stringent terms, by English and French investors. There is a quick and active market for foreign stocks. Transfers are made with little expense.

Some investors are attracted by foreign railways, because of the higher rates of interest, but the stock is always seriously affected by disquieting political rumours and by the absence of any effectual check upon the management.

CHAPTER XVI.

THE TRANSFER OF STOCKS AND SHARES.

VARIOUS methods prevail in the transfer of stocks and shares. They are commonly known as Inscribed Stocks; such as are transferable by deed; and those to Bearer. In the case of Inscribed Stocks no certificates are given, but the names of the holders and the respective amounts are carefully entered, or inscribed, in books kept for the purpose at the Bank of England or by other bankers. They are regarded as the safest form of security. No transfer can be effected without the actual presence of the person whose name is recorded, unless a power of attorney has been executed authorizing some one to act for him. The cost of this is 6s. 6d. for sums less than £20, and 11s. 6d. above that amount. Application has to be made in the Power of Attorney Office, on a form provided for the purpose, which gives all details as to procedure.

The form has to be lodged before 12.30, and will

be ready in the afternoon of the same day. It has then to be signed by the vendor, and again returned to the bank. In any case, the stock-holder or his attorney must be accompanied by some one known to the bank authorities for purposes of identification, unless he be a member of the Stock Exchange or a banker. The object of all these precautions is to prevent the holder of Inscribed Stock being deprived of it without his consent or knowledge. The following stocks are transferable at the Bank of England, in any amount, except those printed in italics, which must be in multiples of £1. The first seven on the list are redeemable in or after the years named.

£2 15s. per cent. Consolidated Stock, 1923 ("Goschens").
£2 15s., ditto, reduced from Three per Cents. in 1884 by Mr. Childers, and redeemable in 1905.
£2 10s. per cent. Annuities, 1905.
£2 15s. per cent. Annuities, 1905.
Local Loans £3 per cent. Stock, 1912.
Metropolitan Police Debenture Stock, 3 per cent., 1920.
India £3 10s. per cent. Stock, 1931.
India £3 per cent. Stock, 1948.
Bank Stock.
Annuities for Terms of Years.
Red Sea and India Telegraph Annuity, expiring August, 1908.
Metropolitan £3 10s. per cent. Stock, 1929.
 „   £3 per cent. Stock, 1941.
 „   £2 10s. per cent. Stock, 1949.
Liverpool £3 10s. per cent. Stock.
Manchester £3 per cent. Stock, 1941.
Birmingham £3 10s. per cent. Stock.

Birmingham £3 per cent. Stock.
Swansea £3 10s. per cent. Stock.
Hull £3 10s. per cent. Stock.
Wolverhampton £3 10s. per cent. Stock.
Nottingham £3 per cent. Stock.
New Zealand £4 per cent. Consolidated Stock, 1929.
„ £3 10s. per cent. Consolidated Stock, 1940.
New South Wales £4 per cent. Stock, 1933.
„ „ £3 10s. per cent. Stock, 1918 and 1924.
Queensland £4 per cent. Stock, 1915 and 1924.
„ £3 10s. per cent. Stock, 1924 and 1930.
Egyptian Government 3½ per cent. Preferred Stock.
Eastern Bengal Railway " A " Annuity, expiring July 30, 1957.
Eastern Bengal Railway " B " Annuity, expiring July 30, 1957.
Eastern Bengal Railway 4 per cent. Irredeemable Debenture Stock.
Scinde, Punjaub, and Delhi Railway " A " Annuity, expiring December 31, 1958.
Scinde, Punjaub, and Delhi Railway " B " Annuity, expiring December 31, 1958.
East Indian Railway 4½ per cent. Irredeemable Debenture Stock.
Oude and Rohilkund Railway 4 per cent. Debenture Stock, 1898.
South Indian Railway Perpetual 4½ per cent. Debenture Stock.

Dividends on the 2¾ per cent. stock are payable on the 5th of January, April, July, and October, until April 5, 1903, when the interest will be reduced to 2½ until 1923, when the Government has the right of redemption at par. This stock is quoted *ex div.* a month previously to the date of payment. Of late years the warrants are transmitted by post under a special form of request, which obviates much trouble in the case of country holders.

Arrangements can also be made for the accruing dividends to be invested in fresh Consols, when the amount of stock held is under £1000. The fee payable on every transfer is 9s. on amounts under £25, and 12s. above £25.

Canada Inscribed Stocks and Cape of Good Hope 4 per cents., with the Victoria Inscribed Stock, are transferable in any amount and by similar procedure, but free of expense, at the London and Westminster Bank, with the exception of the 4 per cent. Canada Reduced 1910, on which there is a stamp duty of 2s. 6d. per cent. South Australians are transferred at the office of the Agent-General for the Colony, 1, Crosby-square; and the Ceylon Inscribed Stock, the Jamaica, the Natal, and the Western Australia at the offices of the Crown Agents for the Colonies, Lothbury.

Another large class of stocks are transferred by deed, involving no personal attendance or identification. The holder is entitled to a certificate under the company's seal, showing the amount held. When it is desired to sell either the whole or a portion another transfer deed has to be prepared, signed by the vendor and the purchaser, and duly registered at the office of the company. Not the slightest alteration or erasure should be passed unless it is initialled by the transferrer, and also that every particular required in the deed is duly supplied. Some companies have special forms of transfer. In any case immediate registration should be seen to. The usage of the Stock Exchange allows ten days for the delivery of registered securities, so as to give sufficient time for execution of the transfers. When a temporary loan is obtained on stock, without the absolute sale being made at the time, it is usual to take a blank transfer, which is held by the bank or the person lending the money as security until the loan is paid off.

In the case of American railway shares the custom is not to register the names of the actual proprietors, but of bankers or other well-known persons, who act as agents in England for the railways, and who undertake to receive and duly transmit the accruing dividends. The latter sign a form in blank on the back of the certificate, which can then be transmitted from one person to another, no transfer deed being necessary; so that they are practically shares to bearer. If a purchaser desires a fresh certificate in his own name, he can obtain it by sending to an agent in America, who will go to the office of the company and exchange the old certificate for a new one. It is quite safe, however, to accept the usual form of certificate endorsed, so long as it is allowed to remain blank.

The third form of transfer is by bonds and shares payable to bearer; requiring neither registration nor any legal document. The usual name given is Scrip Stocks, and they include all foreign Government stocks and most American railway bonds and shares. The former have attached to them a sheet of coupons. Care should be taken to see that they are intact, so far as regards future dividends. They bear a distinguishing number, which is the only mode of identification. However convenient for purposes of expedition and inexpensive transfer, there is, of course, the danger of their being lost or stolen.

It may not be unnecessary to suggest as a cautionary remark that the deeds should be kept in the owner's possession, or in a box with a Safe Deposit Company, of which he alone retains the key. He should only remove the coupons when they fall due, paying them into his bankers for collection; and should never allow the original documents to pass out of his hands, unless for purposes of raising a loan upon them. Constant difficulties arise in administering the estates of deceased persons through missing securities, the custodians being unknown; and they are sometimes misappropriated.

CHAPTER XVII.

BROKERS AND JOBBERS.

DIFFERENT branches of commerce have their Exchanges, or places in which dealers meet to transact business. The Royal Exchange in London was founded by Sir Thomas Gresham, in the time of Queen Elizabeth, on the model of the Continental Bourses. Merchants assemble to dispose of various commodities in bulk; and ship-owners, financiers, and agents of all kinds meet them. Coal, corn, wool, metals, and different sorts of produce or of manufactured goods have their respective centres and marts; regulated by settled rules and customs, to which usage has given the force of law. Stocks and shares are bought and sold under like conditions, in a place devoted exclusively to such matters. The presence of a stranger is regarded as an intrusion in England; but the New York and Paris Stock Exchanges have visitors' galleries, whence the busy, excited, clamorous scene can be surveyed.

Stock Exchange transactions date back more than two hundred years. As a matter of convenience, buyers and sellers of stocks and shares met for business at first in the parlour of the Bank of England, and then in Change Alley and in the Royal Exchange, as an open market, to which all had access. In 1801 the stone of a permanent Exchange was laid. Recently, after repeated enlargements, the present commodious structure was built. The members, some 3600 in number, are tenants of the shareholders, are elected by ballot, pay an entrance fee of £525 and an annual subscription of thirty guineas, and elect a Committee for General Purposes, whose decision on all internal matters is final. About 2600 clerks are admitted on special terms. Stringent regulations are framed, and those members who cannot meet their engagements on settling-day are "hammered" in the midst of the day's business, and proclaimed as defaulters.

The members, who form a private club, or close corporation, as rigid as any trade union, make it their business to buy and sell securities, either on their own account or on commission. The House is divided into markets for various kinds of business. The leading provincial Exchanges are those of Liverpool, Manchester, Leeds, Birmingham, Sheffield, Edinburgh, Glasgow, and Dublin. On the Continent special regulations are framed by Government, which do not concern these pages. The procedure of the Stock Exchange has formed the subject of numerous litigations and judicial proceedings, treated at large by Melsheimer and Gardner in *The Law and Custom of the Stock Exchange,* and in Royle's *Laws Relating to English and Foreign Funds.*

With the rapid expansion of business, and with the growth of the accommodation, numbers of persons have been tempted into the ranks of stockbrokers and stockjobbers, in the hope of quickly realising a fortune amidst the noisy and excited scenes. Stories, freely circulated and credulously accepted, of lucky individuals making fabulous sums before noon on a given day, have lost nothing in the process of narration, as they served to arouse admiring envy, and promised a short and easy cut to riches. The widening area of securities, the growth of companies, the increase in investors, and the accumulating wealth of the community of late years, have opened up new methods and have provided greater facilities for investing.

It is no longer possible to keep the Stock Exchange as a close preserve for the exclusive transaction of business. Just as physicians and surgeons object to any outside their professional monopoly being allowed to treat patients, and just as lawyers rigorously maintain their traditions against all intrusion of what they call "the lay mind," so the members of the Stock Exchange resent and forbid, as far as they can, any operations by persons who are not in "the House."

Whatever may be thought of the rule, the question arises, and will have to be met, why the public should be expected to conduct financial business in a particular way and only through one set of men? Do the public exist for their special benefit, or should not the advantage of the individual or of a limited class be subordinated to the good of the whole community? There are good and bad, both within and outside the portals of the Stock Exchange, and no reason exists why a really sound business should not be conducted beyond the charmed circle.

Members of the Stock Exchange are known as jobbers and brokers. The former are merchants. The latter are agents, who act for the outside public; buying and selling stocks and shares on commission. Their practice is to resort to a jobber, or merchant, who keeps a supply of stocks, usually of a specific class, and who is ready to buy or sell, as the case may be. He quotes two prices; the one price being that at which he is willing to purchase, and the other that for which he will sell. But he does not know whether the broker is an intending buyer or seller. Whichever he elects to be, the jobber must deal with him at the quoted price. He makes his own profit on the "turn," or difference between the two, and he determines the price, in competition with other jobbers, by the supply or demand at the moment. Having made a price, he is bound to deal, if required, though in the less negotiable kinds of stock he will probably decline to make a price.

It is obvious that the supply or demand on the part of the public controls the prices of all stocks. If, for instance, on any given morning the total amount of orders received by brokers to sell North Western Railway Stock amounted to £400,000, while the total amount of orders to buy amounted to £1,200,000—although of course the total would be unknown to any one—the brokers would apply to the jobbers for quotations, and the price might be, say, 190 to 190¼. As, however, there would be more buyers than sellers the jobbers would soon run short of the stock, and would thereupon become reluctant to sell, and make higher quotations; the price rising exactly in the proportion of the demand, and as long as it continued. If, on the other hand, there were more sellers than buyers the reverse result would follow. Hence, as all buying and selling are carried on for the general public, jobbers are practically driven to make higher or lower quotations, and thus it is that the law of supply and demand influences prices.

When prices are quoted, as Consols, $111\frac{7}{8}$-$112\frac{1}{8}$, the meaning is that an intending purchaser would have to give £112 2s. 6d. for every £100 of stock, while a seller would receive only £111 17s. 6d. This is the "turn of the market," which forms the jobber's profit. In addition, the broker's commission must be met, if the bargain is made through him. A jobber does not, or should not, charge commission, for that would be making a second profit, in addition to the one which he makes out of the difference between purchasing and selling prices. The rules of the Stock Exchange permit commission to be charged on the actual value, but brokers seldom exercise this right, because, over a large number of transactions, a natural average adjustment takes place between stocks above and below the nominal value.

Much has been written in the public Press relative to the want of uniformity in the commissions on Stock Exchange dealings. In one case a correspondent uttered a plaintive complaint that his broker, without any risk to himself, makes almost as much profit on a transaction as the one who has to run all the risk. He wrote: "On looking through my accounts I cannot help being struck by the size of the amounts representing my broker's charges, which seem to me quite disproportionate to the services rendered." He then gave specific instances where he made about $7\frac{1}{2}$ per cent. in six weeks on one transaction, and 6 per cent. in about three months on another transaction; whereas the broker's gains work out at 29 per cent. and 26 per cent. respectively. In another instance a firm of family solicitors, having to employ different brokers from time to time, said that they were struck with the want of uniformity in the commissions charged, adding that "there are no two scales alike." "In a recent case where we had to sell some Brewery Preference Shares the broker charged 9d. for partly paid shares, and 1s. for fully paid shares; but our own regular brokers informed us that their charges would have been 6d. and 9d. respectively."

As the Stock Exchange Committee does not profess to lay down any rule as to brokers' charges, it is only natural that much discrepancy should prevail, owing to the inevitable competition. It is pointed out that a difference arises between permanent investment charges and those for temporary investments. It would be well for clients to inquire beforehand what a broker intends to charge, and if they consider his commission unreasonable they can take their business elsewhere. There is said to be a vicious system which has come up in recent years, under which lawyers and bankers who introduce business to a broker expect a share of the commission; and, therefore, the broker has to make a higher charge.

One reason of the excessive charges is that in many cases a provincial broker is employed, who, in his turn, has to employ a London broker, who again transacts his business with a jobber, so that there are three middlemen who have to be repaid out of the transaction. The root of the difficulty, however, lies in the fact that people have got into the habit of supposing that they cannot deal direct with a jobber. This is quite a fallacy. The Universal Stock Exchange buys from and sells to principals direct, ignoring the broker, thereby saving any intermediate expenses.

Any client wishing to deal receives from his broker a written contract, setting forth the name of the stocks or shares and particulars of the bargain. In addition, he pays the commission, the rate of which exhibits a gradual tendency to rise. In theory, the broker is required to set forth on the contract the name of the jobber with whom he has carried out the transaction, but this is not always done. Perhaps it is not too much to say that it is very often omitted. Thus the object is defeated of enabling customers to verify the accuracy, if they choose, by reference to the jobber. If the broker refuses to give the information, he can be held responsible for any loss on the transaction, or it may be cancelled. His client has the right to go to a jobber, when named, and ask to see his book, in order to verify the figures. Probably this is not done once out of a thousand cases.

The contract-note specifies the day on which the settlement is to take place. This usually comes once a fortnight, as regulated by the Committee of the Stock Exchange. If all transactions were for cash, and for actual delivery, the process would be simple; but, as already stated, nine-tenths are for a "carrying over." Arrangements are generally made for doing this on agreed terms; in other words, for deferring until the next settlement the completion of the sale or the purchase. This process is carried on again and again, and may be done indefinitely. The postponement is regulated by the medium price—*i.e.*, the one between the buying and selling price ruling at noon on the day for carrying over. In addition to the broker's commission for buying and selling, he sometimes charges for carrying over, and also the Contango. Whether any ultimate profit is realised by the investor depends upon the final selling price and the length of the deferred procedure. Anyway, the broker is sure to gain, as is shown in the next Chapter.

CHAPTER XVIII.

EIGHT MILLIONS WASTED YEARLY.

THE vast business of the Stock Exchange is conducted under conditions and circumstances that are perpetually fluctuating. Therefore the greatest accuracy is needed in making contracts and in keeping the accounts. The details of each transaction are carefully set forth in the contract, which every one should insist on receiving, as it forms the basis of the negotiation, and is the only standard for determining the accounts. A jobber's contract always bears upon its face that certain stock was bought of or sold to the purchaser.

The contract with a broker, on the other hand, always sets forth that the stock was bought or sold by order of and for account of the client. It is essential to remember that a broker is not responsible for the proper fulfilment of the contract. If the jobber fails with whom he has dealt, any money is lost that a client may have advanced. The only responsibility attaching to the broker is in a case where he has omitted to give the name of the jobber.

On settling day a statement is delivered, in which the investor is debited with the cost price of the stocks, and with commissions, and also with any Contangoes, if the stocks have been carried over. He is credited with the amount realised, less commissions on the sales, which commissions may vary from $\frac{1}{8}$ to $\frac{1}{2}$ per cent., with a charge of from 6d. to 1s. per share on American railways, and from $1\frac{1}{2}$d. to 2s. 6d. on mines, according to value. If he chooses to exact the full amount allowed by the rules of the Stock Exchange, he can do so. The Contango charges vary in amount; and on certain kinds of securities they are very high. By dealing with the Universal Stock Exchange direct, the whole of the profits are secured to the customer.

Supposing A. to have bought £10,000 Brighton "A" Stock at 160, and sold the same later on at $161\frac{1}{4}$, employing a broker to do the transactions, who charges him $\frac{1}{4}$ per cent. commission—which is only one-half of what the rules of the Stock Exchange permit to be charged—his account, when rendered, would be as follows :—

A.B., in account with John Jones, broker.

Dr.					Cr.			
		£	s.	d.		£	s.	d.
£10,000 Brighton "A" @ 160		16,000	0	0	£10,000 Brighton "A" @ 161¼	16,125	0	0
Commission on buying ⅛ per cent.		25	0	0				
Do. on selling ⅛ per cent.		25	0	0				
Cr. balance		75	0	0				
		£16,125	0	0		£16,125	0	0

The profit is £75, whereas, had he dealt direct with the Universal Stock Exchange, it would have been £125, as he would have had no commission to pay, which amounts in this case to £50. This is supposing that the purchase had been completed during the account then running, without carrying over the stock from one settling day to the next.

A customer also sent up the following account, and asked us to let him know the result if carried out for forward delivery on our Three-Monthly Settlement System as compared with the result if done through a broker. He sold 100 shares Rio Tinto on June 20, at $24\frac{3}{4}$ for delivery, but the price going down somewhat, he postponed the delivery from account to account and repurchased the shares later on at $23\frac{7}{8}$, thus making a clear profit—if it had been done for forward delivery on our Three-Monthly Settlement System—of £87 10s., as there would of course be no interest charged, as no purchase money was advanced. If this had been done through a broker it would have extended over six accounts, the commissions amounting in all to £43 15s., *i.e.*, 2s. 6d., per share for the original sale, and five times 1s. 3d. per share for postponement of delivery. The Contangoes amounted altogether to £15 3s. 10d., thus making the total of unnecessary charges £58 18s. 10d., which deducted from his total profit, left only £28 11s. 2d. to go into his pocket, instead of the £87 10s. if he had conducted the business through us. On this one little transaction alone it will be seen the broker netted over double the amount that the investor had for himself.

In another case, B bought £5,000 Dover A. at 111, £1,000 District at 28, and £2,000 Denver Preferred at \$41½, making the total purchase money £6,660. Ten days later he sold the above at $113\frac{3}{8}$, $27\frac{1}{4}$, and \$44 respectively, which yielded £6,821, showing a profit of £161 5s. The interest, at 5 per cent. on the actual purchase money, for as many days as the stock remained undelivered or unsold, amounted to £8 10s. 9d. Deducting this from the £161 5s. left a total profit to the investor of £152 14s. 3d. Had this business been done through a broker, the commission—charged only at $\frac{1}{8}$, which is the lowest charge, it being sometimes $\frac{1}{4}$

—and Contangoes would have amounted to £36 2s. 2d. as against the £8 10s. 9d. on the Three-Monthly Settlement, making the total profit to the investor only £125 2s. 10d. as against £152 14s. 3d. by dealing with us.

In another case, on business amounting to £50,000, B received, as the result of Fortnightly Settlements, £748 5s. 3d. as profit from his broker, who on his part pocketed £248 15s., at his customer's expense in the shape of commissions and Contangoes. In other words, the man who had to bear the entire risk had three-fourths, while the broker had one-fourth for his perfunctory and unnecessary services. The result of the same transaction for the same amount, dated from precisely the same period, if carried on direct with the Universal Stock Exchange, would have been expenses on the 5 per cent. rate, £92 16s., while the investor's profits would have amounted to £903 9s. In this way he would have gained 22 per cent. more on the identical transaction.

These are, no doubt, somewhat startling statements, but that they are borne out by the figures can easily be tested and proved by every reader for himself. If any reader, who has been dealing with a broker, will only work the matter out, he will be able to see that this is in no way exaggerated. Of course it will not always show the same difference. But undoubtedly it will always show a great difference, amounting exactly to the excess of the broker's Contangoes and Commission over the small amount of interest charged on the Three-Monthly System for the use of the money, and it represents no alterations in price or in duration of time. It may be again pointed out for the sake of emphasis that the 5 per cent. charge is made only for as many days as the purchase remains undelivered or unsold, while the Contangoes on the fortnightly system are for the full account. On a purchase made just before the account day and sold on the day following, as is often the case when small quick profits are taken, the Contango would be charged for the whole period of from fourteen to nineteen days, according to the duration of the account, even though the transaction was open for only two days. It will probably never have struck the investor that he is paying a large percentage of his profits to his broker for the honour of having him conduct his account. Directly he begins to see it in this light, it will appear to him, as it has done to many intelligent readers, that to continue dealing in the same costly way would show that he had more money than sense.

It will be seen that brokers are middlemen. Like other intermediaries they increase expenses without enhancing actual values. The great and just complaint in all business is that the prime cost of the producer and the manufacturer, with their legitimate profits, are doubled or quadrupled by middlemen before reaching the consumer, who has to bear the whole burden, just as the taxation of all commodities ultimately falls on him. Why should not the public deal direct with the jobber or merchant, instead of having to employ these middlemen, with the added risk of having to invoke the aid of law to enforce payment of money alleged to be due from another broker on an entirely different account, as in the case of Anderson *v.* Sutherland, in January, 1897? The only answer to the question is that such is the pleasure of the ruling powers in the Stock Exchange; just as an unwritten but inexorable law forbids a client consulting with a barrister excepting through the costly medium of a solicitor.

Some idea of the extent and costliness of brokers' charges, all of which the investing public have to bear, may be gathered from the fact that the brokers on the London Exchange, and the large number in provincial Exchanges, are said, on a moderate computation, to derive £8,000,000 per annum from their transactions as agents. Without impugning the honour of a great body of men, it is obvious that under existing methods a broker can, if so disposed, sell or buy stock for his clients and charge them with the lowest or the highest prices of the day, retaining for himself the difference at which the transaction was actually carried out. The broker is a needless but costly luxury. He does not add one iota to the intrinsic worth of the commodities in which he deals. The services rendered, such as they are, could as easily and more advantageously be performed by the investor in direct dealings with a jobber.

It may be asked, What would become of the thousands of brokers if the plan of direct dealing with jobbers came into vogue? The obvious reply is that they would have to find some other direction for their talents and energies. It is sometimes said that thirty-nine millions of people do not exist for the benefit of forty-two thousand lawyers; although the latter seem to think otherwise. A similar remark may be made of brokers, without implying any disrespect for individuals. It may be objected that the fees are small, and only infinitesimal compared with the magnitude of the sums dealt in. But they speedily mount up in a series of transactions, and absorb an appreciable portion of the profits. It is not surprising that the Stock Exchange has been likened to a barn where the fowls repair daily to pick up golden grain freely flung in by the public.

The sure way of conducting investment accounts economically, and with the greatest chance of profit, is to deal directly with a well-known and responsible firm of jobbers, like the Universal Stock Exchange, and thus avoid the numerous charges made by the brokers, or middlemen. Care must be exercised in the selection, and in ascertaining the financial strength and the standing of the firm or the company. The fullest confidence ought to prevail on both sides. The company must be satisfied of their customers' ability to meet engagements, and also that they will honourably carry out mutual transactions and treat the Company with confidence. Customers, on their part, should take the utmost pains to be convinced of the stability and rectitude of the jobber to whom such important matters are entrusted, that orders will be diligently executed, the stocks promptly delivered, and the accounts cheerfully settled. Time is an essence of the contract.

Whether the dealer selected, after such cautious inquiry, be an individual, or a private partnership, or a registered company, there should be on their part a thorough knowledge of all the ramifications of a most intricate business; observance of all instructions received; a business record that is unimpeachable; and sterling integrity and promptness in every transaction. Moreover, there should be frankness in giving needful particulars and in satisfying legitimate inquiries.

CHAPTER XIX.

INEVITABLE FLUCTUATIONS.

IT has been already pointed out that changes in the value of stocks and shares are mainly determined by the universal law of supply and demand, and thus the Stock Market affords unlimited scope for judicious investments, particularly in good dividend-paying stocks. It has as many possible combinations as the letters of the alphabet. Not a day, and scarcely an hour, passes without some fluctuations in prices, which furnish opportunities to intelligent investors. Attentive observation, accompanied by sound judgment, will perceive that occasions are constantly presented for buying good stocks at a low figure, which are certain to advance. Great changes seldom come as a surprise. They are foreseen, and their effects are discounted long before they occur. Hundreds of investors make it their business to watch prices and to study events, and thus are able as by intuition to calculate to a certain degree the immediate course of business on the market. At the same time they take care to avail themselves of such intermediate fluctuations as are sure to happen, knowing that a stock rarely, if ever, moves straight up or straight down for any period, but vacillates widely and frequently between extreme points.

Nothing is more certain or remarkable than the periodicity of prices. They run in cycles of varying intervals and duration. Tooke was one of the first to point this out in his *History of Prices*. It applies not only to stocks, but to all commodities. At one period the range of prices falls lower than it has been for some time. This lasts for a few months, or a year or so, and complaints of dulness and depression are general. Then prices begin to rise in one market, and others are speedily affected, until the ascending movement becomes general, and at length a high range is established for a longer or shorter period. Again there is a reaction, and the reverse process is again brought about. As a rule, however, there is a permanent tendency to a rise, provided the existing state of affairs is favourable, through a lack of suitable new outlets for accumulating capital, or from the necessity for a large amount being kept in securities that are quickly realisable. The steady appreciation in Consols during recent years illustrates this tendency.[1]

[1] See Appendix C.

The price, or realisable value of every article, let it be what it may, is regulated by the supply and demand of the moment; that is to say, it is fixed by the number of buyers and sellers. At one time the investing public seem suddenly to discover that the best possible investments are English railways. Thereupon they rush in to buy these stocks, thus creating a demand, and, as a consequence, sending up the prices. At another time they arrive at the conclusion that the mining market shows the best chance of a profitable investment. Hence they neglect the other markets and turn their attention to mines, with the same results that prices are driven up. A shrewd investor will always make use of these temporary fluctuations, and on the system of short, quick profits will doubtless reap a very great advantage over those who only think it worth their while to take notice of larger movements.

We may point out here that, as a general rule, it is a mistake, when sending his order, for an investor to strictly limit the price at which he wishes to buy or sell, as, with the constant fluctuations, changing every moment, he may just miss the market by a small fraction, and not get an early opportunity of such an advantageous price again. At the same time it is as well to make up his mind beforehand as to *about* what figure he intends to give or take. The principal point, however, is to know when to buy and when to sell. Some people do not think of buying until a stock has experienced a considerable rise. In like manner, when it has greatly fallen, and probably has reached the lowest point, then they sell. The chances are, in both cases, that a turn is about to take place, and they find themselves in the unpleasant predicament of being too late. They have purchased at the highest and sold at the lowest. Naturally, they lose their money and then attribute it to ill-luck.

Luck, as a matter of fact, has far less to do with business in general, and with investing in particular, than is commonly supposed. What is often attributed to luck, or chance, or to fate, is really the product of prompt judgment and common sense. Careless inquiries, erroneous information, haste or hesitancy, are the real causes of failure, and the result is exactly what reasonable persons might have anticipated.

There is no secret in successful investments, except the art of buying at a low price before the rise sets in, or of selling on the eve of a fall, and thus reaping the benefit of the upward or downwad movement. If it be asked, How is the critical juncture to be known? the obvious reply is that the knowledge is to be attained, and can alone be attained, by the exercise of average intelligence; as is the case with all other affairs of daily life. In no way can experience be gained so easily and so profitably as by the judicious purchase of one or two good dividend-paying securities for forward delivery on the Three-Monthly Settlement plan.

Yet money might often be made and more money gained by seeking available information and taking ordinary care in the choice of stocks. Many of these which appear unlikely are favourable at some time or other, the precise period being determined by the special circumstances of each case. No invariable rule can be laid down, but a careful and regular study of the highest and lowest prices, as published in the Universal Stock Exchange weekly *Market Report*, compared with former prices over a lengthened time, will enable any person of average discernment to decide as to the most likely securities in which to invest. It is well to learn to form one's own opinion, and to trust to one's own judgment. The man who shrinks from entering the water will never learn to swim.

CHAPTER XX.

BOOMS AND PANICS.

A FALSE alarm of fire, the escape of a little gas, the slamming of a door, or the cracking of plaster in a public building, suffices to cause a multitude of people to lose their heads, and to give way to wild alarm. It is then a struggle for *sauve qui peut*, and the weakest are sure to go to the wall. A little thing suffices to create a scare or to get up a panic in the Money Market and the Stock Exchange. They are sensitive to every breath that stirs. A remarkable illustration was furnished in December, 1895, in the case of President Cleveland's message to Congress respecting Venezuela. For a few hours it was supposed that he had the whole of the United States with him; but Nemesis was swift and certain.

The aboriginal inhabitants of Australia have a weapon known as the "boomerang," made out of a flat, curved piece of wood, which cleverly flung, returns to the feet of the person who throws it. In the case of the United States the financial boomerang recoiled with deadly results. When the first excitement, however, passed by, the common sense of the great body of the American people came to the rescue. Bankers and business men in particular instantly perceived the disastrous effects of the Presidential message. Within three days a panic suddenly burst upon Wall-street. Before noon 400,000 shares were flung upon the market for realisation at any price, and nearly double the number were dealt in before that night. Prices kept dropping, until in some cases they reached 14 points. From 50 to 75 per cent. was demanded and paid for money. Even the soundest railway properties, like New York Central, the Pennsylvania, and the Illinois Central, lost from 6 to 10 points of the market value of three days before.

Mr. Chauncey Depew, president of the New York Central Railway, speaking to a gathering of leading business men, said that the depreciation in American securities amounted in three days to $400,000,000. Another great financial authority estimated the total loss to bankers, stock-holders, and to commerce during the week at $1,000,000,000, or £200,000,000. Probably both these conjectures were much in excess, but in all such cases a long period elapses ere confidence can be restored. Nothing is easier than to create a panic; but nothing is more difficult to allay. When public suspicion or timidity is aroused, and there are apprehensions of impending loss, the alarm spreads like fire on a common, and a sure method is taken to accomplish what is dreaded. A run takes place on a bank. Every one demands his money. It is ignorantly supposed that the coffers can be made suddenly to overflow with gold; as if bankers locked up their customers' balances and deposits for the pleasure of handing them back at a moment's notice.

No institution, however solvent and well-managed, could bear such a strain. Not even the Bank of England would be equal to it. Hence, in all such cases of ridiculous panic, a number of sound institutions and firms are certain to be brought down, through no fault of their own, but solely owing to the childish dread that precipitates a crash. In 1892, one of the largest, wealthiest, and best-conducted building societies in London—the Birkbeck—experienced a sudden run upon its funds. How the rumour of insolvency originated no one was able to explain, but in the course of a few hours the office was besieged by an excited, impatient, clamorous crowd, all wishing to withdraw their money at once. The adjacent streets were filled from early morning for several days, and enormous sums were paid out as fast as the accounts could be verified. Fortunately, there were large available resources in Consols and in other liquid securities. Then a reaction gradually set in. Some who had withdrawn their money in a fright paid it in again when they saw the actual coin and bank-notes forthcoming, but of course they forfeited interest and entrance fees. A similar scene was witnessed in Lombard Street in January, 1879, during an equally senseless run upon the London and County Bank.

At such a time it behoves all who can exert a salutary influence to do their utmost to stem the rising tide of foolish and unreasoning panic, and to show how absurd and suicidal it is. Calmness and firmness will do much to allay the fears of the timid; and a display of confidence will inspire it in others. Some years ago, during a spasmodic run upon the London banks, a wealthy and well-known merchant did much to check it by driving up to his bank in a cab with £20,000 in gold, which was carried through the noisy crowd and openly paid in as a proof of his own confidence in the stability of his bankers. Some of the would-be withdrawers paused, reflected, and then decided to allow their money to remain. New arrivals, seeing the turn in the tide, altered their intentions. The panic was checked, and in a few days it wholly ceased. In another instance, the manager had the reserve of gold brought from the strong room, and placed in glittering heaps beside the cashiers; the sight of uncounted wealth, which seemed to be fabulous and inexhaustible, produced a similar effect.

A sudden elevation or depression is easily caused in the Stock Market. Disquieting rumours about foreign affairs; reported or anticipated bankruptcies; the bursting of a reservoir; a great railway collision; a sudden and extensive withdrawal of bullion; or mere vague street talk that a panic is impending, serves to bring it about. Timid holders of stocks and hesitating investors become alarmed. They hear that others are about to sell, and so they press in, hoping to be first. It is like pouring oil on flames. The excitement spreads, and prices go down with a rush. Those who know this, and the convulsions to which it leads, learn to act accordingly.

The number of commercial panics in the last half century, since the great one of 1825-6, when 770 banks stopped payment, mainly through the number of bubble companies, were the following: in 1847, through the railway mania; in 1857, through the American failures; in 1859, owing to the fear of a European war; in 1866, through over-speculation in limited companies; in 1870, through the Franco-Prussian War; in 1885, through the Russian attack on Afghanistan; in 1887, by the war panics in Paris and London ; and in 1895, as before cited, in the case of the United States and Venezuela.

Ordinary prudence suggests a preliminary survey and a calm inquiry before yielding to and increasing the alarm. Are the suggested adverse causes likely to operate? Do they even exist otherwise than in the imagination? If they do exist, is there any true relation between them and the apprehended results? Will the supposed evils be averted by people frantically rushing hither and thither and proclaiming that things are going to the bad? Are not the evils, if real, likely to be aggravated? If imaginary, will not the fiasco overwhelm every one with vexation and remorse, when fancied danger brings actual loss and disaster? It is well to ponder questions like these before yielding to a panic; notable instances of which have occurred within living memory ; although advising men to be calm and collected under such circumstances is like Shakspere's famous illustration about preaching patience, as put into the mouth of Leonato.[1]

Sometimes the process is inverted, for the sake of getting up a "boom." Its object is to inflate prices, and to create an artificial scarcity, so that people may be tempted to buy at enhanced and fancy values. The theory of modern advertising may be

[1] *Much Ado about Nothing*, v. i.

expressed in a formula—" Blow your own trumpet loud enough and long enough, or get a number of persons to blow it for you, and the world will at length take you at your own appraisement." It is the same with a financial "boom." One class of securities may be diligently talked up and written up until the unthinking public are led to believe in what seems to be the universal theme.

Usually, when emphatic and repeated advice is given by unknown and untried persons to invest heavily in a particular thing, it is well to reject the advice, and sometimes to do exactly opposite to the suggested course. A respectable dealer will not jeopardize his reputation by becoming sponsor for shady transactions, and his counsel, when given, may be relied on. Moreover, the Three-Monthly System is a safeguard alike against the ill-effects of booms and panics, while enabling the judicious investor to take advantage of their occurrence. It often happens that the most ready to seek advice are the least disposed to take it. They go first to one oracle and then to another, and if, as is the case with most oracles, they are not mute or enigmatical, the impression made lasts just so long as it takes for another to be produced, which, in its turn, yields to the next in an unending series.

CHAPTER XXI.

PERMANENT AND TEMPORARY INVESTMENTS.

EVERY business venture has in it more or less of the element of uncertainty. It is entered upon in the hope of attaining a success which must, for a time, be problematical. A manufacturer produces new designs on the chance of selling the goods and extending his connection. A merchant brings a cargo from a distant port, or he consigns one to the other side of the world, hoping that a profitable market will be found. A tradesman stocks his shop every season with articles about which he is quite uncertain as to whether they will meet the taste or strike the fancy of his customers; though he trusts that an inclination to purchase will be awakened by the attractiveness of his wares. Caterers of every kind produce or display an endless variety of articles that minister to the needs, or the pleasure, or the vanity of the public. Into all such cases this element of uncertainty or risk largely and necessarily enters. Without it, no business could be carried on; and the same applies to financial transactions.

Philosophers have written lengthy disquisitions, and have carried on wearisome controversies, in order to determine the dew-point, when the thick, viscid, noxious vapours of night are changed into the pellucid, clear, refreshing dew of the morning. In like manner much has been said and written for the purpose of distinguishing between permanent and temporary investments. But they insensibly merge into one another. The border-line is so dim and vague as to be almost impalpable. In theory a permanent investment is supposed to mean comparative safety, if not absolute certainty; but an element of uncertainty enters into every such transaction. Every investor, therefore, runs a certain amount of risk, as it is the unforeseen that frequently happens, If money is placed where the actual value is subject to little or no fluctuation, and if the dividend upon it is regularly paid, though the amount be small, the name of permanent investment is given. But if the money be placed out, not so much with this view as with a reasonable expectation that the market-price of the capital stock will rise, it is temporary investment. The gain in the latter case is styled profit, while in the former case it is styled interest; but the two things are practically identical.

For instance, an investor buys £1,000 South Western Ordinary Railway Stock for forward delivery in three months. The stock perhaps goes down, and he has no opportunity of selling to advantage. On the date of delivery he therefore takes it up, pays for it, and has it transferred into his name; being content to hold for the sake of the dividend regularly paid upon it. This is clearly a "permanent" investment.

Another investor buys £1,000 Brighton Deferred Stock for delivery in like manner. Just before the date of delivery, however, the price suddenly rises several points. He thereupon seizes the opportunity and sells his stock at a good profit. As this happens before the date of delivery, he does not need, of course, to have the stock transferred into his own name. This is a "temporary" investment. The only difference is that the latter investor has the opportunity of selling to advantage before the date of delivery, and may probably repeat the transaction over and over again, making considerable profit; while the other simply allows the stock to lie in his safe, and is content with the comparatively small advantage of the dividend. The intention of both in the outset, however, was exactly the same.

Another group of investments may be designated

as fluctuating. They include most of the commercial joint-stock enterprises, with banks and insurance companies having considerable uncalled capital, and ordinary railway stocks. In dealing in such matters, three points have to be borne in mind, viz., the security of the capital, the amount of further liability, and the interest likely to be secured. The purchasing price necessarily varies with circumstances. It is so even with gilt-edged securities like railway debentures and Consols. The former, though paying a uniform 5 per cent., have been known to vary in price as much as 14 per cent. in five years. Consols, though displaying, on the whole, an upward tendency, have also been subject to disturbing influences. During the last eight years they have ranged from $93\frac{3}{8}$ to $113\frac{7}{8}$.

It is not to be expected, therefore, that other investments will have a fixed value, nor is it desirable. The secret of success is to know when to buy at the ebb, and to sell out at or near to the flood. Taking a wide range of circumstances, spread over a period, if the general trend is downwards, a particular stock has no attractions. But if against a downward tendency on the whole a much larger rise can be observed at some stages, the conclusion is that an investment may be made with a fair prospect of success. Not to burden these pages with minute and complicated tables, a selection will be found in Appendix F.

Some persons prefer a settled investment, such as Consols, or corporation stock, or railway debentures, from which a small but fixed income is derivable. Of late years the market prices of such securities have risen, and they yield only about 3 per cent., or even less. The tendency is towards yet higher prices, with a corresponding diminution in the return. It seems to be becoming "fine by degrees and beautifully less," until it threatens to reach the vanishing-point. As a result, persons of this description spend their lives and resources in what Cowper describes as the profitless toil

> "Of dropping buckets into empty wells,
> And growing old in drawing nothing up."[1]

What are termed "gilt-edged securities" have obvious uses. They will always be in demand for what are regarded as permanent investments. Under the existing stringent law of trusteeship, those who occupy a fiduciary position, and have no personal interest in the amount of income secured, will, naturally enough, protect themselves and avoid all risk and anxiety by investing trust-money in such securities, even if they barely yield $2\frac{1}{2}$ per cent. It is a moot point whether the drastic law applied

[1] *The Task*, bk. iii.

to trustee investments does not effect more harm than good, and whether some less stern and rigid exaction of their liability would not prove better in the long run for the community. Existing regulations, especially when money is abnormally plentiful, and therefore cheap, foster an unfounded and pernicious belief in the minds of other people as to the peculiar safety supposed to attach to the investments defined by the law; thus producing an artificial inflation in values. So long as the fashion lasts, it will be well for the general public to avoid investing in such stocks; because, the more frequent and heavy the transactions, the higher will prices become.

The same remark applies to property held for minors; for persons unable to manage their own affairs; for married women whose husbands would, if they could, speedily dissipate the capital; and for religious and charitable societies, having large bequests and funded property. But such securities as these, with a tendency towards diminishing dividends, are not attractive enough for a large investment to men of business who wish to obtain the best return. Many families are struggling to live on restricted incomes which might be increased 20, 50, or 100 per cent. by other and judicious investments, without any diminution in security. For lack of the requisite knowledge or of good advice they fail to reap advantages enjoyed by others.

If a man chooses to take refuge under rules laid down by the Court of Chancery for the protection of property to a *femme covert*, or to children, lunatics, and imbeciles, and allows his money to lie almost dormant and useless in what are known as trustees' securities, he must not be surprised when his more sagacious and enterprising neighbours reap the reward of their knowledge and courage in returns compared with which his own are infinitesimal. He may, if he will, amuse himself by endeavouring to spin ropes of sand, or by ploughing the sea-shore, instead of watching for the opportunity that always waits on vigilant aptitude, and that comes to the man who is ready to seize it.

Much perplexity exists as to how and why profits are made on the purchase and sale of stocks, which rise and fall while the apparent conditions remain unaltered. The change is mainly determined by the demand and supply at the moment. In other words, it is fixed by the number of buyers and sellers and by their needs or convenience. The same economic law operates universally. Prices of goods, rent of houses or land, wages and hours of labour, cannot be determined by Acts of Parliament, or even by a combination of individuals; whether producers or consumers, employers or workpeople.

Legislative unwisdom tried for centuries to fix

such things by drastic Statutes, all of which failed, though enforced by heavy penalties. If two masters desire the services of one man, or if two purchasers are competing for the same article, wages and prices will advance by an inevitable law. On the other hand, if two men are seeking employment from a master who requires only one, or if there be a superfluity of articles and few purchasers, wages and prices will fall. No artificial rules and restrictions can hinder the operation of this natural law. It applies to Stock Exchange investments, and regulates market values.

The essential principle of commerce, wholesale or retail, in civilized life or in barbarian barter, is to purchase in a cheap market and to sell as quickly as possible at an advance. No commodities are so facile for dealing in as stocks and shares. They require no warehouse room. They involve no expense for carriage. The market is practically unlimited. Buyers and sellers are always to be found. The demand and supply are known, and prices are recorded and easy of access.

Persons seeking thoroughly sound investments should prefer the best dividend-paying Home Railways and American Railways. These are infinitely preferable to many of the projects that have been so freely launched during recent years, and which are certain to end in disaster for the unfortunate shareholders. It is needful to give an emphatic warning against the delusive schemes that have been so assiduously propounded. Instead of embarking in such projects, it is much wiser and safer to buy considerable blocks of dividend-paying stocks, especially when, from temporary causes, the market prices fluctuate. This is greatly preferable to applying for shares in new and unknown ventures.

CHAPTER XXII.

HOW AND WHERE TO SECURE THE BEST RESULTS.

THAT Stock Exchange investments can be rendered very profitable, if carried out on a sound system, as laid down in these pages, is capable of easy proof, and every intelligent observer should be competent to ascertain for himself the truth of the matter. Having shown that it is not at all difficult for any one to acquire such knowledge as may enable him to profitably invest in Stock Exchange securities, it is desirable now to point out where he can best put his knowledge into practice.

It will be patent to every one who has carefully studied the foregoing Chapters that to deal with a thoroughly responsible jobber, and thus avoid unnecessary commissions, is the only proper and successful way of conducting a Stock Exchange account, and nowhere can this be done to better advantage than with the Universal Stock Exchange.

This Company was established many years ago, to meet the constantly increasing demands for a more convenient and economical system of buying and selling Stock Exchange securities, whereby unnecessary formalities and expenses could be avoided, and investors obtain additional facilities for the transaction of their business.

The Company met with such an immediate response from the public, and was so successful in the first few years of its operations, that it removed into larger premises, and was then reconstructed under the present title of the Universal Stock Exchange, Limited. It was again reconstructed in 1895, increasing its capital from £100,000 to £300,000, of which amount £270,099 is paid up. A Reserve Fund of over £50,000 is judiciously invested, as set forth at the end of this work.

In 1890 the Company purchased the lease of its present extensive premises, then known as the front part of Waterloo House. This imposing site in Cockspur Street, facing the statue in Pall Mall, is one of the best in the West End. The whole of the upper part of the building contains the offices of the Company.

Many customers have maintained a connection during a lengthened period, and have entrusted the Company with repeated and growing transactions. Those who have engaged in various transactions with the Universal Stock Exchange testify that it always acts in a considerate and honourable manner. Otherwise, so large and thriving a business could not have been built up. Out of many letters received—which can be shown to *bonâ fide* applicants intending to do business—the following passages are taken ; the names of persons and of places being suppressed, for obvious reasons :

> "During the years I have done business with the Universal Stock Exchange I have never found them otherwise than perfectly honourable and straightforward."

> "In going through my accounts I find that I have received from you over 1,000 per cent. more cash than you have from me. I might thank you for the honourable and straight manner you have always dealt with me, but you do not wish for any thanks. I am sure all you desire is that your customers deal with you as you do with them."

> "If ever a reference as to honest and fair dealing is required, I am at your service, for I deeply appreciate your consideration, and would like to reciprocate."

> "It is only right that I should state that all the business you have transacted for me has been executed in a singularly straightforward and satisfactory manner, and so far very much to my advantage."

> "I have always found your dealings with me fair, or, of course, I should have complained and discontinued, but I have always spoken up for you."

"One thing I like especially in your mode of business—that is, the prompt sending of certificates of stocks and shares which you have bought for me, and which compares very favourably with ordinary brokers' custom of keeping them."

The Exchange is able to deal instantly with any amount or variety of stocks, and delivers the certificates with promptitude. Its financial standing is well known. The salient principles are as follows:—

> The abolition of all commissions and unnecessary charges;
> Special Three-Monthly Settlements, as subsequently explained;
> Only one charge, which is a uniform rate of interest;
> A prompt and straightforward attention to all instructions and communications received from customers;
> And the rendering of clear and concise contracts and accounts, which can be readily understood and checked by the recipients.

The larger portion of the business has been built up on the recommendations of its regular customers to their friends, and this is the best proof of appreciation. The Company transacts business either for forward delivery on the Three-Monthly Settlement System, or for immediate delivery against cash on the Fortnightly System, as fully explained in Chapter XXIV.

In taking up or delivering stock, customers must give a banker's guarantee that the stock will be delivered against the cash at the appointed time or *vice versâ*. In lieu of that the order must be accompanied by at least 20 per cent. of the purchase money, in case of purchase, or scrip, in case of sale, in order to prevent the possibility of any mistake or misunderstanding. All orders must be sent in by wire or letter, no orders being taken over the counter except from old and well-known customers of the Company. Any customer who is able to satisfy the Directors as to his business responsibility is eligible for dealing. The terms for opening accounts are easily accessible to all responsible people. The Directors only desire to know that customers are in a position to meet their engagements. Full particulars will be sent on application.

Orders are promptly attended to and executed at the price ruling on receipt thereof, unless any special limit as to price, either for purchase or sale, is given, in which case, if practicable, the instructions are carried out accordingly. As the Company has its own telegraphic instruments, there is no delay whatever in the delivery of a telegram; but every message is timed at the minute it is received, so that every price can be checked by the *Evening Standard*.

It is erroneous to suppose that customers must be on the spot in order to obtain good results. There is no such necessity. The telegraph enables orders from a distance to be acted upon as promptly as orders given in London. The customer has only to say in his telegram, "I buy or sell so much stock at such and such a price, or sell and buy back at such a price." As soon as his desired price is reached his orders are executed without the necessity of his presence. These remarks are made because correspondents occasionally write that they would gladly adopt the principle of temporary investments as set forth herein, if they were not precluded from doing so by their residence being situated too far from London. Long experience has proved that customers at a distance from the Stock Market are better off in the long run than those who can sit all day long in a stock-dealer's or broker's office, watching the fluctuations of prices.

Full information concerning market movements is contained in the weekly *Market Report* of the Universal Stock Exchange, furnishing in a tabular form the latest prices, and supplying well-written and authoritative original articles on financial and

HOW AND WHERE TO SECURE THE BEST RESULTS. 173

investment subjects of the day, and on allied topics. It is supplied, post free, to subscribers, at a nominal charge of five shillings per annum. Another valuable and original compilation issued by the Universal Stock Exchange is *A Special List for Investors of Perfectly Sound Securities, paying from 2 to 6 per Cent.* Particulars will be found at the end of this book. These are grouped under the heads of Corporation Stocks, Government Securities, Railways, Breweries, Industrial Companies, &c. A bird's-eye view is presented of their respective positions, with the highest, lowest, and mean prices last year.

The Universal Stock Exchange is quite independent of any similar business, and is in direct touch with some 380,000 Shareholders in all parts of Great Britain and Ireland, embracing Investors in Railways, Banks, Mines, Gas and Water Companies, Government and Corporation Stocks, Foreign and Colonial Bonds, Docks, Shipping, Insurance, Telegraphs, Cycles, Tramways, Breweries, and all the principal Manufacturing and Industrial Limited Companies. Out of this vast number of Shareholders in every class of business transacted on the Stock Exchange, securities are constantly offered for sale or desired to be purchased every day, and the Company offers exceptional facilities to such. It is the oldest established, largest, and most extensive firm of dealers in the world, transacting business not only in Great Britain, but on the Continent and abroad, having at times actual accounts open in the following countries :—United States of America, Africa, India, Italy, France, Germany, Belgium, Portugal, and Gibraltar.

CHAPTER XXIII.

HOW TO START AN ACCOUNT.

WE frequently receive letters from correspondents intimating their desire to open an account were it not for the difficulty they find in starting. It is astonishing how many of the letters commence in this way: " I should very much like to open an account with you on your Three-Monthly Settlement system, but do not know exactly how to begin, &c." This difficulty is found very often, not only in this particular case, but in many and various other instances. Persons seem to know how to proceed, but the thing is how to start. To those, however, who have written to us on the subject, or have felt a similar difficulty without writing, we give the following information.

We are prepared to open an account on being satisfied as to a customer's financial responsibility and repectability, and this satisfaction the customer can furnish us in whichever way he pleases, either by references (bankers', solicitors', or trade), or by sending us a statement of his holdings and financial position, or by forwarding cash to be applied as part purchase money of the purchases he wishes to make. We know that many people object to giving references, because they do not care for their business friends to know too much of their personal affairs. To avoid this, we have arranged for all enquiries to be made through a high-class firm of solicitors, so that it is practically impossible for the nature of the business for which the enquiries are made, or our name, to transpire in any way.

Naturally, however, references take some considerable time to enquire about, and notwithstanding our arrangement, a customer may still have an objection; or he may not have any lock-up securities, and therefore has no list of holdings to send. The simplest and easiest way, therefore, for him is to send up some cash as part purchase money. He can either send it as a percentage with each order, ranging from 5 per cent. to 20 per cent., according to the value of the stock he wishes to purchase, or, what is certainly less troublesome, an amount to be applied as part purchase money of purchases generally. We may mention that we allow 5 per cent. interest on the money so sent, and naturally, therefore, the more purchase money a customer has on his account, the less the charge for interest on his transactions will amount to.

It may happen, however, that a customer may not find it convenient to send part purchase money, but he has considerable capital locked up in securities which he does not wish to sell, although he would like to use the money they represent in purchasing other securities. This can easily be done, as we would arrange to procure a loan for him, on most easy terms, on these securities—providing they are marketable—which loan could be placed to his credit, and be used in precisely the same way as though he had sent part purchase money in the first instance. (See page 187.)

Instead, therefore, of writing to us about any difficulty in opening an account, an intending customer, willing to give references, has only to write as follows: " I wish to open an account with you, and herewith give names of my bankers, solicitor, or trade references—as the case may be—through whom I wish you to make enquiries." We then make the necessary enquiries with all possible speed, write the result to the customer, and, if satisfactory, as they no doubt would be, he is at liberty to send his orders. In the second case, where particulars are given, " I wish to open an account with you, and herewith send you a list of my holdings and financial position generally. Kindly let me know if this is satisfactory." In the third mode, where cash is sent, the order can accompany the cash, and will be executed at the price ruling on receipt thereof; so that in this case no time is lost. It will be seen, therefore, that it is, after all, a very simple matter to start an account, as the only point on which we desire to be assured is that every intending customer can and will meet his liability as promptly as we ourselves do; in plain words, that he will treat us as we treat him.

We may also mention here that though we are always ready and willing to make any suggestions, or to give an opinion, or any market information of which we may be in receipt at the time, we cannot and do not act on our own discretion for any customer, but only on his or her distinctly written orders. It sometimes happens that a new customer says: "I am ready to open an account with you, and herewith send, etc., etc., but must ask you to please select the stock you think it would be best for me to invest in, and let me know what you have done."

Now this it is obviously impossible for us to do. Being jobbers, were we to act on an order like this, and it were to turn out an unprofitable transaction, we place ourselves under the suspicion of having chosen that stock for some reason of our own, no matter how carefully our selection might have been made, whereas it is absolutely impossible for us to tell (except by general observation, the same as anyone else can do) how the stock will move; but, as already stated, we are always ready to suggest or to assist the customer in any way that we can.

We hope that this chapter will remove some of the difficulties of starting new accounts, and we shall be much obliged to our readers if they will kindly let us know any other points likely to prove difficulties also, and we will do our best to explain them.

CHAPTER XXIV.

THREE-MONTHLY SETTLEMENTS.

SEVERAL methods are followed in dealing in stocks and shares. On the Cash Cover system, they are bought or sold by depositing with the broker or jobber a certain amount of money, on the understanding that until it is exhausted no more liability shall arise. This is termed "cover," or "margin," and is a percentage on the nominal value of the stock in question; varying from 1 to 10 per cent. A grave disadvantage consists mainly in forced closings. Another is that the usual Contangoes are charged, and must be paid on account days to keep the cover intact. A very little liability, however, often proves disastrous, owing to a sudden and temporary fall in prices. The system is not one to be recommended, and does not concern these pages.

On the Fortnightly plan, stocks can be bought or sold without "cover" or restriction. The dealer has no right to close any transaction without ex-press orders, or unless the customer makes default. Accounts are made up fortnightly, or thereabouts, according to the settling-days on the Stock Exchange, and settled either by payment, or by delivery of the stocks dealt in. If any stocks are open on the first day of the account they are carried over at the making-up price ; Contangoes being charged at the prevailing rates.

Fortnightly Settlements, however, are open to the objection that their regular and swift recurrence is often inconvenient, and may prove disastrous. There is always a danger that some particular stock cannot be carried over. Besides this, on the method pursued by most brokers, their heavy commissions for buying, selling, and carrying over on repeated transactions swallow up most of the profits, and, in many instances, convert a possible profit into an actual loss.

The third system, and manifestly the most advantageous one, is that of the Three-Monthly Settlement, originated many years ago by the Universal Stock Exchange. On this system fixed periods are appointed for settlement, so that investors know the time available for the completion of their investments. Instead of an arbitrary rate of Contango, with the scales of brokerage, a charge is made at the rate of 5 per cent. per annum, reckoned on the actual purchase-money of the stock, from the date of purchase to that of delivery or sale. During the account, the investor can buy back what he has sold, or sell what he has bought.

The period of a Three-Monthly Settlement having been fixed, all transactions are entered upon the statement of account rendered, with interest on each purchase, stated separately, so that it may be seen what each transaction involves for the exact period of its duration.

On this plan the investor has perfect freedom to buy and sell as he likes for three months, giving ample time for every purchase or sale to develop. In addition to the actual saving in money, there is an untold gain in time, trouble, and perplexity, which are avoided through not having to master an intricate series of accounts, largely made up of arbitrary charges, which it is impossible to escape. Moreover, a broker is irresponsible in the event of a loss, and the investor has no voice in the selection of the jobber; whereas by dealing with a large, well-known, and established company, no delay and no risk occur, and there can be no dubious apprehensions as to the completion of the transaction.

The public are beginning to find out wherein their own advantages lie. Viewed in all its bear-

THREE-MONTHLY SETTLEMENTS. 183

ings, the Three-Monthly Settlement system is far the best of any prevailing system of dealing in stocks and shares. The interval is not too long, and yet it is long enough. Advantages similar to those of the Fortnightly System are offered, with other greater advantages which it does not possess, while the manifest disadvantages are avoided. Especially, it may be repeated, is the interest chargeable much less, and other charges are impossible. In extensive investments hundreds of pounds may be saved in a year in this way.

One very important point for an investor to thoroughly understand is how to word his orders for the various classes of securities. It frequently happens that, through ignorance on this point, he buys more than he intended, and is saddled with stock he does not want; or, on the other hand, he buys less, and cannot get the remainder at such an advantageous price. For instance, in ordering Home Rails, an investor may say, "I buy five North Easterns," meaning five hundred pounds nominal value stock; or he may say, "I buy five shares North Eastern," meaning five one hundred pounds, equalling five hundred pounds stock. In the former case, he would be wrong, as, in ordinary Stock Exchange parlance, "five" stands for five thousand pounds nominal value; "one" for one thousand pounds; "ten" for ten thousand pounds' and so on. In the second case, it would be also wrong, as Home Rails are quoted in one hundred pounds stock, not in shares, but if the order read, "I buy five thousand pounds North Eastern," there could be no mistake.

American securities are more confusing, if not understood, but they are quite clear when this is done. Most American Railways issue their capital in shares of one hundred dollars (equalling twenty pounds per share), and the quotation is therefore so many dollars per one hundred dollars share. Fifty shares are nominally equal to one thousand pounds stock, and the price is then reckoned at so many pounds per cent., in the same way as English stock. Thus, " one Denver Preference at 40," means one thousand pounds nominal value at 40 per cent, equalling four hundred pounds. The only exceptions to this rule are Pennsylvania and Philadelphia and Reading shares, which are not one hundred dollars per share, but fifty dollars per share as required by the State law. Thus fifty shares of these would be only equivalent to five hundred pounds, instead of one thousand pounds as in the other cases.

Mines, again, are quoted so much per share; therefore they must be ordered in shares. Thus, "20 Associated Gold at $2\frac{1}{2}$," would mean twenty shares at two pounds ten shillings per share; or, "500 Rio Tinto at 25," would mean five hundred shares Rio Tinto at twenty-five pounds for every share.

CHAPTER XXV.

PERMANENT INVESTMENTS UTILISED FOR IMMEDIATE PROFIT.

EVERY investment has a twofold value, that is, its dividend-earning power and the constant fluctuations in the price or their actual value. Some investors are satisfied with one, some with the other, but the man who uses his capital to the extent of its money-making power is the one who looks after both values and secures his dividend at the same time he is taking advantage of the fluctuations in the price of the security he holds, or of some other as good.

This may sound difficult perhaps, but it is in reality very simple. There are doubtless many investors who are anxious to take advantage of the favourable opportunities constantly presenting themselves for profitable purchases on the system of short, quick profits, but as they have large sums of money practically locked up in permanent in-

PERMANENT INVESTMENTS UTILISED FOR PROFIT. 187

vestments—which they do not wish to disturb as they are solid and dividend-paying ones—they have never seen their way to doing so without realising. To any such we make the following suggestion, which they can see for themselves can easily and advantageously be carried out, and by following up our plan, they can get the twofold value out of their investment; that is, the dividend on the investment itself and the advantage of fluctuations in the prices, at the same time without having to sell their original investment. The plan is as follows :—

We will arrange to procure for them a loan on any good marketable security on satisfactory terms —say, for the purposes of example, four per cent., although of course the rate would fluctuate from time to time according to the value of money. This done, the loan so raised would be used as part purchase money for the purchase of several good dividend-paying stocks on the plan of temporary investments for forward delivery on the Three-Monthly Settlement System. As already explained, there is on this system only one charge, which is interest at 5 per cent. on the actual purchase money, only for as many days as the purchase remains incomplete, and therefore the more purchase money in hand against the purchases, the less the interest charge will be.

The stocks purchased in this way must of course be carefully chosen, giving thought to the promise they show of advancing in price or of a good dividend to be paid on them, but in order to work advantageously, it must be done on the small, quick profit system, securing it directly it is shown, and not running the risk of losing several small turns while waiting for a large profit which may never come. Now-a-days events happen so quickly and communication all over the world is so easy, that movements are shorter and more rapid than in former times, when communication was difficult and tedious.

The successful man of the present day is he who trades upon the maxim of small profits and quick returns, whether in Stock Exchange investments or in any other kind of business. In order to render this plan of taking short, quick profits quite easy to our customers, we are always prepared to take an order for the sale of their stock—at the same time the purchase is made, if they wish— provided the instructions are definite and unmistakable. We then watch the market closely, and as soon as their price is practicable we execute the order.

To fully illustrate this method of utilising permanent investments for immediate profits, we give the following example, based upon actual figures taken from our books :—

A. B. held £1,000 Guinness's Brewery 5 per cent. debentures which he did not wish to sell. Their market value was £1,220, and as he wanted to take advantage of the many opportunities he saw in the fluctuation of prices, but had no available capital, he raised a loan of £1,000 on this security, for three months, at the rate of 4 per cent. This £1,000 he left in our hands as part purchase money on the purchase of the following :—

> Jan. 2nd, £3,000 Dover A, at 106.
> Jan. 11th, £1,000 N. British Def., at 46¾.
> Jan. 16th, £1,500 Consols, at 112¼.
> Jan. 19th, £5,000 Mexican 6%, at 95¾.

which he afterwards sold as follows :—

> Jan. 14th, £3,000 Dover A, at 106⅝, being a profit of £18 15s.
> Jan. 14th, £1,000 N. British Def., at 45¾, being a loss of £10.
> Feb. 4th, £1,500 Consols at 113¼, being a profit of £15.
> Jan. 26th, £5,000 Mexican 6%, at 96¼, being a profit of £25.

It will be seen that he made a profit of £58 15s. on three of his purchases, and a loss of £10 on one = £48 15s. profit on the whole. He then had to deduct interest on the loan of £1,000 at 4 per cent. for three months = £10, added to interest on the purchase money (less interest at 5 per cent. on the part purchase money) = £11 17s. 1d. He meantime received the three months' dividend on the £1,000 Guinness 4 per cent., his original investment, amounting to £12 10s., the whole being as follows :—

CREDIT.	£ s. d.	DEBIT.	£ s. d.
Profit on stocks	58 15 0	Loss on stock	10 0 0
Three months' dividend on investment	12 10 0	Interest on loan	10 0 0
Interest on £1,000 part purchase money	12 10 0	Interest on purchase money	14 7 1
	£83 15 0		£34 7 1
	34 7 1		
	£49 7 11		

so that by utilising his permanent investment he makes nearly £50 in three months, while had he simply held it in his safe, it would only have yielded £12 10s. This process repeated several times during the year would considerably increase his income.

CHAPTER XXVI.

UNPROFITABLE INVESTMENTS.

THERE is but a very small percentage out of the 380,000 shareholders on our list, compiled from Somerset House, who do not hold some unprofitable investments, that is to say, non-dividend-paying ones. Many of them, too, paid excessive prices for their holdings, which now show considerable loss, in fact, there is in the United Kingdom alone, millions of money invested in securities which would come under this heading.

Some people may remark, upon reading the previous Chapter, "Yes, that is all very clear, and it may be profitable to those holding good dividend-paying investments, but what about some which pay me no dividend and only go down in price instead of up?" In reply, we would suggest they should work on the same plan, and earn a dividend in another way. This means that the plan just set forth can be as well applied on non-dividend-paying investments, as on such as actually pay a dividend.

Of course, it will be understood that in all cases the security must be one which has a free market value, even if depreciated.

To those who hold securities which have gone out of existence, or are not marketable, we are afraid we cannot give any assistance. They must regard their lost money in the light of experience dearly bought. But those who hold investments which, although they have been so far unprofitable, and yet have a ready market value, can always utilise them, as was fully explained in the preceding chapter.

For instance, at the present time many people have part of their capital locked up in Railway, Mining, Exploration, and Industrial shares, which they do not like to realise at a loss, as they are undoubtedly good though unprofitable securities, and look as if they will have to be held for years before yielding any profit. While this class of investors have had their capital locked up in this way, they have felt debarred from taking advantage of the constant fluctuations day by day, in the same manner as those who had their capital free. This is quite a mistake, as we proceed to show by the following example :—

A customer of ours held some Mexican Second

Railway stock for years, having bought it at 42, but as the traffics were good, and the state of the country on the increase, he did not wish to sell until he could do so at a good profit, which looked very probable indeed, if he held still longer. This stock, however, lay in his safe all the time, thoroughly unproductive, and he saw no way of utilising such an unprofitable investment unless he realised.

Supposing, however, he heard of our plan, and obtained a loan of £500 at 4½ per cent. interest for three months on his Mexican Second, and with the money so obtained purchased £5,000 District at 28½, £500 Midland at 170, £1,500 Caledonian Def. at 54¼. These he could have sold as follows: —Districts, ten days later at 29½ = £50 profit; Midland, five days later at 170⅝ = £3 2s. 6d. profit; and Caledonian Deferred, 18 days later at 55⅛ = £13 2s. 6d. profit, making altogether a profit of £66 5s.

The interest at 5 per cent. on the purchase money would have amounted to £4 10s. 4d., and being deducted left £61 14s. 8d. From this also must be deducted the interest on the loan of £500 for three months = £5 12s. 6d., leaving a profit of £56 2s. 2d.

This is therefore what he would have made on his

unprofitable investment by carrying out our plan. Of course it does not always happen exactly as we have depicted, because the time may not always be so advantageous, but by careful purchases of good stocks, taking short quick profits, and not following a loss too far, the result is almost sure to be satisfactory. It must, however, be borne in mind that to work this profitably on the system of short profits and quick returns, it must be done direct with a jobber like the Universal Stock Exchange, where the charge is known and fixed, and not through a broker, where the repeated Commissions and Contangoes would greatly reduce the various little profits, and in some cases turn a profit into a loss.

CHAPTER XXVII.

SHORT AND QUICK PROFITS.

A LEGEND is occasionally seen in tradesmen's shop windows, "Small profits and quick returns." Where this is honestly and thoroughly carried out the results are always highly satisfactory, alike to buyer and seller. The tradesman who by shrewd purchases and nimble sales turns his capital over four or five times in a year is contented with a moderate rate of profit. He will realise much more in the twelve months than his neighbour who exacts double the profit, but whose shop is crowded with unsaleable goods. The chances are that he will have to dispose of much of his stock at a sacrifice, because it has outlived the market, or has spoiled in the keeping.

The same rule applies to Stock Exchange investments. Few persons have any conception of the sure results of steady arithmetical progression, or of the way in which compound interest, even at a low rate, swells the principal sum. A few thousand pounds judiciously invested, and realised with similar care every few weeks, and sometimes every few days, although yielding on an average only one-half per cent. at each transaction, will aggregate to an incredible amount in the course of a year.

The precise method of investing in stocks must be determined by their specific character, by the conditions of the hour, and by relative circumstances. There are times when a large and judicious purchase is wise and safe; and every man must judge for himself, as guided by the state of the market. No uniform rule can be laid down. Each must be a law to himself, as experience and common sense may dictate at the moment. Ordinarily, however, and in the absence of anything special or abnormal, it is safe to advise the flying of the kite with a short line, so that it may be easily and quickly drawn in.

The best choice possible having been made, with all reasonable care and judgment, and with a fair prospect of a rising price, advantage should be taken of a fractional rise. Another investment should at once be made, and the operation repeated whenever the chance arises. If there be courage to hold on during a temporary depression, and, still more, during a passing panic, the results must be satisfactory, on a system of averages, always sup-

SHORT AND QUICK PROFITS. 197

posing the original purchases to be in good sound securities.

All this, however, presupposes that the investor does not resort to the customary transactions through an ordinary broker, restricting himself to the usual settling-days on the Stock Exchange, and paying repeated Commissions and Contangoes that will certainly absorb the chief part of any accruing profits. Instead of this it is essential to watch the market, so as to sell and re-purchase, or invest in other securities, with promptitude. Though the fluctuations may be slight, the frequent repetition of the process is certain to eventuate in a considerable gain, always on the supposition already made, that a careful choice has been exercised.

Here is an actual example, and many such might be given: Brighton "A" Stock was bought at a time when there was a reasonable prospect of the price rising. The average amount paid was $157\frac{1}{8}$, and the sum invested was £10,000. It was sold the next day at an increase of a-half. Five days later it was re-purchased at $156\frac{7}{8}$. The process was continued for four months, the total number of purchases and sales being thirty each. Allowing for slight loss and for interest, the net profit on this series of transactions was £1,292, or nearly 13 per cent. on the four months. Now it is possible that, under favouring circumstances, by a master-stroke of prudence, a large profit on £10,000 might have been realised; but, on the other hand, there might have been a heavy loss. In this actual instance, the small but quick accretion of profit, averaging only ½ per cent., or £50, on the whole series of transactions, resulted in the realisation of the handsome return of £1,292 in four months.

The principles above enunciated, and the methods recommended, are applicable to every kind of investment for which a market exists. The great thing is to turn over the money as often as possible, always, of course, exercising vigilance in closely watching the fluctuations of the market, and then taking prompt action. We repeat that the essence of the matter lies in the frequency of the turnover. A small and immediate certainty is far better than large problematical gains that may never be secured. To buy promptly when prices are cheap, to sell as promptly when the market rises, even to a fractional degree, and to go on repeating the process *ad infinitum*, is the secret of success. To be reproductive, money must be in constant use. It will not fructify in the pocket. But a constant outgoing and returning, even though the actual gain on each transaction seems to be infinitesimal, mounts up to an extraordinary degree when repeated over a lengthened period.

It is the old story of the nimble ninepence multiplying itself by frequent repetition, while the tardy pound was dormant and unproductive. "Small profits and quick returns," is safe and certain when applied to judicious investments. Of course, all this implies, as it may be not altogether unnecessary to repeat, that ordinary prudence is exercised in the selection of stock for purchase, and in seizing upon the right moment for sale and re-investment. Decision and promptitude are also essential, so as to be contented with a small and certain rise, instead of waiting or hesitating in the hope of something better being offered next week or next month.

It is strictly true in business of this kind that a bird in the hand is worth two in the bush. A fractional profit every few days, and repeated eighty or ninety times in a year, if suitable occasions offer, is far more advantageous than waiting, and watching, and hoping for a large rise that may never come. "Little and often" is a simple but safe rule. It has borne the strain of experience, and may be confidently recommended for adoption. True, the markets are not always in a condition to allow of such profits being taken, but such is the case very frequently. By going in promptly, and being content with a small profit, it is almost impossible to be in the wrong, on the law of averages.

The near prospect of a rising market is a time to buy, so as to be prepared to reap the advantage. Those who are astute enough and courageous enough to buy when prices seem to have reached their lowest limit, and who are prepared to hold until the higher limit approaches, may reasonably hope to secure considerable profits. They hold blocks of securities which are increasing in value, and by watching their opportunity and seizing upon the auspicious moment to realise, they may expect to reap the reward.

CHAPTER XXVIII.

THE CHOICE OF STOCKS.

FASHION, personal preference, or accident largely determine the choice of stock. Sometimes the swing of the pendulum is towards Consols or English railways ; then towards foreign railways ; or to mines, or breweries, or manufacturing companies. The reasons for the choice cannot always be defined. Political complications, impending war, bad weather, a good harvest, failure in crops, the outbreak of a pestilence, a serious railway accident, storms and shipwrecks, the state of trade, and various other causes, produce fluctuations in market prices, while intrinsic values remain the same. A general disposition is manifested to favour or to reject certain securities, for no particular reason, but because everybody else is doing so. They are talked about in society, they form the theme of newspaper articles, or they seem to be in the air, and the man in the street has something to say concerning them. The fashion is set ; no one exactly knows how or by whom ; but it is sure to be followed.

An intending investor has relatives or friends residing in a country or who are engaged in some manufacture, industry, or trade which happens to be prominently before the public. Or he may possess special knowledge which induces a belief that the chances are good and that the occasion is opportune. Some acquaintance has done well in a similar undertaking, or he himself had a stroke of good fortune in it a few months ago, and he concludes that he may make an experiment. One man is enamoured of mines. Another will not look at them, but holds by railroads. A third rejects both, but pins his faith to banks, while a fourth deals only in American or in Colonial securities. Sometimes this is a result of deliberate choice. In other cases it is the child of habit or of accident. It is as mysterious as the caprices of the palate, or as the unconquerable aversion occasionally shown to certain colours or odours, or as the causes that determine political and religious opinion with the multitude.

It is well, at the outset, to limit the effort to some good dividend-paying stock. It is impossible to know everything at once; whereas, by studying one at a time, difficulties will vanish and everything essential can be learned. Its past history, its recent fluctuations, its highest and lowest prices, with the reasons that influenced them, and the probable conditions in the near future, should be carefully and patiently investigated, so as to form a just estimate of the prospects of an early or an ultimate movement upwards or downwards. All this will aid in a solution of the problem whether, at current prices, it is better to buy or to sell. Experience of this kind can easily be acquired by practice, and by use of personal effort and common sense. The swift runner must first have learned to walk. To seek to know everything at once ends in nothing being really known; nor can any one hope, even if it were necessary, to become acquainted with the fluctuations of all the securities dealt with on the Stock Exchange.

Some of them present a margin for tolerably safe investment. By taking the average of prices over a series of years it is possible to make a reasonable forecast, after noting the influences which affected values. Others fluctuate so often, and to such extremes, that profits can be made only by a careful study of each rise or fall, and of its special causes. This enables a careful investor to anticipate similar movements under similar circumstances, and to turn his knowledge and observation to good account.

It is as true in such matters, as in politics and in domestic life, that "coming events cast their shadows before"; but watchfulness and sagacity are required to read and interpret the signs that infallibly denote impending changes. Hence the paramount necessity for acting upon the advice already given, and to make a close and careful study of the particular stock ; noting the extent of fluctuations, and gathering all possible information, so as to compare and judge.

By the exercise of care and patience, it will become an easy matter to select and watch any stock, so as to learn all about it. This, it may be necessary to repeat, is the first step to success ; and, if followed up with intelligence and prudence, will bring its ultimate reward. Knowledge will teach when stock is dear and when it is cheap ; in other words, when to buy and when to sell, so as to be enabled to secure profits. Some such investments as the following may be confidently recommended. They are all good dividend-paying stocks. In investing in them the risk is less, and the results must be more satisfactory :—Consols, Brighton Ordinary and Deferred, Caledonian Ordinary and Deferred, Chatham First Preference, Great Northern "A" and Deferred, Great Western, Lancashire and Yorkshire, Metropolitan Consolidated, Midland, North British Preferred and Deferred, North Eastern, North Western, South Eastern Ordinary and Deferred, Chicago and Milwaukee, Illinois Central, Lake Shore, New York Central, and Pennsylvania.

CHAPTER XXIX.

CONSOLS, AND WHY THEY SHOULD BE BOUGHT.

IT is erroneous to suppose, as many people do, that only investors with large capitals can deal to advantage in Consols. On the contrary, they are accessible to all—particularly adaptable for temporary investment on the system of short, quick profits, and are thoroughly suitable to small investors, being, as they are, one of the safest investments in the market. They can at any time be bought at a minimum cost and risk, with a prospect of maximum profit. We have found through a long experience that those of our customers who purchase Consols on the short, quick profit system, acting also on the law of averages should the price decline, are generally satisfied with the result of their transactions.

The quotation is a close one; the difference between the buying and selling price being as a rule only $\frac{1}{8}$ or a $\frac{1}{4}$, and the fluctuations generally steady, not being given to any rapid and large depreciation. This of course for repeated purchases and sales is a great advantage. Then, again, it is a security at all times readily marketable, and can always be bought and sold without any difficulty and with little expense. Being so safe, too, and the cost of purchase so small, an investor can buy very much larger amounts with less risk than half the amount he would purchase of other securities; but in order to work to advantage he must be content with small profits, which must be secured as soon as shown, ranging, say, from $\frac{1}{4}$ to $\frac{3}{4}$ per cent.

Taking the last $3\frac{1}{2}$ years, the range of prices in Consols is as follows:

RANGE OF PRICES FOR ONE QUARTER.	1894.	TOTAL FLUCTUATIONS.	1895.	TOTAL FLUCTUATIONS.	1896.	TOTAL FLUCTUATIONS.	1897.	TOTAL FLUCTUATIONS.
1st Quarter	$\{98\frac{3}{4}, 100\frac{1}{8}\}$	$1\frac{7}{8}$	$\{103\frac{1}{8}, 105\frac{1}{4}\}$	$2\frac{1}{8}$	$\{105\frac{1}{4}, 110\}$	$4\frac{3}{4}$	$\{111\frac{1}{8}, 113\frac{3}{4}\}$	$2\frac{5}{8}$
2nd Quarter	$\{99\frac{5}{8}, 101\frac{3}{4}\}$	$2\frac{1}{8}$	$\{104\frac{1}{2}, 107\frac{1}{2}\}$	3	$\{109\frac{5}{8}, 113\frac{3}{4}\}$	$4\frac{1}{8}$		
3rd Quarter	$\{101\frac{1}{8}, 102\frac{3}{4}\}$	$1\frac{5}{8}$	$\{106\frac{3}{4}, 108\frac{5}{8}\}$	$1\frac{3}{8}$	$\{109, 113\frac{3}{4}\}$	$4\frac{3}{4}$		
4th Quarter	$\{101, 103\frac{3}{8}\}$	$2\frac{3}{8}$	$\{105\frac{5}{8}, 107\frac{3}{4}\}$	$2\frac{1}{8}$	$\{107\frac{3}{8}, 112\frac{1}{4}\}$	$5\frac{1}{4}$		
Total fluctuations for year		$4\frac{7}{8}$		$4\frac{5}{8}$		$8\frac{3}{4}$		

The total fluctuations being, as shown, $4\frac{7}{8}$ for the year 1894, $4\frac{5}{8}$ for 1895, $8\frac{3}{4}$ for 1896, and $2\frac{3}{8}$ for the first three months of 1897, any one can readily see how many repeated purchases and sales could have been profitably made on these fluctuations. Another great advantage to the investor in purchasing Consols is that he can do so with very little fear, for he is perfectly secure either way the price may go. Should it advance, he can then secure his profit and repeat the transaction; should it go down, he can then purchase a like quantity at the lower price, thus reducing his purchase price on the average, and this averaging can be repeated over and over again should the decline continue, till, instead of a loss, the investor can make a good profit on his entire holding.

The following examples fully illustrate this, both in the case of purchase with an advance in price, and of a purchase with a decline in price, the figures of which can be verified by the reader for himself :—

On January 21st, 1896, A. purchased £10,000 Consols at $107\frac{1}{4}$, which he sold on February 1st at $107\frac{7}{8}$, thus making $\frac{5}{8}$ per cent. profit, equalling £62 10s On February 6th he again bought the same amount at $108\frac{1}{4}$, which he sold on February 18th at $108\frac{15}{16}$, making a profit of £56 5s.; thus realising no less than £118 15s. in twenty-eight days. As the price touched its highest point at

$113\frac{7}{8}$ during the year, he could have repeated this process over and over again, receiving in addition the quarterly interest.

Now to show the other side of the picture. B. bought, on August 10th, £5,000 Consols at $112\frac{5}{8}$; they remained stationary for some days, then gradually declined until the middle of September, when he purchased a further £5,000 at $109\frac{3}{4}$, thus making his average price $111\frac{3}{16}$; he had no opportunity of selling to advantage then, but on October 12th he bought a further £5,000 at $108\frac{3}{4}$, thus making his total average price $110\frac{3}{8}$. He held the stock until towards the end of November, when, seeing that there was a good profit showing, he secured it by selling out at $111\frac{1}{8}$, making $\frac{3}{4}$ per cent. profit on the whole £15,000, equalling £112 10s. In addition to this, on September 1st, he received the quarterly interest of £33 4s. 7d. on his first purchase of £5,000, bringing his total profit up to £145 14s. 7d. Of course, if his means would allow, he could have doubled the amount of his purchases, making it £10,000 each time instead of £5,000; which would have brought his profit up to nearly £300 in four months, and this on three purchases of Consols alone.

It will therefore be plainly seen what income could be made in the same way during the year by judicious purchases and sales. In fact, we firmly believe that, if investments were extensively carried out in Consols, they could be made to yield—in addition to the yearly interest of $2\frac{3}{4}$ per cent.—a return of from 10 to 20 per cent. per annum, according to circumstances.

CHAPTER XXX.

THE LAW OF AVERAGES.

REMEMBERING just definitions and limits, it may be remarked that Stock Exchange investments have in view a settled return and the keeping intact of the principal. Investors, who cannot or who will not take the trouble to comprehend the laws that govern stock transactions, must be content with a very moderate return. They may, if they choose, learn the character of the risks, and understand the conditions of success, by the exercise of ordinary intelligence. No Prospero's wand is needed in order to avoid failure; but only common sense and common prudence, such as all may cultivate.

On the other hand, there are no short and sure cuts to success. It does not come by wishing and waiting for it. The proper means must be used, likely opportunities turned to advantage, and a careful judgment must be exercised. If it be thought that in one or two transactions of five or ten thousand each a great fortune will be instantly secured, there is certain to be a speedy process of disillusioning. Neither can it be expected that every venture will prove lucrative. "The best laid schemes o' mice an' men gang aft a-gley." No mechanism is so automatically perfect in its working as to be free from all risks of friction. It is the same with investments. However carefully made, it sometimes happens that unexpected complications arise, such as no foresight could have anticipated or guarded against. Yet the law of averages is certain to operate, as is the case with accidents, with fires, and with every business. Its operation may be illustrated by the following instance :—

An investor buys £1,000 North Western Ordinary stock at 195, with a good prospect of an immediate improvement. Owing, however, to a slight accident, the price of the stock unexpectedly falls $1\frac{1}{2}$ per cent. He thereupon promptly purchases a further £1,000 at $193\frac{1}{2}$. Instead of the price recovering, however, it is found on investigation that the accident is more serious than was supposed, and the price falls again $1\frac{1}{2}$ per cent.

The investor is not discouraged, but immediately buys another £1,000 at 192, making his average price $193\frac{1}{2}$. The stock now only has to rise $\frac{1}{2}$ per cent., namely, to 194, to give him a $\frac{1}{2}$ per cent. profit on the whole £3,000 (= £15), whereas on the original purchase it would have to rise to 195½ and then the profit would only be on £1,000 stock (= £5).

Though prices may be variable, and even seem to be fitful and uncontrolled, the eye of the trained observer detects a certain amount of regularity in such eccentric movements; just as the meteorologist deduces certain great principles as to the law of storms or as to the prospect of settled weather, from observations over a wide area and a long period as to the rise and fall of the barometer, from atmospheric currents, from electrical conditions, and other circumstances open to careful deduction.

The general tendency of stocks is in one direction for a time, upward or downward, and then, after an interval of varying length, with what resemble the wayward movements of the magnetic needle, though really regulated by inexorable laws, they tend in an opposite direction until an extreme limit is reached. The principle is that of the pendulum; so that after a rise comes a fall, and *vice versâ*, as is proved by the following illustrations :—

In the issue of our *Market Report* for February 28, 1896, in an article on "Consols at 110," we expressed an opinion they they would go yet higher, and suggested that our readers should watch the

THE LAW OF AVERAGES. 213

market so as to take advantage of a probable rise. We proceeded to give the following advice : " In place of buying railway stock just at the present time, an investor can afford, with little or no risk, to buy double or treble the amount of Consols."

In another article, a fortnight earlier, entitled, " A Time to Buy," we said : " It is a most favourable opportunity for dealing in all kinds of stock. Our opinion is confirmed week by week that before long there will be a considerable increase in prices. . . . So far as it is possible to forecast the immediate future, there is every prospect of activity in the markets with the approach of Spring, and the improvement may come much sooner than the most sanguine venture to hope." We, therefore, repeated the advice already tendered, that it would be well for investors to purchase blocks of good stocks on the short and quick profits system.

Such of our customers as followed the suggestion had every reason to be satisfied with the results. In one case, £10,000 Consols were purchased at 109, and were sold a month later at $110\frac{3}{4}$, yielding a profit of £175. A similar block was bought two days later at $110\frac{1}{2}$, and sold again at $112\frac{1}{2}$, or a further profit of £200. A return of £375 on two transactions within ten weeks cannot but be regarded as eminently gratifying. The investor received, in addition, the quarterly dividends due April 5th. Similar temporary investments were conducted in other amounts in Consols and in other stocks and none of our customers had cause to regret acting upon the hints we gave. It is satisfactory to know that the accuracy of our forecast was so abundantly demonstrated. We do not profess to be wiser than other people, but long experience and constant watching of the markets enable us to draw probable inferences from signs which many fail to notice.

At the close of 1895, and early in 1896, a panic in American securities was caused by a message to Congress from President Cleveland with regard to Venezuela. Within twenty-four hours the stock markets throughout the world were flooded with railway and other securities offered for sale. Prices fell rapidly; in some cases as much as fourteen points; and it was estimated that the depreciation in one week amounted to £200,000,000.

We were confident that a rally would soon occur, and we advised immediate and extensive purchases for the improvement in prices that was bound to come. We wrote, in our *Market Report* of January 3, 1896:—" Now is the time. Every door is open to wise and profitable investment. Money is cheap. Dividends are accruing. Outlets must be found for accumulations. Both English and American securities should be bought, and held for the present ; care being, of course, taken in the selection, on which we shall be pleased to place our knowledge and experience at the disposal of our customers."

In this instance, also, advantage was promptly taken of the favouring conditions, and substantial profits accrued. We repeat, with added emphasis, advice given a year ago, to buy when things are cheap, and to sell when they are dear.

CHAPTER XXXI.

HIDDEN PITFALLS.

STOCKS have a small and sluggish or a large and quick market. In some it is possible to deal at any moment, with a difference of $\frac{1}{4}$, $\frac{1}{8}$, or even $\frac{1}{16}$, while in others it amounts to 1, or 2, or more, and even then a sale is not easy. Investing in a stock where a close price can be obtained promptly enables a bad bargain to be retrieved at a trifling loss, which would otherwise be heavy. Some markets are so small that an investor, once in, gets "roasted" before he can extricate himself.

No difficulty need be experienced by any one possessing average intelligence, and willing to acquire the requisite knowledge, in order to invest in Stock Exchange securities in such a manner as to ensure good results. Before engaging in any transaction its wisdom should be assured, with a likelihood of its being profitable. After having resolved on a certain course, its issue should be patiently awaited.

Charles James Fox used to speak of "the elegant simplicity of the Three per Cents." The Duke of Wellington is credited with the dictum that "high interest always means low security." Like many other wise saws and modern instances, these maxims, however sound within just limitations, are often pressed to an extreme and made to bear a forced meaning. A wise man will be reasonably careful, while seeking to obtain for his money the largest return compatible with safety. Yet caution may end in timidity or torpor. Investment is an art. It might even be termed a science. Like other arts and sciences, knowledge is only to be acquired by study and effort. Judgment comes from experience. Sometimes it springs from failure. But a man must learn to compare and discriminate. He needs to follow a course deliberately chosen after careful inquiry, and promptitude in decision to avail himself of sudden and transient changes.

In the commercial world it sometimes happens that injudicious purchases result in disaster; but this is also induced by excessive timidity or by slowness to seize upon the favouring conditions of the hour, which wait upon the convenience of no one. Washington Irving's Rip van Winkle woke up from his prolonged slumber to find a world altogether changed, and he could not adapt himself to the new state of things. The same is true of mercantile affairs and of Stock Exchange investments.

It is not difficult for persons possessing ready money, good securities, or good credit, and having sound judgment, to invest profitably in stocks and shares. The conditions of the market vary from day to day. Hence a rule, however sound and excellent at one time, may not be applicable in a week or in a month. Speaking in general terms, there are but two distinct plans, each of which possesses its own advantages. They comprise (1) temporary investment, which is buying stock and selling it again quickly at a small profit; and (2) permanent investment, or buying to hold. The first requires but little knowledge of the intrinsic value of stocks; their daily fluctuations being principally taken into account; but the second demands greater knowledge of intrinsic values, and but little of daily fluctuations. Two maxims of vital importance must be borne in mind, however; never to engage in an investment which does not, on a careful estimate, show chances of a good profit; and never to go beyond one's means.

To be dissatisfied with a moderate profit, risking it for the chance of gaining much more, is a sure sign of incapacity. A profit of $\frac{1}{2}$ per cent. may be offered, but it is not taken because of a desire to get $\frac{3}{4}$. Should that be reached, another $\frac{1}{8}$ is longed for, with the result that, like the dog in Æsop's fable, in attempting to grasp the shadow, the substance is lost. Innumerable instances of the kind have occurred, showing that sufficient value is never set upon the importance of avoiding a loss, while studying feverishly how to make a problematical profit. "Take care of the pence, and the pounds will take care of themselves," is a trite maxim of wide application. "Never refuse a profit" is a golden rule which many have not the courage to adopt. "End your losses" may appear a counsel of perfection, unattainable by ordinary mortals, yet it is sound and wise.

In the foregoing pages, the practical experience acquired during a prolonged connection with Stock Exchange transactions has been placed at the disposal of our readers. It will not be our fault if any business entrusted to us, to be conducted upon the principles herein expounded, does not result in mutual advantage. Our readers will, we are sure, have every reason to be satisfied with their investments if they adopt the methods and follow the rules laid down. Any additional information that may be required will be furnished on application to "The Manager, Universal Stock Exchange, Cockspur Street, London, S.W."

APPENDICES.

A.—DEFINITIONS OF STOCK EXCHANGE TERMS AND PHRASES.

B.—CLASSIFIED LIST OF THE PRINCIPAL ENGLISH INVESTMENTS.

C.—PRICE OF CONSOLS, THEIR MEAN YIELD, THE BANK RATES OF DISCOUNT AND OF DIVIDEND, AND THE MEAN PRICE OF WHEAT, 1850-1896.

D.—THE NATIONAL DEBT AND THE NATIONAL EXPENDITURE AT PERIODS OF FIVE YEARS, AND THE RATE OF INCOME TAX, WITH THE DEBTS AND THE TAXATION OF OTHER COUNTRIES.

E.—THE PRINCIPAL JOINT-STOCK BANKS, WITH THEIR CAPITAL, THE NOMINAL SHARE VALUES, AND THE LAST DIVIDENDS.

F.—HIGHEST AND LOWEST PRICES OF STOCKS AND SHARES, 1881-1896.

G.—HIGHEST AND LOWEST PRICES OF PRINCIPAL MINES, 1891-1896.

H.—DIVIDENDS ON LEADING STOCKS, 1890-1896.

I.—DIVIDENDS ON PRINCIPAL MINES, 1890-1896.

K.—TABLE FOR COMPUTING DIVIDENDS.

APPENDIX A.

DEFINITIONS OF STOCK EXCHANGE TERMS AND PHRASES.

LORD BRAMWELL used to say that definitions are dangerous. Perhaps he sympathized with another judge, whose decisions were generally sound, though the reasons assigned for them were always wrong. Notwithstanding the legal dictum, it is necessary and convenient to furnish an explanation of terms commonly used in Stock Exchange dealings.

Account Days, three in number, are fixed by the Stock Exchange Committee at intervals ranging from 14 to 19 days, for settling the transactions of the fortnight; when delivery of stocks bought and sold must be made, or arrangements effected for carrying over. (See *Contango*.)

Arbitrage.—The profit made by the difference in the price of securities bought in one country and instantly sold in another.

Averaging.—To secure at a lower price more stock, so as to reduce the total risk on an average of the whole.

Backwardation.—It sometimes happens that a particular

stock is scarce, or a great deal more has been sold than can be delivered. A premium or consideration money, barbarously called Backwardation, has then to be paid, in addition, for leave to postpone actual delivery, or for the loan of stock.

Banging is the opposite of *Rigging* (q.v.), and is done by freely selling stock to induce a fall, so as to buy back at the lower figure.

Bargain.—An agreement for the purchase or sale of any kind of security.

Bear.—An operator for a fall in prices, who sells what he has not got, in the expectation that he can buy it back cheaper, and gain by the difference. Called "short" in America.

Bond.—The sign of title to possession; equivalent to "Debenture" in the case of stocks. (See *Gold: Sterling*.)

Boom.—An American word, denoting an upward rush of prices caused by speculators.

Broker.—An agent who buys or sells stock for another person on commission.

Bull.—An operator for a possible rise in prices, who buys what he does not want, for the contingency of selling at a profit. In America called "long."

Buying-in.—Failure to deliver stocks sold entitles the purchaser to buy elsewhere, and to recover any loss thereby.

DEFINITIONS OF TERMS.

Carrying Over.—Also called "Continuation"; deferring until next account day the completion of a bargain. (See *Contango.*)

Childers.—The 2¾ Consols reduced from Three per Cents. by Mr. Childers in 1884, and redeemable in 1905.

Consideration.—The sum named in a transfer deed to indicate the value of the stock.

Consolidated Stock.—Various 3 per cent. stocks of the National Debt, amalgamated in 1751, and bearing a common name. The phrase is shortened into "Consols."

Commissions vary from ⅛ upwards, with the class of securities. Half-rates are usually charged on Contangoes.

"*Contango.*"—The interest charged to a buyer for the privilege of deferring until the next account the delivery of stocks purchased. Some one has to provide the money to take them up, or has to make satisfactory arrangements, and the charge for this is called Contango. Its rate fluctuates with the Bank rate of discount, and it is charged until the next account day, even though a sale be effected meanwhile. This is one of the multifarious rules of the Stock Exchange, all of which are framed in the interests of the members rather than of the public. The ¼ rate means 5s. for each £100 stock for the fortnight, so far as regards English railways. On other stocks the calculation is at a certain rate per annum; while on mines and some other things it is at so much per share. Practically, it is found that from 3 to 8 per cent. is charged on the best securities; but it may range as high as 30 per cent. upon the more speculative.

Contract.—The formal note sent by a broker to a client to indicate the business done.

Conversion.—Turning one form of security into another; usually with the object of lowering the rate of interest or deferring the date of redemption.

Corner.—A scheme for buying up stock so as to force a rise in price through an artificial scarcity. An Americanism, similar to "Ring."

Cover.—Money deposited by a speculator to ensure his fulfilment of bargains.

Cum Div.—Entitles the buyer to the accruing dividends.

Debentures.—A charge or mortgage on assets, bearing interest, and redeemable at a certain date; transferable like shares, over which they rank in claim. "Debenture Stock" is usually irredeemable.

Differences.—Sums paid to balance accounts carried over.

Discount.—The sum at which the market price of a security stands below the amount paid up.

Exchange, Rate of.—The price of bills or drafts drawn in the standard money of one country and payable in that of another varies with circumstances, and sometimes, as has been the case for a long while with Argentina, the premium for gold rises to as much as 260. *The Theory of Foreign Exchanges* is the title of a book by Mr. G. J. Goschen, which few people can be said to understand.

Ex Div.—Stocks thus sold involves the payment of accruing dividends to the seller, and not to the purchaser.

Ex New, or *Ex Rights.*—New stock or other property apportioned among shareholders, who retain it when parting with the original stock.

Five-Twenties.—United States Government Loans, redeemable at option in five years, and absolutely within twenty years.

Fractions, like $52\frac{1}{2}$ or $84\frac{7}{8}$, stand in English money for £52 10s. or £84 17s. 6d. Most stocks, excepting American, which are reckoned in dollars, are quoted at prices per £100 nominal value. This, and not the actual—that is, the existing—market value, is always understood in matters of purchase and sale.

Gold Bonds.—Debentures of American railways, the interest on which is payable in gold.

Goschens.—The popular name, after the then Chancellor of the Exchequer, for the $2\frac{3}{4}$ Consols, reduced by him from the Three per Cents. After 1903 they will be $2\frac{1}{2}$; redeemable in 1923.

Guaranteed Shares.—Interest pledged irrespective of profits.

Hammered.—Three blows are struck with a mallet in the Stock Exchange when a member is in default, and his name is announced as being unable to meet his engagements. This involves expulsion.

Identification by a known broker or his clerk is necessary to effect a transfer of stock at the Bank of England.

Income Bonds.—A loose and misleading term, of American origin, denoting a kind of Preference Shares which are in no sense Bonds.

Inscribed Stocks have no certificates; but proprietors' names are registered in a book at a bank. Transfers are made by the personal signatures of buyer and seller.

Jobber.—A stock-dealer who buys and sells on his own account for a profit. He is a principal, and not an agent.

Limit.—The price fixed by a client for share transactions with a dealer.

Making-up Prices are those at which stocks are carried over to a new account.

Margin.—The excess percentage, in cash or securities, over the market price for money lent on stocks.

Memorandum of Association.—A statement, signed by at least seven subscribers, and, by implication, signed by all shareholders, setting forth the objects for which a Limited Company is formed.

Nominal Value.—That on the face of certificates, as distinct from Market Value. (See *Fractions*.)

Official List.—Issued daily by the Stock Exchange Committee, and supposed to quote the actual prices of business done; but it does not discriminate between buying and selling, and there is no necessity for a broker or a jobber to register his bargains. Moreover, the prices are loosely entered in the list, and often are erroneous, as appears from a comparison with those given in the best papers. Even these do not always agree with one another, and a fraction may make a considerable difference in large dealings. A remedy is being supplied by the tape quotations of the Exchange Telegraph Company, which are now given in most of the London evening and the provincial morning papers.

Omnium, "of all"; being composed of several distinct stocks.

Options.—The right to buy or sell stock at an agreed price for a given time. The former is a "call option," the latter a "put option," and the right to either is a "double option."

Par.—When the market price and the nominal value are the same.

Pay-Day.—(See *Settlements.*)

Points.—A slang term, with arbitrary meanings, to denote an up or down movement in prices.

Pool.—A number of persons combining for a joint purpose and sharing the risk and the profit.

Power of Attorney.—A legal authority to another person to act for the principal.

Preference Shares rank before Ordinary Shares, but after Debentures or Mortgages.

Premium.—The price above the nominal value at which any security stands in the market.

Prices always consist of two sets of figures; the lower being the selling, and the higher the purchasing.

Registered Stock can only change hands by formal transfer; unlike "Stock to Bearer." (*Ante*, p. 122.)

Rente.—A French term to denote the interest—which alone is saleable—on the National Debt.

Reserve Fund.—Profits set aside to meet contingencies.

Rigging the Market.—Buying up to create scarcity, and so force prices. (See *Banging*.)

Ring.—(See *Corner.*)

Rupee Paper.—Indian Government Certificates of indebtedness for money borrowed.

Scrip.—An abbreviation of "subscription." Temporary certificates exchangeable for Shares and Bonds on payment of calls.

Securities.—A term applied to all marketable stocks, however miscellaneous and unsatisfactory.

Selling out.—The remedy against a dilatory buyer.

Settlements.—The fortnightly accounts embrace three days. The first is for continuation or carrying-over, of which notice must be given to the broker, and mutual arrangements made, before 11.15 a.m. Next is the ticket-day, when the name, address, and description of the purchaser are supplied to the seller, so that transfers may be prepared, if needful. The third is pay-day, when stocks are delivered and accounts are settled; an anxious time for many persons. Stocks to bearer must then be delivered, but for transfers 10 days' grace are allowed. (See *Special.*)

DEFINITIONS OF TERMS. 231

Shares.—The nominal division of the capital, usually into Ordinary, Preference, Deferred, Founders, &c. Share Warrants are certificates of ownership; usually made to Bearer, and passing from hand to hand.

Shrinkage.—An expressive synonym of "depreciation."

Sinking Fund.—A reserve created to pay off a loan at a fixed date, or by periodical drawings.

Special Settlement.—A day appointed by the Stock Exchange Committee, other than the usual fortnightly settlement, for completing transactions in any new stock.

Stag.—One who applies for shares to sell on allotment at a possible premium.

Sterling Bonds.—Those on which the interest is payable in pounds sterling.

Stock.—In the published lists Stock is always quoted at the price per £100. "One" is equivalent to £1000 in value, and "one-half" is £500. Shares have diverse nominal values, and the prices vary accordingly. The former represent the original and titular denomination. The latter represent the market value, which fluctuates from day to day, and sometimes hour by hour.

Tape Machine.—The self-recording instrument of the Exchange Telegraph Company; giving the prices and their times.

Ticket-Day (See *Settlements.*)

Time Bargains.—Transactions for periods beyond the ordinary Account; designed to furnish opportunities for making profits without locking-up capital.

Transfer.—A stamped document, signed by seller and buyer, to show that certain stock has changed hands. (See Chapter xvi.)

Trustees Stocks.—Securities in which trustees may lawfully invest are defined by an Act of 1893, and by the rules laid down from time to time by the Court of Chancery.

Turn.—The difference between the price at which a jobber or dealer will buy a security, and the price at which he will sell.

Uncalled Capital.—The portion not called up for payment, but remaining as a liability by shareholders.

Unlimited Liability.—A company in which the members are jointly and severally liable for the whole of the debts.

Watered Stock.—Bogus capital created by the issue of paper stock without any equivalent payment of cash. (*Ante*, p. 117.)

Besides the above, many names, of a specific or local character, are used among the initiated, and slang terms are applied to denote particular stocks; but they need not be particularized.

APPENDIX B.

CLASSIFIED LIST OF PRINCIPAL ENGLISH INVESTMENTS TO DECEMBER 31, 1896.

CLASS OF SECURITY.	PRESENT AMOUNT.
	£
British Funds, &c.	772,772,594
Corporation Stocks (United Kingdom) ...	108,572,113
Colonial and Provincial Government Stocks	64,306,551
Colonial and Provincial Registered and Inscribed...	221,914,313
Railways—Ordinary Shares and Stocks	
„ Leased at fixed Rentals ...	
„ Debenture Stocks	913,926,862
„ Guaranteed Shares and Stocks	
„ Preference	
Foreign Stocks and Bonds	783,886,953
Indian Railways	109,561,789
Railways—British Possessions...	123,161,823
American Railroad Shares	391,076,917
„ „ Bonds, Currency ...	49,482,938
„ „ „ Gold	387,205,674
„ „ „ Sterling... ...	47,047,610
Foreign Railways	145,324,745
„ Obligations	460,190,641

APPENDIX B.

CLASS OF SECURITY.	PRESENT AMOUNT.
	£
Banks	58,712,600
Breweries and Distilleries...	75,636,865
Canals and Docks	44,499,653
Commercial and Industrial	120,780,589
Corporation Stocks (Colonial and Foreign)	45,823,277
Financial, Land, and Investment	74,149,867
„ Trusts	54,690,453
Gas and Electric Lighting	39,718,180
Insurance	11,815,844
Iron, Coal, and Steel...	13,144,749
Mines	36,475,252
Shipping	12,302,115
Tea and Coffee	4,266,412
Telegraphs and Telephones	35,068,760
Tramways and Omnibuses	15,675,329
Waterworks	16,706,287
Total	5,237,901,755

_{*} The above total does not include Foreign Stocks the coupons of which are payable abroad, and the exact amounts of which are not ascertainable with accuracy, but are estimated by Burdett at £2,038,129,686 on December 31, 1896. Including this conjectural sum, the aggregate of investments is £7,276,031,441.

APPENDIX C.

CONSOLS: BANK RATE AND DIVIDEND: WHEAT.

1850-96.

THE HIGHEST AND LOWEST PRICES OF CONSOLS, WITH THE MEAN RATE OF DIVIDEND YIELDED; ALSO THE HIGHEST AND LOWEST BANK RATE OF DISCOUNT, AND THE MEAN PRICES OF WHEAT.

YEAR.	CONSOLS.					BANK RATE.		DIV. ON STOCK.	MEAN PRICE OF WHEAT.		
	Highest.	Lowest.	Mean Yield.			Highest.	Lowest.				
			£	s.	d.				£	s.	d.
1850	98⅛	94⅜	3	2	1	3	2½	7½	2	0	3
1851	99⅛	95⅝	3	1	4	3	3	7½	1	19	5
1852	102	95⅞	3	0	8	3	2	7½	1	19	10
1853	101	90¾	3	2	6	5	2	8	2	5	7
1854	95⅞	85⅛	3	6	3	5½	5	9	3	12	10
1855	93¾	86¼	3	6	8	7	4½	8	3	11	10
1856	95⅞	85¾	3	6	1	7	4½	9½	3	13	1
1857	94¼	86½	3	6	1	10	5½	10	2	19	2
1858	98⅞	94⅛	3	2	2	8	2½	10	2	6	10
1859	97⅜	88¼	3	4	8	4½	2½	8½	2	3	6
1860	95⅞	92¼	3	3	8	6	2½	9½	2	9	9
1861	94¼	89⅛	3	5	4	8	3	10	2	14	9
1862	94¾	91⅛	3	4	4	3	2½	8½	2	18	3
1863	94	90	3	4	9	8	3	8¾	2	6	8
1864	92	87⅛	3	6	6	9	6	11	2	0	9
1865	91½	86¾	3	7	0	7	3	10½	2	0	3
1866	90½	84⅝	3	8	3	10	3	11¾	2	6	10
1867	96⅜	89⅞	3	4	6	3½	2	10	3	1	7
1868	96⅛	91¾	3	4	0	3	2	8	3	7	9

YEAR.	CONSOLS.					BANK RATE.		DIV. ON STOCK.	MEAN PRICE OF WHEAT.		
	Highest.	Lowest.	Mean Yield.			Highest.	Lowest.				
			£	s.	d.				£	s.	d.
1869	94½	91¾	3	4	7	4½	2½	8¾	2	9	8
1870	94⅜	88½	3	4	10	6	2½	8¾	2	5	11
1871	94	91⅜	3	4	8	5	2	8¾	2	15	1
1872	93¾	91½	3	4	10	7	3	9½	2	16	9
1873	94	91¾	3	4	10	9	3½	10	2	17	8
1874	93⅝	91¼	3	4	10	6	2½	10	2	19	11
1875	95¾	91⅞	3	4	0	6	2	9	2	4	7
1876	97½	93⅜	3	3	2	5	2	9	2	5	9
1877	97⅜	93	3	3	0	5	2	9½	2	15	9
1878	98	93⅝	3	3	10	6	2	9½	2	9	5
1879	99⅝	94⅞	3	1	6	5	2	10½	2	1	10
1880	100¾	97⅜	3	1	0	3	2½	9½	2	5	7
1881	103	98¼	3	0	0	5	2½	9½	2	4	8
1882	102½	99	2	19	8	6	3	10½	2	6	4
1883	102¾	99⅜	2	19	2	5	3	10¼	2	1	9
1884	102¾	98⅞	2	19	4	5	2	9¾	1	17	10
1885	101½	94⅜	3	0	2	5	2	10	1	13	0
1886	102¾	99⅜	2	19	8	5	2	9½	1	10	11
1887	103¾	99⅞	2	19	0	5	2	9¾	1	12	10
1888[1]	103⅜	99⅛	2	16	4	5	2	10	1	11	6
1889	99¼	96½	2	16	3	6	2½	10¼	1	10	1
1890	98¾	93⅜	2	17	3	6	3	10½	1	11	5
1891	97½	94⅜	2	17	8	5	2½	11	1	15	9
1892	100½	96¼	2	17	6	3	2	10	1	13	8
1893	99⅝	97	2	15	10	5	2½	9¾	1	6	7
1894	103⅝	98⅜	2	14	5	2½	2	8½	1	1	11
1895	108⅛	103½	2	14	5	2	2	8¼	1	0	8
1896	113⅞	105⅛	2	5	1	4	2	8½	1	6	1

[1] Reduced to 2¾ per cent. until 1903, when they become 2½.

*** Consols reached the extraordinary price of 112½, April 18, 1896, after Sir Michael Hicks Beach made his Budget statement in the House of Commons. The Two and a Half Per Cents. reached 105¾—106. On June 1, the former rose to 113⅞.

*** The Bank Rate of Discount, after remaining at 2 per cent. since February, 1894, was raised to 2½ on September 10, 1896; to 3 on September 24, 1896; and to 4 on October 22, 1896.

APPENDIX D.

THE NATIONAL DEBT AND THE NATIONAL EXPENDITURE, AND THE RATE OF INCOME TAX AT INTERVALS OF FIVE YEARS, WITH THE DEBTS AND THE TAXATION OF OTHER COUNTRIES. 1850-1895 (FROM APRIL 5 EACH YEAR).

YEAR.	NATIONAL DEBT.		NATIONAL EXPENDITURE.	INCOME TAX IN THE POUND.
	Amount.[1]	Interest.		
1850	787,029,162	28,091,590	50,231,874	7d.
1855	793,375,199	27,647,899	84,505,788	1s. 4d. & 11½d.
1860	821,936,564	26,833,470	69,617,698	10d. & 7d [2]
1865	806,935,963	26,369,398	66,462,207	4d.[3]
1870	800,681,428	27,053,560	68,864,752	4d.[3]
1875	768,945,757	27,094,480	73,116,000	2d.[3]
1880	771,605,908	28,762,874	84,105,871	5d.[2]
1885	740,330,654	29,548,239	89,898,222	6d.[2]
1890	689,944,026	25,226,760	86,723,168	6d.[2]
1895	656,998,941	24,977,912	94,538,685	8d.[4]

The only country the National Debt of which exceeds in absolute amount that of the United Kingdom is France, which stands at £1,085,555,014.

The other large amounts are as follows:—

Russia	£711,074,000
Italy	£513,338,962
United States	£348,148,899
Spain	£263,667,417
Austria-Hungary	£261,031,331
Hungary (Special) ...	£185,322,381
Portugal	£153,990,503
Turkey	£117,581,000
Egypt	£104,636,840

[1] Including Funded and Unfunded Debt and Capital Value of Terminable Annuities, but not including sundry liabilities for barracks, &c., or certain estimated assets, like the Suez Canal. Taking all these into account, the net indebtedness, March 31, 1895, was £628,750,209. [2] Free under £150.
[3] Free under £100. [4] Under £160 exempt.

APPENDIX D.

The Debts of all other countries are under one hundred millions; but, divided by the respective populations, the rate greatly varies per head:—

	£	s.	d.
Portugal	35	15	1
Uruguay	29	4	11
France	28	6	3
Netherlands	19	5	2
Great Britain	17	1	11
Italy	15	19	0
Spain	15	15	1
Egypt	15	7	10
Belgium	15	1	3
Greece	14	11	0
Hungary	10	3	7

The taxation in European countries per head is as follows:—

	£	s.	d.
Great Britain	2	1	0
Netherlands	1	15	9
France	1	8	7
Greece	1	7	9
Spain	1	7	5
Denmark	1	4	6
Hungary	1	4	4
Belgium	1	1	4
Italy	0	18	7
Norway	0	17	2

APPENDIX E.

THE PRINCIPAL JOINT-STOCK BANKS, WITH THEIR CAPITAL, THE NOMINAL SHARE VALUES, AND THE LAST DIVIDENDS. *(See also Appendix F and H.)*

NAMES.	AUTHORIZED CAPITAL.	VALUE OF SHARES.	LAST TWO DIVIDENDS.	
	£	£	Per cent.	
African Banking Cor., Ltd.	2,000,000	10	5 June	5 Dec.
Anglo-Californian	1,200,000	20	6 Sept.	6 March
Anglo-Egyptian	1,200,000	15	6 June	6 Dec.
Australian Joint Stock	3,000,000	10	nil	nil
Bank of Africa	1,575,000	18 15/-	10 & 1 b. Sept.	10 & 1 b. Ap.
Bank of Australasia	2,000,000	40	5 Oct.	5 March
Bank of Bolton	1,000,000	20	5 July	5 Jan.
Bank of British North America	1,000,000	50	4 Oct.	4 Ap.
Bank of China and Japan	1,800,000	8	— [1]	—
Bank of England	14,553,000	100	8¼ Oct.	10 Ap.
Bank of Ireland	2,769,231	100	10¼ Aug.	11 Feb.
Bank of Liverpool	8,000,000	100	10 July & b. 7/6	10 Jan.
Bank of Montreal	$12,000,000	$200	10 June	10 Dec.
Bank of New South Wales	3,000,000	20	9 May	9 Nov.
Bank of New Zealand	2,500,000	3 6/8	nil	nil
Bank of Scotland	4,500,000	Stock.	12 Oct.	12 Ap.
Bank of Tarapaca & London	1,000,000[2]	10	5 Ap.	5 Oct.
Bank of Victoria	3,240,000	10	nil	nil
Barclay & Co., Ltd.	2,000,000	20	—	—
Belfast Banking Co.	2,000,000	125	20 on Old & 8 on New Shrs. Feb.	20 on Old & 8 on New Shrs. Aug.
Birmingham Dist. and Cnties.	4,000,000	20	11¼ Aug.	11¼ Feb.
Bolitho, Williams, Foster & Co.	1,500,000	50	12 Feb.	12 Aug.
Bradford Banking Co.	1,400,000	100	11¾ Aug.	11¾ Feb.
Bradford Commercial Jnt. Stk.	1,500,000	100	8 July	8 Feb.
Bradford District	1,000,000	100	12½ July	12½ Jan.
Bradford Old	1,250,000	50	8 Aug.	8 Feb.

[1] Under reconstruction.   [2] £1,875,000 subscribed.

APPENDIX E.

NAMES.	AUTHORIZED CAPITAL.	VALUE OF SHARES.	LAST TWO DIVIDENDS.	
	£	£	Per cent.	
British of South America	1,000,000	20	8 Oct.	8 March
British Linen Co.	1,500,000	Stock.	17 June	16 Dec.
Capital & Counties	5,000,000	50	16 July	16 Jan.
City	4,000,000	40	8 July	9 Jan.
Clydesdale Bank	5,000,000	50	10 Aug.	10 Feb.
Colonial Bank	2,000,000	100	10 July	10 Jan.
Commercial Bank of Australia	6,000,000	10	nil	nil
Commercial Bank of Scotland	5,000,000	100	15 July	17 Jan.
Commercial Bg. Co. of Sydney	2,000,000	25	8 July	8 Jan.
Craven	1,200,000	30	15 July	15 Jan.
Crompton & Evans Union	1,500,000	20	15 Feb.	15 & b. 1/- Aug.
Devon & Cornwall Bankg. Co.	1,000,000	100	15 Sept	15 & b. £1 March
English, Scottish, & Australian	1,575,000	35	4 on Deb. Jan.	4 on Deb. July
Glamorganshire Bankg. Co.	1,750,000	{30 Ord. / 5 Pf.}	7½ July	10 Jan.
Halifax & Huddersfield	2,000,000	40	8 Aug.	8 Feb.
Halifax Joint Stock	1,000,000	25	10 Aug.	10 Feb.
Hibernian	2,000,000	20	4 Feb.	4 Aug.
Hong Kong & Shanghai	$10,000,000	$125	25/- p. s. Aug.	25/- p. s. Feb.
Huddersfield Banking Cor.	1,700,000	100	10 July	10 Jan., b. of 5/-
Imperial Ottoman	10,000,000	20	6 July	—
International & Mort. of Mexico	$5,000,000	$100	2 Feb.	2 Aug.
International of London	1,200,000	20	nil	3 Ap.
Lancashire & Yorkshire	1,000,000	20	10 July	10 Jan. & b. 4/- p.s.
Lancaster Banking Co.	2,100,000	25	12 Aug.	14 Ap.
Leicestershire	1,100,000	25	10 Aug.	10 Ap.
Liverpool Union	5,000,000	100	10 July	10 Jan. & b. 2½ Oct.
Lloyd's	12,000,000	50	14 July	16¼ Feb.
London & Brazilian	1,500,000	20	10 Oct. & b. 8/- p.s.	10 & b. of 8 Ap.
London & County	8,000,000	80	20 Aug.	20 Feb.
London & Midland	6,000,000	60	15 Aug.	15 Feb. & b. 1 %
London & Provincial	1,200,000	10	17 July	17 Jan.
London & River Plate	2,000,000	25	14 June	22 Dec.
London & South Western	3,000,000	50	10 Aug. & b. 1	10 Feb. & b. 1
London & Westminster	14,000,000	100	10 July & b. 1	12 Jan.
London & Yorkshire	1,500,012	£9 10s.	8 July	10 Jan.
London Bank of Australia	4,000,000	{40 Ord. / 10 Pf.}	5½ June Pref.	5½ Dec Pref.
London Bank of Mexico	1,000,000	10	6 Sept.	10 Mar.
London Joint Stock	12,000,000	100	9 July	10 Jan.
London, Paris & American	1,000,000	20	6 Sept.	8 Mar.
Manchester & County	5,000,000	100	15 July	15 Jan.
Manchester & Liverpool Distr.	6,000,000	60	15 & b. 5 July	15 & b. 5 Jan.
Mercantile of India	1,500,000	25	5 Oct.	5 Ap.
Mercantile of Lancashire	1,000,000	20	£2 10/- p.s. July	£2 10/- p.s. Jan.
Metropolitan of Eng. & Wales	7,500,000	50	12½ Aug.	12½ Feb.
Munster & Leinster	1,000,000	5	10 Aug.	10 Feb.
Natal	2,000,000	10	8 Aug.	8 & 2 b. Feb.
National	7,500,000	50	8 July	9 Jan.
National of Australia	4,000,000	10	5 May on Pref.	5 Nov. Pref.

PRINCIPAL JOINT-STOCK BANKS.

NAMES.	AUTHORIZED CAPITAL.	VALUE OF SHARES.	LAST TWO DIVIDENDS.	
	£	£	Per cent.	
National of China	1,000,000	10	nil	nil
National of India	1,000,000	25	7 Sept.	7 Ap.
National of New Zealand	1,750,000	£7 10s.	5 July	5 Jan.
National of Scotland	5,000,000	Stock.	13 & b. 2 July	13 & b. 3 Jan.
National Provincial	15,900,000	75 & 60	8 & b. 5 July	8 & b. 5 Jan.
North and South Wales	2,400,000	40	10 & b. 2½ July	10 & b. 4 Feb.
North Eastern	1,020,000	20	10 July	10 6/7 Feb.
North of Scotland	2,000,000	20	6¼ May	7¼ Nov.
North Western	2,000,000	20	6 July	6 Jan.
Northern Banking Co.	2,500,000[1]	50	11 "A" shs. Mr.	11 "A" shs. Sep.
Nottingham & Nottinghamshire	1,300,000	20	8 Aug.	8 Jan.
Nottingham Joint Stock	1,000,000	50	5 July	15 Jan.
Oldham Joint Stock	1,000,000	20	10 July	10 Jan.
Pares' Leicestershire	1,000,000	25	12 Aug.	13 Feb.
Parr's	6,000,000	100	19 A. & N.	19 F. & M.
Provincial of Ireland	4,080,000	100 & 20	10 Aug.	10 Feb.
Queensland National	3,000,000	8	nil	nil
Robinson, South African	3,000,000	4	10 Mar.	10 Nov.
Royal of Ireland	1,500,000	50	11 Ap.	11 Oct.
Royal of Queensland	1,425,000	9	2½ July	2½ Mar.
Royal of Scotland	2,000,000	Stock.	8 June	8 Dec.
Sheffield and Hallamshire	1,000,000	100	10 Jan.	10 & b. 1½ act. July
Sheffield and Rotherham	1,200,000	50 & 200	10 Aug.	12½ & b. 4/- Feb.
Sheffield Banking Co.	1,000,000	50	10 July	12½ Mar.
Stamford & Spalding	1,200,000	30	8 Aug.	12 Mar.
Standard of Australia	1,000,000	5	nil	nil
Standard of South Africa	4,000,000	100	10&15/-p.s.Oct.	10&15/-p.s.Ap.
Stuckey's Banking Co.	2,040,000	60	23½ Jan.	23½ July
Town & County	1,260,000	35	12½ Sept.	12½ Mar.
Ulster	3,000,000	15	18 Mar.	18 & b. 1 Sept.
Union of Australia	4,500,000	75	5 Aug.	5 Feb.
Union of London	11,000,000	100	10 July	10 Jan.
Union of Manchester	1,000,000	25	10 Jan.	10 July
Union of Scotland	5,000,000	50	10 May	10 Nov.
West Riding Union Bankg. Co.	2,000,000	50	8/- p.s. July	8/- p.s. Feb.
Williams, Deacon, Man. & Salf.	6,250,000	50	12½ July	12½ Jan.
Wilts & Dorset	2,500,000	50	20 July	20 Jan.
York City & County	1,250,000	10	15 July	18½ Jan.
York Union Banking Co.	1,500,000	60	10 Aug.	24 Feb.
Yorkshire Banking Co.	1,500,000	50	14 Aug.	14 Feb.

[1] 35,000 A £50 Shares; 15,000 B ditto £10 paid.

** In July, 1896, the liabilities of all the banks in the United Kingdom, including private banks, was £827,000,000, for acceptances, deposits, current accounts, notes in circulation, &c., in addition to the paid-up capital and reserve mentioned on page 71.

HIGHEST AND LOWEST PRICES OF

NAME OF STOCKS.	1881. H. & L.	1882. H. & L.	1883. H. & L.	1884. H. & L.	1885. H. & L.	1886. H. & L.
British Gov. Stocks—						
1 Consols 2¾ (Goschen's)	103	102½	102¾	102⅝	101½	102⅜
	98¼	99	99⅜	98⅞	94⅜	99⅜
2 Do. (Childers') ...	101¼	101¾	102⅞	102½	101⅛	102⅛
	96¾	98¼	98	99	93½	99⅛
3 India 3½%	104¼	102¼	103⅝	107½	103¾	102¾
	100	99½	101⅜	101½	96	99⅛
4 Do. 3%	...	...	...	...	92¼	91½
	...	...	...	...	85¼	85½
5 Do. Rupee Paper 3½%	...	...	...	...	...	74¼
	...	...	...	...	...	64½
Corporation Stocks—						
6 Birmingham 3½% ...	103	101⅛	101	104¼	101⅜	105
	98⅝	97¾	97¾	99¼	98½	100
7 Do. 3%	...	...	...	...	...	...
	...	...	...	...	...	...
8 Bradford 3½%	...	...	...	...	...	...
	...	...	...	...	...	...
9 Cardiff 3½%	...	...	...	...	98½	99½
	...	...	...	...	98	96¾
10 Liverpool 3½%	103⅞	102¼	101½	105¼	102	104¾
	99	98⅜	99½	98⅜	98½	100
11 Manchester 3%	...	...	..	...	...	...
	...	...	...	...	...	...
12 Metro. Cons. 3½% ...	108⅝	107¼	107¾	113	109⅞	110
	104	104⅜	103¾	104⅜	101	107

DIX F.

STOCKS AND SHARES, 1881—1896.

1887.	1888.	1889.	1890.	1891.	1892.	1893.	1894.	1895.	1896.	
H. & L.	H. & L.	H. & L.	H. & L.	H. & L.	H. & L.	H. & L.	H. & L.	H. & L.	H. & L.	
$103\frac{3}{4}$	$103\frac{3}{8}$	$99\frac{1}{4}$	$98\frac{3}{4}$	$97\frac{1}{2}$	$100\frac{1}{2}$	$99\frac{5}{8}$	$103\frac{5}{8}$	$108\frac{1}{4}$	114	1
$99\frac{7}{8}$	$99\frac{3}{8}$	$96\frac{1}{2}$	$93\frac{3}{8}$	$94\frac{3}{8}$	$96\frac{1}{4}$	97	$98\frac{3}{8}$	$103\frac{1}{2}$	$105\frac{1}{8}$	
$102\frac{7}{8}$	$101\frac{1}{2}$	$100\frac{1}{4}$	100	$99\frac{3}{8}$	$100\frac{1}{2}$	$102\frac{1}{4}$	$103\frac{5}{8}$	$106\frac{3}{4}$	$108\frac{3}{8}$	2
$99\frac{5}{8}$	97	$98\frac{3}{8}$	$95\frac{5}{8}$	$95\frac{7}{8}$	$96\frac{1}{4}$	$99\frac{7}{8}$	$100\frac{5}{8}$	103	$103\frac{1}{4}$	
$104\frac{1}{2}$	$108\frac{3}{8}$	$109\frac{5}{8}$	$109\frac{1}{4}$	110	$109\frac{7}{8}$	$110\frac{1}{2}$	$113\frac{1}{4}$	$118\frac{5}{8}$	$122\frac{1}{8}$	3
100	$103\frac{3}{4}$	$106\frac{1}{4}$	$104\frac{1}{2}$	$103\frac{3}{4}$	105	$106\frac{1}{2}$	$108\frac{5}{8}$	$112\frac{5}{8}$	$114\frac{1}{2}$	
94	100	102	$101\frac{1}{2}$	$99\frac{5}{8}$	$98\frac{1}{2}$	$100\frac{1}{4}$	$103\frac{1}{4}$	110	$115\frac{1}{4}$	4
$84\frac{1}{2}$	$93\frac{3}{4}$	$97\frac{5}{8}$	$94\frac{1}{2}$	$93\frac{1}{8}$	$94\frac{7}{8}$	$96\frac{5}{8}$	98	$102\frac{3}{4}$	105	
$71\frac{3}{4}$	$73\frac{3}{8}$	$69\frac{5}{8}$	$90\frac{5}{8}$	$82\frac{1}{2}$	$74\frac{1}{2}$	$71\frac{1}{2}$	$58\frac{1}{8}$	$62\frac{3}{4}$	$66\frac{1}{8}$	5
$66\frac{1}{4}$	65	$63\frac{1}{4}$	68	$72\frac{1}{2}$	62	$61\frac{1}{8}$	$54\frac{1}{2}$	$52\frac{5}{8}$	$59\frac{1}{4}$	
$105\frac{3}{4}$	$112\frac{3}{8}$	$112\frac{7}{8}$	$111\frac{5}{8}$	$112\frac{3}{8}$	$115\frac{5}{8}$	$116\frac{7}{8}$	$120\frac{1}{4}$	$124\frac{1}{4}$	131	6
$102\frac{1}{2}$	$105\frac{1}{2}$	$110\frac{5}{8}$	$107\frac{3}{4}$	$107\frac{3}{8}$	109	$112\frac{1}{4}$	114	$118\frac{3}{4}$	$116\frac{1}{2}$	
$94\frac{1}{2}$	101	102	102	$101\frac{1}{2}$	$102\frac{1}{4}$	$104\frac{1}{2}$	108	$113\frac{1}{2}$	117	7
$91\frac{3}{4}$	$94\frac{3}{8}$	$98\frac{3}{4}$	$99\frac{3}{4}$	98	$98\frac{3}{4}$	$100\frac{1}{2}$	$102\frac{1}{4}$	$105\frac{1}{4}$	111	
...	...	...	...	...	...	...	...	121	127	8
...	...	...	...	...	...	...	...	$118\frac{1}{2}$	$119\frac{1}{2}$	
$103\frac{3}{4}$	$109\frac{3}{4}$	$110\frac{1}{4}$	$109\frac{3}{4}$	$109\frac{1}{2}$	$112\frac{3}{8}$	$115\frac{5}{8}$	$117\frac{3}{4}$	120	$127\frac{3}{4}$	9
$96\frac{3}{4}$	$103\frac{1}{8}$	$107\frac{1}{4}$	106	$104\frac{1}{2}$	$106\frac{1}{4}$	$111\frac{1}{4}$	$112\frac{1}{4}$	$116\frac{1}{4}$	$117\frac{3}{4}$	
$105\frac{3}{4}$	112	$114\frac{5}{8}$	$114\frac{3}{4}$	$112\frac{1}{2}$	$116\frac{1}{4}$	119	$125\frac{5}{8}$	133	$143\frac{1}{2}$	10
$102\frac{5}{8}$	$105\frac{1}{2}$	$110\frac{1}{2}$	$110\frac{1}{2}$	$108\frac{5}{8}$	$111\frac{1}{4}$	$115\frac{1}{4}$	$116\frac{5}{8}$	125	130	
...	...	...	...	$97\frac{1}{2}$	$100\frac{3}{4}$	$102\frac{1}{4}$	$107\frac{5}{8}$	$110\frac{3}{4}$	$116\frac{1}{2}$	11
...	...	...	...	96	95	$98\frac{5}{8}$	101	$104\frac{3}{4}$	$107\frac{1}{2}$	
111	$115\frac{1}{2}$	$113\frac{1}{4}$	113	$111\frac{1}{2}$	$113\frac{3}{8}$	$115\frac{5}{8}$	$119\frac{7}{8}$	$123\frac{1}{4}$	$128\frac{1}{4}$	12
106	$110\frac{5}{8}$	111	109	$107\frac{3}{8}$	110	112	$114\frac{3}{8}$	$118\frac{1}{2}$	$115\frac{1}{4}$	

APPENDIX F.

NAME OF STOCKS.	1881. H. & L.	1882. H. & L.	1883. H. & L.	1884. H. & L.	1885. H. & L.	1886. H. & L.
13 Met. Cons. 3%	$99\frac{5}{8}$ / $95\frac{3}{4}$	$99\frac{1}{4}$ / $96\frac{1}{4}$	$98\frac{1}{4}$ / $95\frac{1}{2}$	$103\frac{5}{8}$ / $96\frac{3}{8}$	$100\frac{1}{4}$ / 94	$100\frac{1}{4}$ / 94
14 Do. 2½%	... / ...	... / ...	... / ...	... / ...	... / ...	.. / ...
Colonial Gov. Stocks—						
15 Canada 3½%	... / ...	... / ...	... / ...	... / ...	94 / $89\frac{1}{8}$	$99\frac{3}{4}$ / $92\frac{3}{4}$
16 Do. 3%	... / ...	... / ...	... / ...	... / ...	... / ...	... / ...
17 Cape of Good Hope 3½%	... / ...	... / ...	... / ...	... / ...	... / ...	... / ...
18 Natal 4½%	... / ...	... / ...	... / ...	... / ...	... / ...	... / ...
19 Do. 3½%	... / ...	... / ...	... / ...	... / ...	... / ...	... / ...
20 New South Wales 3½%	... / ...	... / ...	... / ...	... / ...	... / ...	... / ...
21 New Zealand 3½%	... / ...	... / ...	... / ...	... / ...	... / ...	... / ...
22 Queensland 3½%	... / ...	... / ...	... / ...	... / ...	... / ...	... / ...
23 Tasmania 3½%	... / ...	... / ...	... / ...	... / ...	... / ...	... / ...
24 Victoria 3½%	... / ...	... / ...	... / ...	... / ...	... / ...	... / ...
Foreign Securities—						
25 Argentine 6% Funding	... / ...	... / ...	... / ...	... / ...	... / ...	... / ...
26 Chilian 4½% 1886	... / ...	... / ...	... / ...	... / ...	... / ...	$99\frac{1}{8}$ / $98\frac{1}{4}$
27 Do. 5% 1892	... / ...	... / ...	... / ...	... / ...	... / ...	... / ...
28 Egyptian Daira Sa.	$79\frac{3}{8}$ / $68\frac{7}{8}$	$73\frac{3}{4}$ / $48\frac{1}{4}$	$76\frac{1}{4}$ / $60\frac{5}{8}$	$68\frac{5}{8}$ / 56	$67\frac{3}{4}$ / $53\frac{1}{2}$	75 / $61\frac{3}{8}$
29 Do. Pref.	$100\frac{1}{4}$ / $90\frac{5}{8}$	$96\frac{1}{2}$ / 73	$99\frac{1}{4}$ / $85\frac{1}{4}$	$94\frac{5}{8}$ / $80\frac{1}{4}$	$91\frac{5}{8}$ / $75\frac{1}{2}$	$98\frac{1}{4}$ / $87\frac{1}{4}$
30 Do. Unified	81 / $69\frac{1}{4}$	$73\frac{3}{4}$ / $47\frac{1}{2}$	$76\frac{5}{8}$ / $61\frac{1}{4}$	$69\frac{3}{8}$ / $56\frac{1}{2}$	$69\frac{3}{8}$ / $58\frac{5}{8}$	$77\frac{3}{8}$ / $63\frac{1}{2}$
31 Do. State Domain	$100\frac{3}{4}$ / $89\frac{3}{4}$	$94\frac{1}{4}$ / $70\frac{1}{4}$	$98\frac{7}{8}$ / $83\frac{3}{4}$	$93\frac{1}{2}$ / 80	90 / $74\frac{1}{4}$	98 / $87\frac{1}{2}$

1887. H. & L.	1888. H. & L.	1889. H. & L.	1890. H. & L.	1891. H. & L.	1892. H. & L.	1893. H. & L.	1894. H. & L.	1895. H. & L.	1896. H. & L.	
102	106¾	104¾	102¾	103⅞	104⅞	106½	110½	114¼	120	13
96	100¼	101⅝	98¾	99⅞	100⅞	102⅝	105½	109¼	107¼	
...	...	...	91¼	89⅞	90¾	92⅞	99¼	104	107	14
...	...	...	85	86⅜	87	88¼	91½	99¼	98	
103¼	109	107¼	106	104½	105⅝	106	107¾	111	111⅞	15
96½	101⅝	103⅛	101¾	100	101¾	101¼	102¼	104⅜	101	
...	95	97¾	96⅞	95¾	96	96¾	101⅛	103¼	107¼	16
...	92½	93⅜	91¾	91⅝	91⅞	92	93⅜	97¼	98⅛	
...	...	104⅝	103½	100¼	100¾	103½	111½	120¼	119½	17
...	...	100¾	98½	96¾	95½	99¼	100⅛	110¼	108½	
...	...	...	114½	112¼	109¾	110¾	115	124¼	126	18
...	...	...	109	106½	106¼	106½	107½	113	119½	
...	...	101¼	101½	98⅞	95⅞	98⅞	107	109¾	113¼	19
...	...	98¾	96¼	90¼	91¼	94⅞	95¾	105¼	102½	
...	107¾	106	103¾	103⅞	97½	97⅛	103⅛	109¼	112¼	20
...	99⅛	101¼	98	94	92¾	83⅛	95⅛	99¾	103⅝	
...	...	...	98⅝	98¼	98	97½	103½	107½	110⅜	21
...	...	...	93¼	91⅛	91½	90	96¼	100	101½	
...	100⅜	103	101¾	98¾	95⅛	92¼	100¼	107¼	111½	22
...	95¾	100	96¾	90⅛	87¾	75	90⅜	97	101	
...	...	101	100⅜	98¾	98	96	102¼	107⅝	112	23
...	...	98⅞	94½	92⅛	92¾	84	91	98¼	102¾	
...	...	105	103⅛	100½	98	93⅛	99⅞	105⅜	109¼	24
...	...	102⅜	97	93¼	89⅞	79	91¾	91¾	99⅝	
...	...	...	...	71½	73⅞	75⅛	74¼	80⅝	88	25
...	...	...	...	47	49	59½	62⅞	66	77½	
101¾	103⅛	106⅞	105¼	99¾	94	89½	96⅝	99⅞	95⅞	26
97⅜	97½	100⅜	98½	74½	87½	75	80⅜	92½	86	
...	...	...	...	...	97¾	96¾	102½	104¾	103½	27
...	...	...	...	...	97¼	82¼	88¾	98	92	
74¼	80⅝	88⅛	88⅛	98¾	99	103½	105½	105	104¾	28
64⅞	69½	79	79½	91½	93	98¼	102	98⅞	99¾	
100¼	104	105¾	105⅞	95	95⅞	98¼	103	104	104	29
91⅝	98⅜	101	100	85¼	87⅝	92½	97¼	96⅜	98	
77	85⅝	94⅛	99	98¾	99⅝	102⅞	105⅛	105¼	105⅜	30
67½	72⅝	83¼	92½	91½	93⅞	97⅞	100⅛	99¾	101	
98½	103	105½	105⅞	104	105½	106	106¾	107½	106	31
88	94	100½	100	101⅛	100¾	102	102⅞	102	101	

APPENDIX F.

NAME OF STOCKS.	1881. H. & L.	1882. H. & L.	1883. H. & L.	1884. H. & L.	1885. H. & L.	1886. H. & L.
32 French 3% Rentes	$86\frac{1}{2}$ / $81\frac{1}{2}$	$83\frac{5}{8}$ / $79\frac{7}{8}$	$81\frac{1}{2}$ / $74\frac{3}{4}$	79 / $74\frac{3}{4}$	$82\frac{1}{4}$ / $75\frac{1}{4}$	$83\frac{1}{4}$ / $79\frac{1}{4}$
33 Greek 1881	85 / $67\frac{1}{4}$	85 / 71	$72\frac{3}{8}$ / 65	74 / $66\frac{3}{4}$	$69\frac{7}{8}$ / 51	69 / $48\frac{3}{8}$
34 Greek 4% Rts.	... / ...	... / ...	... / ...	... / ...	... / ...	... / ...
35 Hungn. Gold Rts.	$103\frac{3}{4}$ / $91\frac{5}{8}$	$102\frac{3}{4}$ / $97\frac{5}{8}$	$103\frac{1}{8}$ / $98\frac{1}{2}$	$103\frac{3}{4}$ / $99\frac{3}{4}$	$83\frac{1}{4}$ / $72\frac{3}{4}$	$87\frac{3}{4}$ / 79
36 Italian 5%	$93\frac{1}{4}$ / $85\frac{1}{2}$	$90\frac{1}{4}$ / 83	$92\frac{5}{8}$ / 85	98 / $88\frac{7}{8}$	$97\frac{1}{2}$ / 88	$101\frac{1}{4}$ / $95\frac{1}{4}$
37 Mexican 6% 1888	... / ...	... / ...	... / ...	... / ...	... / ...	... / ...
38 Peruvian Deb.	... / ...	... / ...	... / ...	... / ...	... / ...	... / ...
39 Do. Pref.	27 / $16\frac{1}{4}$	$20\frac{1}{4}$ / $13\frac{1}{2}$	$18\frac{9}{16}$ / 14	$14\frac{7}{8}$ / $10\frac{7}{8}$	$16\frac{3}{8}$ / $9\frac{7}{8}$	$15\frac{1}{4}$ / $10\frac{5}{16}$
40 Russian 4%	$95\frac{5}{8}$ / $86\frac{1}{2}$	87 / $80\frac{3}{4}$	$88\frac{1}{2}$ / $81\frac{7}{8}$	$96\frac{1}{2}$ / $73\frac{1}{4}$	$97\frac{3}{4}$ / $80\frac{1}{4}$	$101\frac{1}{4}$ / $93\frac{1}{8}$
41 Spanish 4%	... / ...	... / ...	$64\frac{3}{4}$ / $55\frac{5}{8}$	$61\frac{1}{4}$ / $54\frac{3}{8}$	$62\frac{3}{8}$ / $50\frac{7}{8}$	$68\frac{1}{4}$ / $52\frac{3}{4}$
42 Ottoman 3½% Cons.	$95\frac{3}{4}$ / 71	$93\frac{5}{8}$ / $52\frac{1}{4}$	94 / $62\frac{3}{8}$	$91\frac{1}{4}$ / $64\frac{1}{4}$	$93\frac{3}{4}$ / $58\frac{3}{8}$	97 / 66
43 Do. Group A	$25\frac{5}{8}$ / $15\frac{1}{2}$	$28\frac{1}{2}$ / 20	$24\frac{1}{4}$ / 17	$36\frac{1}{2}$ / $23\frac{3}{4}$	$38\frac{1}{2}$ / 25	27 / 20
44 Do. do. B	... / ...	... / ...	... / ...	... / ...	... / ...	$15\frac{1}{2}$ / $13\frac{1}{2}$
45 Do. do. C & D	$20\frac{1}{4}$ / $12\frac{5}{8}$	$17\frac{7}{8}$ / $10\frac{3}{8}$	15 / $8\frac{1}{4}$	$17\frac{1}{4}$ / $13\frac{1}{2}$	$17\frac{1}{16}$ / $12\frac{1}{2}$	$15\frac{1}{4}$ / 12
46 Do. 4% 1891	... / ...	$90\frac{1}{4}$ / $60\frac{1}{4}$	$90\frac{7}{8}$ / 74	$83\frac{7}{8}$ / $76\frac{5}{8}$	$86\frac{1}{8}$ / $68\frac{3}{4}$	$89\frac{3}{4}$ / $77\frac{3}{4}$
47 U. S. 4% Fund	$122\frac{3}{8}$ / 115	124 / 119	127 / 120	128 / 121	127 / 124	$132\frac{1}{8}$ / $125\frac{1}{8}$
48 Uruguay 3½% Cons.	$39\frac{5}{8}$ / $33\frac{1}{2}$	$46\frac{1}{2}$ / $32\frac{3}{4}$	$57\frac{1}{4}$ / $36\frac{1}{2}$	60 / 51	$52\frac{3}{8}$ / $43\frac{1}{2}$	$50\frac{5}{8}$ / $36\frac{3}{4}$
Home Rails—						
49 Brighton Ord.	$145\frac{1}{2}$ / 136	147 / 119	$129\frac{3}{4}$ / $116\frac{1}{2}$	122 / 112	120 / 105	133 / $115\frac{1}{4}$
50 Do. Def.	$148\frac{1}{4}$ / $127\frac{3}{8}$	$146\frac{7}{8}$ / $106\frac{1}{8}$	$122\frac{7}{8}$ / $99\frac{3}{8}$	$108\frac{5}{8}$ / $89\frac{1}{4}$	$104\frac{7}{8}$ / 79	$119\frac{3}{4}$ / $93\frac{3}{8}$
51 Caledonian	$115\frac{3}{4}$ / $100\frac{1}{4}$	$112\frac{5}{8}$ / $100\frac{1}{4}$	$110\frac{3}{4}$ / $100\frac{3}{8}$	$103\frac{7}{8}$ / 92	$103\frac{3}{8}$ / $90\frac{7}{8}$	$105\frac{5}{8}$ / $96\frac{1}{4}$

HIGHEST AND LOWEST PRICES.

1887.	1888.	1889.	1890.	1891.	1892.	1893.	1894.	1895.	1896.	
H. & L.	H. & L.	H. & L.	H. & L.	H. & L.	H. & L.	H. & L.	H. & L.	H. & L.	H. & L.	
$81\frac{3}{4}$	83	88	95	$95\frac{1}{4}$	100	$98\frac{3}{4}$	$103\frac{5}{8}$	103	$102\frac{1}{2}$	} 32
75	$79\frac{1}{2}$	$81\frac{5}{8}$	$86\frac{1}{4}$	92	94	$93\frac{1}{4}$	$95\frac{1}{4}$	$98\frac{3}{4}$	100	
$75\frac{3}{4}$	$86\frac{1}{4}$	$95\frac{1}{4}$	$96\frac{3}{4}$	$91\frac{1}{4}$	83	$76\frac{5}{8}$	35	36	$32\frac{1}{2}$	} 33
$54\frac{1}{4}$	$66\frac{1}{4}$	$81\frac{3}{4}$	87	$72\frac{1}{2}$	$56\frac{1}{4}$	$28\frac{7}{8}$	$28\frac{1}{2}$	27	$28\frac{1}{4}$	
...	...	78	76	74	62	60	$28\frac{1}{8}$	$29\frac{7}{8}$	$27\frac{1}{2}$	} 34
...	...	73	68	$49\frac{3}{4}$	$44\frac{7}{8}$	24	23	24	23	
$82\frac{3}{4}$	$86\frac{5}{8}$	$88\frac{3}{4}$	$92\frac{3}{4}$	$92\frac{3}{4}$	$96\frac{1}{2}$	$96\frac{3}{4}$	102	$104\frac{1}{4}$	105	} 35
$72\frac{1}{2}$	$74\frac{3}{4}$	$82\frac{1}{2}$	$84\frac{3}{4}$	86	$90\frac{1}{4}$	$90\frac{1}{2}$	$92\frac{3}{8}$	99	100	
$99\frac{3}{8}$	$98\frac{3}{8}$	$97\frac{3}{4}$	$97\frac{1}{4}$	$94\frac{1}{4}$	$93\frac{7}{8}$	$92\frac{7}{8}$	$86\frac{7}{8}$	90	91	} 36
90	$91\frac{1}{8}$	$90\frac{3}{8}$	$90\frac{3}{4}$	$85\frac{1}{2}$	86	$77\frac{7}{8}$	$71\frac{1}{8}$	$82\frac{3}{4}$	$75\frac{1}{2}$	
...	...	...	$100\frac{1}{2}$	$93\frac{3}{4}$	$87\frac{1}{4}$	$85\frac{1}{2}$	$72\frac{1}{2}$	$97\frac{1}{4}$	$96\frac{5}{8}$	} 37
...	...	...	84	79	$76\frac{3}{4}$	52	57	$69\frac{3}{4}$	$87\frac{3}{4}$	
...	...	...	79	$85\frac{1}{2}$	$88\frac{1}{2}$	$83\frac{3}{8}$	$56\frac{3}{4}$	$59\frac{1}{2}$	$41\frac{1}{2}$	} 38
...	...	...	78	$71\frac{1}{2}$	$79\frac{1}{4}$	$52\frac{3}{4}$	$42\frac{7}{8}$	$36\frac{1}{2}$	$34\frac{3}{8}$	
$20\frac{1}{2}$	$18\frac{3}{4}$	20	$31\frac{1}{4}$	$37\frac{1}{2}$	$42\frac{1}{2}$	$35\frac{7}{8}$	16	$20\frac{3}{16}$	10	} 39
$13\frac{5}{16}$	$14\frac{7}{8}$	14	$31\frac{1}{4}$	$18\frac{3}{4}$	$34\frac{1}{4}$	$13\frac{3}{4}$	$8\frac{1}{2}$	7	$5\frac{5}{8}$	
99	$101\frac{1}{4}$	94	100	$100\frac{1}{2}$	$99\frac{1}{2}$	$101\frac{1}{4}$	$103\frac{5}{8}$	$104\frac{1}{2}$	105	} 40
89	$88\frac{3}{8}$	90	$92\frac{1}{2}$	$86\frac{1}{2}$	$91\frac{1}{2}$	$95\frac{1}{8}$	97	$99\frac{5}{8}$	100	
$68\frac{1}{4}$	$75\frac{5}{8}$	$77\frac{3}{4}$	$79\frac{1}{2}$	$78\frac{9}{16}$	$68\frac{3}{4}$	$67\frac{1}{2}$	$74\frac{1}{4}$	$78\frac{7}{8}$	$65\frac{1}{2}$	} 41
$58\frac{3}{4}$	$65\frac{3}{4}$	$71\frac{1}{16}$	$70\frac{5}{8}$	$61\frac{5}{8}$	$56\frac{3}{4}$	$58\frac{5}{8}$	$62\frac{1}{2}$	$60\frac{1}{8}$	$56\frac{1}{4}$	
98	102	$104\frac{1}{2}$	105	105	105	$106\frac{1}{2}$	$99\frac{3}{4}$	$100\frac{3}{8}$	97	} 42
67	$71\frac{3}{4}$	$83\frac{1}{4}$	$93\frac{1}{4}$	$87\frac{7}{8}$	92	$95\frac{5}{8}$	96	$91\frac{1}{4}$	$90\frac{1}{2}$	
23	26	$38\frac{7}{8}$	$46\frac{5}{8}$	$45\frac{1}{2}$	$43\frac{1}{2}$	53	$56\frac{5}{8}$	66	66	} 43
18	$21\frac{3}{4}$	$35\frac{1}{8}$	$37\frac{1}{4}$	$38\frac{1}{2}$	$32\frac{1}{4}$	$35\frac{1}{2}$	$46\frac{1}{2}$	55	55	
$14\frac{1}{2}$	$14\frac{1}{2}$	$23\frac{3}{8}$	$27\frac{1}{2}$	$26\frac{3}{4}$	$32\frac{1}{4}$	$35\frac{3}{4}$	$46\frac{1}{2}$	$48\frac{3}{8}$	39	} 44
$12\frac{3}{8}$	$14\frac{1}{2}$	$21\frac{1}{4}$	$21\frac{1}{8}$	$19\frac{3}{4}$	24	$29\frac{3}{8}$	$35\frac{3}{8}$	$24\frac{1}{2}$	$26\frac{3}{4}$	
$15\frac{3}{16}$	$15\frac{5}{8}$	$17\frac{13}{16}$	$19\frac{3}{16}$	$19\frac{3}{8}$	$23\frac{1}{4}$	$24\frac{1}{2}$	$29\frac{3}{8}$	$30\frac{5}{8}$	$22\frac{3}{8}$	} 45
$12\frac{1}{8}$	$12\frac{3}{4}$	17	$17\frac{5}{16}$	$16\frac{3}{8}$	$18\frac{1}{4}$	$20\frac{5}{8}$	$22\frac{1}{2}$	$16\frac{7}{8}$	$17\frac{3}{4}$	
$90\frac{1}{8}$	$98\frac{3}{4}$	$104\frac{1}{4}$	$105\frac{3}{8}$	$104\frac{1}{4}$	$94\frac{1}{4}$	$99\frac{1}{2}$	$104\frac{3}{8}$	105	$102\frac{7}{8}$	} 46
78	85	$95\frac{3}{8}$	$99\frac{3}{8}$	$101\frac{1}{4}$	$84\frac{3}{4}$	$93\frac{1}{2}$	98	$97\frac{3}{4}$	$97\frac{1}{8}$	
$132\frac{1}{2}$	$131\frac{3}{4}$	132	$129\frac{3}{4}$	$124\frac{1}{8}$	$120\frac{3}{4}$	$117\frac{1}{4}$	118	116	113	} 47
$127\frac{1}{8}$	$126\frac{3}{4}$	129	$123\frac{1}{4}$	119	116	112	$114\frac{1}{2}$	$112\frac{1}{2}$	108	
$73\frac{1}{4}$	$76\frac{1}{4}$	$75\frac{1}{2}$	$78\frac{1}{2}$	$55\frac{1}{2}$	$40\frac{1}{4}$	$38\frac{7}{8}$	$50\frac{1}{2}$	$53\frac{3}{4}$	$52\frac{1}{8}$	} 48
$44\frac{3}{8}$	65	$68\frac{1}{4}$	38	$29\frac{1}{2}$	27	$29\frac{1}{4}$	$34\frac{1}{4}$	$44\frac{1}{4}$	$45\frac{1}{8}$	
137	145	$162\frac{1}{2}$	$166\frac{1}{2}$	$165\frac{1}{2}$	$170\frac{1}{2}$	$169\frac{1}{2}$	$173\frac{1}{2}$	178	197	} 49
125	135	144	154	$150\frac{1}{2}$	157	$158\frac{1}{2}$	163	169	174	
$122\frac{1}{2}$	$133\frac{3}{4}$	$164\frac{3}{4}$	$169\frac{3}{4}$	164	$163\frac{3}{4}$	$159\frac{5}{8}$	$161\frac{1}{8}$	$166\frac{3}{4}$	$185\frac{3}{4}$	} 50
$106\frac{5}{8}$	$111\frac{1}{2}$	$131\frac{1}{4}$	$149\frac{5}{8}$	$137\frac{1}{2}$	$145\frac{1}{4}$	142	$147\frac{1}{2}$	$152\frac{3}{4}$	$161\frac{1}{4}$	
105	$118\frac{3}{4}$	$129\frac{1}{2}$	132	$123\frac{1}{4}$	$123\frac{3}{4}$	$121\frac{3}{4}$	132	$149\frac{3}{4}$	166	} 51
$93\frac{1}{2}$	$99\frac{1}{2}$	$114\frac{5}{8}$	$114\frac{1}{8}$	$111\frac{1}{4}$	$115\frac{1}{2}$	$111\frac{1}{4}$	$112\frac{1}{2}$	$125\frac{1}{2}$	143	

NAME OF STOCKS.	1881. H. & L.	1882. H. & L.	1883. H. & L.	1884. H. & L.	1885. H. & L.	1886. H. & L.
52 Caledonian Def. ...	...	...	...	...	...	...
	...	...	...	...	...	...
53 Chatham & Dover ...	34⅞	32⅜	29¼	24¼	20¼	26¾
	28¾	27⅜	22	17¾	13¼	18⅛
54 Do. Pref.	106½	109	106¾	106⅛	98	103⅜
	100¼	102½	100¼	94	73½	87½
55 Do. 2nd do.	...	...	...	77	70[1]	72
	...	...	...	51	50	47
56 District	82	65⅝	62⅛	72¼	60½	44½
	63½	54¼	51½	55½	34⅞	37
57 East London	35⅛	27½	26½	24¾	17	17⅜
	27	18⅞	19	17¼	9¾	8
58 Furness	152¾	163	149	118	107	106½
	136¼	135	118½	105½	98½	86¼
59 Great Eastern	74	79	78	69¼	69¼	74¼
	64⅜	69⅛	60⅞	56⅞	57⅞	62¼
60 Great Northern... ...	133½	132½	124¾	116	114½	117¾
	120	123½	111½	109	104½	108
61 Do. "A"	145½	143½	134½	112	106⅝	113¼
	122⅞	133	107¼	95½	92½	102
62 Do. Def.	...	...	...	...	...	...
	...	...	...	...	...	...
63 Great Western	139⅛	149	148½	145⅝	140⅞	139⅞
	122¾	133¼	132¾	132⅝	124⅞	126½
64 Hull & Barnsley ...	...	...	...	...	...	29¼
	...	...	...	...	...	14½
65 Lancas. & Yorkshire...	137⅞	135¾	132⅝	118⅜	117½	115¼
	130½	127	109	111¾	104¼	99¼
66 Metropolitan Cons. ...	125	124	121	118	113	118
	118	117	115	110	98	102¼
67 Do. Surplus Lands...	...	...	...	...	...	...
	...	...	...	...	...	...
68 Midland	143	143	140	137	134	131⅛
	132	134	131	129	125	122⅜
69 North British Pref. ...	...	...	...	...	...	...
	...	...	...	...	...	...
70 Do. Def.	...	...	...	...	...	...
	...	...	...	...	...	...
71 North Eastern	178	179	175	171	160	159¾
	157	163	165	153	142	142⅛
72 North Staffords... ..	89⅝	85¾	93¼	92½	92¾	94¼
	79½	77	83	86	81½	88¾

[1] Approximate

HIGHEST AND LOWEST PRICES.

1887. H. & L.	1888. H. & L.	1889. H. & L.	1890. H. & L.	1891. H. & L.	1892. H. & L.	1893. H. & L.	1894. H. & L.	1895. H. & L.	1896. H. & L.	
...	...	...	$54\frac{3}{8}$	$47\frac{1}{4}$	$47\frac{1}{8}$	$39\frac{1}{4}$	$46\frac{1}{2}$	$55\frac{1}{4}$	$64\frac{1}{2}$	} 52
...	...	...	$41\frac{3}{4}$	35	$36\frac{3}{4}$	$30\frac{7}{8}$	$32\frac{3}{8}$	40	$49\frac{7}{8}$	
$25\frac{1}{4}$	25	$29\frac{1}{8}$	$26\frac{1}{2}$	$20\frac{5}{16}$	$20\frac{5}{8}$	18	$18\frac{1}{8}$	$21\frac{1}{2}$	$21\frac{1}{16}$	} 53
$19\frac{3}{4}$	$19\frac{3}{4}$	$22\frac{1}{4}$	$18\frac{3}{8}$	$15\frac{3}{8}$	$16\frac{1}{4}$	$12\frac{3}{4}$	$12\frac{3}{8}$	$14\frac{1}{2}$	$14\frac{3}{4}$	
$102\frac{5}{8}$	$103\frac{1}{4}$	117	$115\frac{1}{4}$	$111\frac{1}{4}$	$109\frac{1}{4}$	$108\frac{1}{2}$	$119\frac{1}{2}$	$125\frac{1}{2}$	$138\frac{1}{2}$	} 54
$95\frac{1}{4}$	$95\frac{1}{4}$	$102\frac{1}{2}$	$106\frac{1}{4}$	$100\frac{1}{2}$	104	$93\frac{1}{2}$	$93\frac{1}{2}$	117	$118\frac{3}{4}$	
$67\frac{1}{4}$	$65\frac{1}{4}$	76	75	61	$57\frac{7}{8}$	$50\frac{1}{2}$	$59\frac{1}{2}$	$74\frac{1}{2}$	75	} 55
50	54	$61\frac{1}{2}$	$61\frac{1}{4}$	$47\frac{1}{2}$	48	35	33	$55\frac{1}{2}$	63	
$43\frac{1}{4}$	37	39	$34\frac{3}{4}$	$33\frac{5}{8}$	33	$34\frac{3}{4}$	$32\frac{3}{4}$	$31\frac{1}{4}$	$34\frac{1}{2}$	} 56
$33\frac{1}{4}$	$29\frac{3}{4}$	$30\frac{3}{8}$	$28\frac{3}{4}$	$28\frac{3}{8}$	$28\frac{1}{4}$	$22\frac{3}{16}$	$26\frac{5}{16}$	$24\frac{1}{2}$	$24\frac{5}{8}$	
$13\frac{3}{4}$	$12\frac{5}{8}$	$15\frac{1}{2}$	$11\frac{1}{2}$	$11\frac{1}{4}$	$10\frac{1}{2}$	9	8	$10\frac{1}{4}$	8	} 57
$7\frac{1}{2}$	$8\frac{1}{2}$	$9\frac{1}{2}$	$9\frac{1}{4}$	8	8	$6\frac{11}{16}$	6	$6\frac{1}{4}$	$6\frac{3}{4}$	
108	$106\frac{1}{2}$	$119\frac{1}{2}$	$119\frac{3}{4}$	$104\frac{1}{2}$	93	$75\frac{7}{8}$	85	$71\frac{1}{2}$	78	} 58
$88\frac{1}{4}$	$92\frac{1}{4}$	$102\frac{7}{8}$	98	85	$73\frac{1}{4}$	$65\frac{1}{2}$	65	$61\frac{3}{8}$	$59\frac{1}{2}$	
$70\frac{5}{8}$	$72\frac{1}{4}$	$84\frac{1}{4}$	$94\frac{1}{2}$	$97\frac{1}{2}$	$91\frac{1}{4}$	$86\frac{3}{8}$	$83\frac{3}{4}$	$88\frac{3}{4}$	$109\frac{1}{4}$	} 59
$64\frac{1}{4}$	$63\frac{3}{4}$	$68\frac{5}{8}$	$80\frac{3}{8}$	$86\frac{3}{4}$	$82\frac{1}{4}$	$73\frac{3}{8}$	$70\frac{5}{8}$	$74\frac{5}{8}$	$86\frac{1}{2}$	
...	...	$132\frac{1}{2}$	$128\frac{1}{4}$	113	$114\frac{3}{8}$	$117\frac{1}{2}$	$116\frac{1}{2}$	$119\frac{1}{4}$	$127\frac{3}{4}$	} 60
...	...	$117\frac{1}{2}$	$113\frac{1}{4}$	$106\frac{3}{4}$	108	$109\frac{1}{2}$	$109\frac{1}{2}$	$112\frac{1}{4}$	$117\frac{1}{2}$	
109	$106\frac{1}{4}$	$116\frac{5}{8}$	$110\frac{1}{2}$	$90\frac{1}{2}$	$78\frac{3}{4}$	68	$65\frac{1}{2}$	$56\frac{3}{4}$	$57\frac{1}{2}$	} 61
$96\frac{1}{2}$	$96\frac{1}{2}$	103	91	$70\frac{1}{2}$	$59\frac{1}{4}$	50	49	$44\frac{1}{2}$	$47\frac{7}{8}$	
...	...	...	87	$86\frac{1}{2}$	$76\frac{1}{2}$	$68\frac{1}{4}$	$65\frac{1}{2}$	$57\frac{7}{8}$	$61\frac{1}{8}$	} 62
...	...	...	87	$67\frac{1}{2}$	$58\frac{3}{8}$	$49\frac{1}{2}$	48	$44\frac{5}{8}$	$48\frac{7}{8}$	
$140\frac{3}{4}$	$152\frac{1}{8}$	172	$170\frac{7}{8}$	$166\frac{1}{4}$	$168\frac{5}{8}$	$168\frac{3}{8}$	$169\frac{1}{4}$	$165\frac{5}{8}$	$187\frac{1}{4}$	} 63
$132\frac{1}{4}$	$138\frac{5}{8}$	151	$159\frac{7}{8}$	$152\frac{5}{8}$	$156\frac{1}{4}$	$150\frac{5}{8}$	$150\frac{1}{2}$	$155\frac{1}{4}$	$159\frac{1}{4}$	
$41\frac{1}{4}$	$42\frac{1}{2}$	$39\frac{3}{4}$	$41\frac{1}{4}$	41	$41\frac{1}{4}$	$33\frac{5}{8}$	35	$39\frac{5}{8}$	43	} 64
16	$24\frac{1}{2}$	$32\frac{3}{4}$	$34\frac{1}{4}$	31	$31\frac{1}{4}$	20	26	$30\frac{1}{2}$	$32\frac{3}{4}$	
$123\frac{1}{2}$	$121\frac{1}{4}$	$127\frac{5}{8}$	$125\frac{1}{4}$	118	112	$109\frac{1}{4}$	116	$130\frac{1}{4}$	$153\frac{5}{8}$	} 65
$113\frac{1}{2}$	114	$116\frac{5}{8}$	$115\frac{1}{2}$	$105\frac{1}{2}$	$103\frac{1}{2}$	$102\frac{1}{4}$	102	$113\frac{1}{4}$	$127\frac{1}{2}$	
$72\frac{1}{2}$	$77\frac{3}{4}$	$92\frac{1}{2}$	$84\frac{1}{4}$	92	$90\frac{1}{4}$	$89\frac{3}{8}$	$93\frac{3}{4}$	$96\frac{1}{2}$	117	} 66
62	64	$74\frac{1}{4}$	$74\frac{1}{4}$	$75\frac{1}{2}$	$85\frac{1}{2}$	$81\frac{1}{4}$	$79\frac{3}{4}$	88	$90\frac{3}{4}$	
75	$72\frac{1}{2}$	71	68	$74\frac{1}{2}$	76	$77\frac{3}{4}$	86	91	$95\frac{1}{2}$	} 67
$64\frac{3}{4}$	$65\frac{1}{2}$	67	62	$62\frac{1}{2}$	72	$72\frac{5}{8}$	$73\frac{1}{2}$	$80\frac{3}{4}$	88	
$129\frac{3}{4}$	$136\frac{1}{2}$	$150\frac{1}{4}$	$150\frac{1}{2}$	$163\frac{1}{2}$	$164\frac{1}{4}$	$162\frac{5}{8}$	$162\frac{1}{4}$	159	$174\frac{7}{8}$	} 68
$121\frac{1}{2}$	$124\frac{1}{2}$	$135\frac{5}{8}$	$139\frac{1}{4}$	147	$152\frac{1}{4}$	$146\frac{5}{8}$	$145\frac{1}{4}$	$150\frac{1}{4}$	154	
...	$77\frac{7}{8}$	$80\frac{1}{4}$	$79\frac{1}{4}$	$76\frac{3}{4}$	$72\frac{1}{2}$	$73\frac{1}{4}$	$79\frac{1}{4}$	$85\frac{5}{8}$	$94\frac{3}{4}$	} 69
...	73	$74\frac{1}{4}$	$73\frac{1}{4}$	$63\frac{3}{4}$	$67\frac{1}{4}$	$65\frac{1}{2}$	$70\frac{1}{4}$	76	$79\frac{1}{4}$	
...	$56\frac{1}{2}$	$65\frac{3}{4}$	$74\frac{7}{8}$	$52\frac{5}{8}$	$48\frac{1}{4}$	$40\frac{5}{8}$	$43\frac{5}{8}$	$46\frac{3}{4}$	$53\frac{5}{8}$	} 70
...	$50\frac{3}{4}$	$54\frac{5}{8}$	$51\frac{1}{4}$	$36\frac{1}{2}$	$36\frac{3}{8}$	30	$32\frac{1}{2}$	36	$38\frac{7}{8}$	
$158\frac{5}{8}$	163	178	$175\frac{1}{2}$	$168\frac{1}{2}$	$163\frac{3}{4}$	$161\frac{1}{4}$	$166\frac{7}{8}$	$169\frac{5}{8}$	$184\frac{7}{8}$	} 71
$149\frac{1}{4}$	150	$162\frac{1}{2}$	$161\frac{3}{4}$	$153\frac{1}{2}$	$151\frac{1}{8}$	$151\frac{1}{2}$	$154\frac{1}{2}$	$158\frac{1}{2}$	$162\frac{1}{4}$	
$100\frac{5}{8}$	114	$119\frac{1}{4}$	$120\frac{1}{2}$	$126\frac{1}{4}$	130	$128\frac{1}{4}$	$136\frac{1}{2}$	$131\frac{1}{2}$	$134\frac{1}{2}$	} 72
$90\frac{1}{4}$	$99\frac{1}{2}$	$112\frac{1}{2}$	$110\frac{1}{4}$	$120\frac{1}{4}$	$122\frac{1}{2}$	120	122	$123\frac{1}{2}$	126	

prices only.

NAME OF STOCKS.	1881. H. & L.	1882. H. & L.	1883. H. & L.	1884. H. & L.	1885. H. & L.	1886. H. & L.
73 North Western	172	180	178	174	170	167
	157	165	169	162	153	151½
74 Sheffield Def.	63¾	58	55⅜	45⅞	39	41
	43⅛	48	44⅞	34½	29	32⅞
75 South Eastern	145	141¾	132½	128½	123	130½
	131	127	121	119	110	117
76 Do. "A"	134	132	122	111	101	114
	121	114	108	95	77	92⅜
77 South Western	141½	138⅞	136	131½	129½	128¾
	132¼	131	128	122¾	119½	118¼
78 Taff Vale	...	...	...	...	...	...
	...	...	...	...	...	...
79 Tilbury & Southend...	179½	167	158	153½	159	157¾
	120¼	142	144	137½	143	140½
Col. & Ind. Rails, &c.—						
80 Bengal, Nagpur... ...	...	...	...	...	...	...
	...	...	...	...	...	...
81 Bombay, Baroda & Cen.	142	148	148	156½	154½	170
India	131¾	136	140	143¼	132	150½
82 Canadian Pacific ...	...	...	67⅞	59½	65	75¾
	...	...	51⅝	41¼	36½	63¼
83 Do. 3½% 50-year Land	...	...	...	...	...	...
Grant	...	...	...	...	...	...
84 Do. 4% Cons. Deb.	...	...	...	...	...	...
	...	...	...	...	...	...
85 Delhi, Umballa & Kalka	...	...	...	...	...	...
	...	...	...	...	...	...
86 Grand Trunk	26	29	28	18	12	17⅜
	15	15	16	7	6	9
87 Do. Guaranteed ...	...	...	...	82½	73⅛	79
	...	...	...	70⅞	50	54
88 Do. 1st Pref.... ...	106¾	110	108½	104¼	78⅝	85⅜
	93¾	96	100¼	71½	42⅝	52¼
89 Do. 2nd Pref. ...	98	101	99	88	48	70¾
	76	76	81	43	29	35½
90 Do. 3rd Pref. ...	54½	64⅜	62⅜	45¼	25½	41
	33	32⅜	38¾	20¼	14	10⅛
91 Great Indian Peninsula	140¼	147¼	148	152	145¾	153
	126¾	134	140	139	126	141
92 Hudson's Bay Shares .	27⅝	40¾	33⅜	26	24⅛	26 11/16
	17⅞	25⅝	20¾	21¼	14 15/16	21 11/16

HIGHEST AND LOWEST PRICES. 251

1887.	1888.	1889.	1890.	1891.	1892.	1893.	1894.	1895.	1896.	
H. & L.	H. & L.	H. & L.	H. & L.	H. & L.	H. & L.	H. & L.	H. & L.	H. & L.	H. & L.	
$169\frac{1}{4}$	173	189	$185\frac{1}{4}$	$180\frac{3}{4}$	$177\frac{1}{4}$	$176\frac{1}{4}$	$179\frac{3}{4}$	$187\frac{1}{4}$	$209\frac{5}{8}$	} 73
160	$163\frac{1}{4}$	$178\frac{1}{4}$	174	$167\frac{3}{4}$	$170\frac{1}{4}$	162	$161\frac{1}{2}$	$174\frac{7}{8}$	$185\frac{1}{4}$	
$44\frac{1}{4}$	40	$49\frac{1}{4}$	$53\frac{3}{4}$	39	39	$33\frac{7}{8}$	$32\frac{1}{4}$	$30\frac{5}{8}$	$29\frac{1}{4}$	} 74
$33\frac{3}{4}$	$32\frac{3}{4}$	$37\frac{7}{8}$	$34\frac{1}{4}$	$31\frac{1}{4}$	32	$22\frac{7}{8}$	20	$23\frac{1}{2}$	$22\frac{1}{2}$	
132	135	$138\frac{1}{2}$	134	128	122	126	133	$139\frac{1}{2}$	$150\frac{1}{4}$	} 75
124	124	130	125	114	107	111	112	131	$135\frac{1}{4}$	
$113\frac{3}{8}$	$114\frac{1}{4}$	$117\frac{5}{8}$	$107\frac{3}{4}$	$97\frac{1}{4}$	$90\frac{1}{4}$	89	$91\frac{7}{8}$	$95\frac{1}{4}$	$105\frac{1}{8}$	} 76
97	$98\frac{1}{2}$	$104\frac{1}{4}$	$95\frac{5}{8}$	$79\frac{3}{4}$	$69\frac{1}{4}$	$68\frac{3}{8}$	$65\frac{3}{4}$	$83\frac{3}{4}$	$83\frac{7}{8}$	
133	144	160	167	164	178	195	197	204	217	} 77
123	$131\frac{1}{2}$	$143\frac{1}{2}$	$150\frac{1}{2}$	153	161	$175\frac{7}{8}$	180	194	$197\frac{1}{4}$	
...	...	$87\frac{1}{2}$	90	$79\frac{5}{8}$	$81\frac{3}{4}$	88	$83\frac{1}{8}$	84	95	} 78
...	...	80	63	$69\frac{1}{2}$	69	$75\frac{1}{2}$	$75\frac{1}{2}$	77	78	
$143\frac{1}{2}$	$135\frac{1}{2}$	$133\frac{3}{4}$	128	$110\frac{1}{4}$	$118\frac{1}{2}$	$114\frac{1}{4}$	117	$123\frac{3}{4}$	$136\frac{3}{4}$	} 79
132	$121\frac{1}{2}$	$118\frac{1}{2}$	$102\frac{1}{2}$	95	108	104	$104\frac{1}{2}$	115	118	
$110\frac{3}{8}$	117	120	$120\frac{1}{2}$	120	119	118	121	$122\frac{1}{2}$	126	} 80
105	$107\frac{3}{4}$	$115\frac{3}{4}$	115	$109\frac{1}{2}$	114	113	$113\frac{3}{4}$	118	$117\frac{1}{4}$	
$171\frac{1}{4}$	$176\frac{1}{2}$	190	$191\frac{1}{4}$	$189\frac{1}{2}$	$192\frac{1}{2}$	$196\frac{1}{2}$	$208\frac{1}{2}$	$229\frac{1}{2}$	$253\frac{1}{2}$	} 81
160	$160\frac{1}{2}$	173	179	$179\frac{1}{2}$	181	$184\frac{1}{2}$	187	203	219	
$70\frac{1}{2}$	$64\frac{1}{2}$	$76\frac{5}{8}$	$86\frac{1}{2}$	$95\frac{5}{8}$	$97\frac{1}{2}$	93	$75\frac{7}{8}$	$65\frac{5}{8}$	$65\frac{1}{8}$	} 82
$52\frac{1}{8}$	$52\frac{1}{2}$	$48\frac{1}{2}$	$66\frac{7}{8}$	$74\frac{7}{8}$	$87\frac{1}{8}$	$66\frac{1}{2}$	59	35	51	
...	...	...	$100\frac{1}{4}$	$99\frac{1}{4}$	$102\frac{1}{4}$	$105\frac{1}{4}$	107	$109\frac{1}{2}$	$110\frac{3}{4}$	} 83
...	...	...	$94\frac{3}{4}$	96	$96\frac{1}{2}$	$100\frac{7}{8}$	103	97	$99\frac{1}{2}$	
...	...	...	$103\frac{1}{2}$	$105\frac{1}{4}$	106	$107\frac{1}{2}$	$108\frac{1}{2}$	$104\frac{7}{8}$	$112\frac{1}{2}$	} 84
...	...	,,	$97\frac{5}{8}$	$98\frac{1}{4}$	$100\frac{3}{4}$	$101\frac{1}{4}$	$103\frac{3}{4}$	$90\frac{1}{4}$	98	
...	...	...	$121\frac{1}{4}$	$115\frac{1}{2}$	106	$99\frac{1}{2}$	$96\frac{1}{2}$	112	120	} 85
...	...	...	110	99	85	$88\frac{1}{2}$	83	96	110	
$17\frac{3}{4}$	$13\frac{1}{4}$	$13\frac{7}{8}$	$12\frac{3}{4}$	$11\frac{1}{4}$	$11\frac{9}{16}$	$9\frac{5}{8}$	7	7	$6\frac{3}{16}$	} 86
$11\frac{1}{16}$	$9\frac{1}{4}$	$9\frac{5}{8}$	$8\frac{1}{2}$	$8\frac{3}{4}$	$8\frac{1}{4}$	$5\frac{5}{8}$	5	$4\frac{3}{8}$	$4\frac{3}{16}$	
$82\frac{1}{8}$	$76\frac{1}{4}$	$80\frac{7}{8}$	$81\frac{1}{4}$	$77\frac{1}{4}$	$78\frac{1}{4}$	$75\frac{5}{8}$	$62\frac{1}{4}$	$54\frac{1}{8}$	$48\frac{1}{8}$	} 87
70	$64\frac{1}{4}$	$70\frac{1}{2}$	$68\frac{1}{2}$	$68\frac{1}{2}$	$67\frac{1}{2}$	$56\frac{7}{8}$	$44\frac{1}{2}$	35	$36\frac{3}{4}$	
$85\frac{3}{4}$	$78\frac{3}{4}$	$80\frac{3}{8}$	$81\frac{1}{8}$	74	$73\frac{1}{4}$	$65\frac{1}{8}$	$46\frac{3}{4}$	$44\frac{1}{2}$	$38\frac{1}{4}$	} 88
$72\frac{1}{2}$	$56\frac{3}{4}$	$65\frac{5}{8}$	$54\frac{3}{4}$	55	$56\frac{5}{8}$	$41\frac{1}{8}$	$34\frac{3}{4}$	$26\frac{1}{8}$	$27\frac{3}{8}$	
$74\frac{1}{4}$	$60\frac{1}{2}$	61	60	$54\frac{1}{4}$	$54\frac{5}{8}$	$44\frac{3}{4}$	31	28	$24\frac{5}{8}$	} 89
$52\frac{1}{2}$	$37\frac{1}{2}$	$45\frac{1}{8}$	34	$34\frac{1}{2}$	$36\frac{5}{8}$	$26\frac{5}{16}$	23	$17\frac{7}{8}$	$16\frac{1}{4}$	
$41\frac{1}{4}$	$30\frac{1}{4}$	$35\frac{3}{4}$	$32\frac{1}{4}$	$29\frac{5}{8}$	$30\frac{1}{4}$	$23\frac{5}{8}$	$17\frac{1}{4}$	$16\frac{5}{16}$	$13\frac{1}{4}$	} 90
$25\frac{3}{4}$	$21\frac{1}{8}$	$25\frac{1}{4}$	$19\frac{1}{2}$	$19\frac{1}{4}$	$19\frac{5}{8}$	$14\frac{7}{8}$	$12\frac{1}{2}$	$9\frac{3}{16}$	9	
$161\frac{1}{2}$	174	179	178	178	$177\frac{1}{2}$	$174\frac{1}{2}$	175	179	$191\frac{3}{4}$	} 91
144	155	$166\frac{3}{4}$	$161\frac{1}{2}$	168	167	$158\frac{1}{2}$	155	$166\frac{3}{4}$	$166\frac{1}{2}$	
$25\frac{9}{16}$	$23\frac{1}{2}$	$22\frac{7}{16}$	$22\frac{1}{2}$	$19\frac{5}{16}$	$16\frac{7}{8}$	17	$15\frac{1}{8}$	$16\frac{7}{8}$	16	} 92
$20\frac{5}{8}$	$16\frac{1}{4}$	$18\frac{5}{8}$	$17\frac{5}{8}$	$14\frac{3}{16}$	$13\frac{1}{2}$	$12\frac{3}{4}$	$12\frac{1}{2}$	$12\frac{5}{8}$	$13\frac{1}{4}$	

NAME OF STOCKS.	1881. H. & L.	1882. H. & L.	1883. H. & L.	1884. H. & L.	1885. H. & L.	1886. H. & L.
93 Indian Midland ...	...	...	...	...	...	$110\frac{1}{2}$
	...	...	..	...	...	$106\frac{1}{2}$
94 Madras	131	$130\frac{1}{2}$	130	131	$129\frac{1}{2}$	$131\frac{1}{2}$
	$123\frac{1}{2}$	123	124	124	113	$125\frac{1}{2}$
95 Nizam State Railway...	...	...	...	19	$18\frac{3}{4}$	109
	...	...	...	$17\frac{3}{8}$	$14\frac{7}{8}$	$100\frac{1}{2}$
96 Southern Mahratta ...	...	...	...	...	..	106
	...	...	...	...	...	$99\frac{1}{4}$
97 Suez Canal...	...	...	...	$86\frac{1}{8}$	$88\frac{1}{4}$	$88\frac{3}{4}$
	...	...	...	$71\frac{7}{8}$	$71\frac{1}{8}$	$77\frac{7}{8}$
Foreign Rails—						
98 Buenos Ayres & Rosario	...	...	...	...	$114\frac{3}{4}$	$164\frac{1}{4}$
	...	...	...	...	$86\frac{1}{2}$	114
99 Central Argentine ...	$24\frac{3}{8}$	124	$160\frac{1}{2}$	183	$179\frac{1}{2}$	$179\frac{1}{8}$
	$19\frac{5}{8}$	$102\frac{1}{4}$	$122\frac{1}{2}$	$150\frac{1}{2}$	$154\frac{1}{2}$	154
100 Central Uruguay of	...	...	...	...	...	...
Montevideo... ...	...	...	...	...	...	...
101 Gt. Western of Brazil	...	$28\frac{1}{4}$	$27\frac{1}{8}$	$26\frac{1}{4}$	$22\frac{7}{8}$	21
	...	25	$22\frac{3}{4}$	$21\frac{1}{2}$	$19\frac{1}{2}$	$16\frac{1}{8}$
102 Mexican Cent. 4 %	...	...	...	...	...	...
Cons. Mort.... ...	...	..	...	...	...	...
103 Mexican Rails... ...	$99\frac{3}{4}$	$149\frac{1}{8}$	$146\frac{3}{4}$	$64\frac{3}{8}$	$37\frac{1}{2}$	$57\frac{5}{8}$
	11	$81\frac{3}{4}$	$60\frac{1}{2}$	25	$20\frac{11}{16}$	$25\frac{1}{8}$
104 Do. 1st Pref. ...	$141\frac{7}{8}$	157	$145\frac{3}{4}$	117	$94\frac{3}{8}$	$118\frac{5}{8}$
	$120\frac{5}{8}$	$129\frac{1}{2}$	$114\frac{1}{2}$	68	$71\frac{1}{2}$	$78\frac{1}{4}$
105 Do. 2nd Pref. ...	$104\frac{3}{8}$	$119\frac{1}{2}$	109	$76\frac{3}{4}$	$53\frac{1}{2}$	$77\frac{1}{2}$
	$82\frac{1}{2}$	$89\frac{1}{4}$	$74\frac{1}{2}$	35	$33\frac{1}{4}$	$37\frac{1}{2}$
106 North West. of Uru-	...	...	...	...	$47\frac{1}{2}$	79
guay	...	...	...	...	19	37
American Rails—						
107 Atchison, Topeka, and	...	...	...	...	...	...
Santa Fé	...	...	...	...	...	...
108 Do. Adjustment Mort-	...	...	...	...	...	...
gage	...	...	...	..	...	...
109 Baltimore & Ohio Com.	...	...	...	...	...	...
Cap. Stock	...	...	...	...	...	...
110 Cent. of New Jer. Gen.	123	117	$117\frac{1}{2}$	$117\frac{1}{2}$	111	$120\frac{1}{2}$
Mort.	115	$109\frac{3}{4}$	111	100	$95\frac{1}{4}$	$107\frac{1}{2}$
111 Central Pacific ...	$105\frac{1}{2}$	$100\frac{3}{4}$	$91\frac{3}{4}$	$68\frac{7}{8}$	51	$52\frac{1}{8}$
	87	$88\frac{3}{4}$	$63\frac{3}{4}$	$29\frac{7}{8}$	$27\frac{1}{2}$	$38\frac{3}{4}$

1887. H. & L.	1888. H. & L.	1889. H. & L.	1890. H. & L.	1891. H. & L.	1892. H. & L.	1893. H. & L.	1894. H. & L.	1895. H. & L.	1896. H. & L.	
110¾	118	122½	124	120¼	119	118	120¾	121¼	123	93
103	108⅜	116	115½	110	113	113	113½	117½	117½	
134¾	146	150	151½	153½	151	151⅝	159½	171½	180½	94
125½	131⅜	143½	145½	139	142½	142	145¼	156½	165	
113¾	118½	121½	126	124¾	120½	119½	123	130	131½	95
106¼	108½	112½	117	113½	115½	115½	114½	120	123	
111½	116½	118⅞	117½	116½	116½	116	122	129	131	96
101½	107¾	112	112	109	110	109½	112¾	119½	122½	
83⅞	89½	97½	97½	116	113	109½	125	135	138	97
75	81½	85¼	90	94	102½	100½	106	121½	128	
169	181	185½	172½	138	84	80	71	69¼	73½	98
138	157	162	119	61	56	46	50	55	53	
200	218	219	185½	94½	75¼	72⅜	73⅝	74½	87½	99
164	165	172	85	40	40	50	56	65	62½	
...	...	...	160	113	80½	80¾	102¾	114¾	107½	100
...	...	...	104	72½	55¼	60	69¼	96	89½	
20⅛	22¼	21⅞	17¾	17	13½	14¼	18⅛	18¼	16½	101
18⅛	19¼	16	14½	11⅞	10⅜	10	11½	13¾	13	
...	74½	75	81¼	77	75½	68⅛	61½	73¾	73¾	102
...	64¾	66½	68¾	70¼	66	45	49½	55¼	63½	
67½	54¾	58	67¾	52	34¼	24⅝	20¼	26¾	21 13/16	103
34⅞	37¾	39⅛	31⅛	27⅞	20¾	10½	12⅞	14	15⅝	
131⅝	127⅝	133⅝	134¾	125⅝	113	87¾	78	87¼	78¾	104
107¼	109½	112⅜	109¾	102⅜	76¼	54½	55¼	57	62	
90	86⅛	93½	95⅜	85½	58⅛	50	44½	44½	36	105
65	67½	68¼	67½	46⅞	35½	36½	27⅝	28	27	
81	84	91¼	88	57	37¼	28½	36	33	25	106
60½	66½	77¼	57	25	24¼	19¼	19¾	25	18½	
...	...	...	...	49	48	37½	16½	24	18 3/16	107
...	...	...	...	25¼	43¼	12¾	3	3½	9	
...	...	...	73½	69½	69⅞	59⅛	40¼	38	46⅜	108
...	...	...	48⅞	41	54¼	31	15½	15½	28½	
...	...	...	...	...	100¼	100⅛	83½	68	46	109
...	...	...	...	...	95¾	58	60⅞	30	12½	
122	...	118	116½	115	116¾	116½	121	124	123½	110
111¼	...	108	110	110¼	111½	108	114½	113	112¼	
52⅛	45⅛	38	38⅛	36½	36¾	30½	19	21⅜	18¼	111
38¾	28	34¼	27	27½	28	14¼	10½	12⅜	13	

APPENDIX F.

NAME OF STOCKS.	1881. H. & L.	1882. H. & L.	1883. H. & L.	1884. H. & L.	1885. H. & L.	1886. H. & L.
112 Chesapeake & Ohio 4½% 1892	... ...	... ...	... ...	... ...	... ...	... ...
113 Chicago & Milwaukee	$130\frac{3}{4}$ 107	$131\frac{1}{4}$ 102	$110\frac{7}{8}$ $95\frac{1}{8}$	97 61	$101\frac{7}{8}$ $66\frac{1}{2}$	$101\frac{3}{4}$ $84\frac{3}{8}$
114 Do. Pref.	... ...	... ...	... ...	... ..	... ...	$129\frac{1}{4}$ 119
115 Do. Gen. Mort. ...	... ...	... ...	... ...	... ...	... ...	... ...
116 Cleveland & Pitts ...	... ...	... ...	... ...	... ...	$75\frac{1}{2}$ $70\frac{3}{8}$	$80\frac{1}{4}$ $75\frac{3}{4}$
117 Denver & Rio... ...	... ...	76 $40\frac{1}{8}$	$52\frac{3}{8}$ $23\frac{1}{2}$	$26\frac{1}{16}$ $7\frac{1}{2}$	$24\frac{3}{4}$ $4\frac{1}{4}$	$19\frac{7}{8}$ 16
118 Do. Pref.	... ...	... ...	... ...	... ...	... ...	... ...
119 Erie	54 $42\frac{1}{4}$	$44\frac{3}{4}$ 34	42 $28\frac{3}{8}$	$29\frac{1}{16}$ $11\frac{1}{2}$	$29\frac{1}{4}$ $9\frac{1}{2}$	$39\frac{3}{8}$ $22\frac{1}{4}$
120 Do. 1st Cons. Mort.	$136\frac{1}{2}$ $129\frac{1}{4}$	136 127	133 $125\frac{1}{2}$	... ...	132 144	$140\frac{1}{4}$ 131
121 Illinois Central ...	150 129	155 131	$152\frac{3}{8}$ $128\frac{5}{8}$	142 113	$143\frac{3}{8}$ 122	$146\frac{1}{2}$ $135\frac{1}{2}$
122 Do. 4%	... ...	... ...	.. ...	... ...	... ...	... ...
123 Lake Shore	... ...	... ...	$118\frac{3}{8}$ $97\frac{3}{8}$	$106\frac{1}{2}$ $61\frac{1}{8}$	93 ...	$103\frac{5}{8}$ $77\frac{3}{8}$
124 Lehigh Valley 1st Mort. 4½%	... ...	... ...	... ...	... ...	$52\frac{1}{2}$ ...	... ...
125 Louisville & Nashville	... ...	... ...	... ...	50 $23\frac{1}{4}$	$53\frac{3}{4}$ $23\frac{1}{8}$	$70\frac{1}{2}$ $34\frac{5}{8}$
126 Missouri, Kansas, and Texas	... ...	... ...	... ...	... ...	30' 25	$39\frac{5}{8}$ 24
127 Do. 1st Mort. Gld.	... ...	... ...	... ...	... ...	... ...	... ...
128 New York Central ...	$159\frac{3}{4}$ $135\frac{1}{4}$	$140\frac{1}{2}$ 127	133 $116\frac{1}{2}$	$120\frac{5}{8}$ $86\frac{1}{2}$	$110\frac{3}{4}$ $83\frac{1}{2}$	$120\frac{1}{2}$ $101\frac{1}{4}$
129 New York & Ontario	... ...	... ...	... ...	$17\frac{5}{8}$ $8\frac{1}{4}$	22 $6\frac{1}{2}$	$23\frac{5}{8}$ $15\frac{1}{4}$
130 New York O. & W., Cons. 1st Mort. ...	... ...	... ...	... ...	... ...	... ...	... ...
131 Norfolk & West. Pref.	... ...	$59\frac{5}{8}$ 50	$51\frac{1}{2}$ 35	$42\frac{5}{8}$ 21	$35\frac{1}{2}$ $14\frac{1}{4}$	$60\frac{1}{2}$ 26
132 Do. 100 years old 5%	... ...	... ...	... ...	... ...	... ...	... ...

[1] Approximate

1887. H. & L.	1888. H. & L.	1889. H. & L.	1890. H. & L.	1891. H. & L.	1892. H. & L.	1893. H. & L.	1894. H. & L.	1895. H. & L.	1896. H. & L.	
...	...	...	...	...	...	86 1/2	80 1/4	86 1/4	78 1/2	112
...	...	...	...	...	...	70 1/4	75	65	66	
101 3/4	97 1/2	76 1/2	81 1/2	84 7/8	86 3/4	85 1/8	69 1/4	80	83	113
84 3/8	72 1/4	62 1/8	45	52 1/2	77 1/2	50	59 3/4	54 3/8	61 3/4	
130 3/4	120 1/4	118 1/8	125 3/4	127	131 1/4	128 1/2	126 1/4	133	134	114
116 1/2	103	98 1/2	108	113	122	110	119 1/2	117	126 1/2	
...	...	...	99 1/2	91	95 3/4	98	94 1/4	99 1/2	100	115
...	...	...	89 1/4	84 7/8	90 1/2	92 1/2	91 1/4	89	90 1/2	
81 3/4	82 3/4	83 1/2	82 1/2	80	82 1/4	81 3/4	82 1/4	88 1/2	85	116
78	79 3/4	79 3/4	78 3/4	74	77 3/8	73 1/4	77 3/8	78 3/4	78 7/8	
19 7/8	33 7/8	23 7/8	22 3/4	21 1/4	19 3/8	19	13 1/2	18 3/8	14 11/16	117
16	21 1/4	14 5/8	14	13 1/2	15 7/8	7 3/4	7 1/2	9 7/8	10	
70 1/8	56 5/8	54 3/8	63 3/4	65 3/4	56 3/8	58 7/8	38	56 5/8	51 7/8	118
54	43 7/8	42 5/8	46 1/2	41 1/8	46 1/4	26	24 5/16	33 5/8	37	
36 3/4	31 3/8	31 5/8	30 3/8	35 1/2	36	27 3/4	19 1/2	15 5/8	18 1/4	119
25 1/2	22 7/8	26 1/8	16 1/4	18	23 3/4	8 7/8	9 3/4	7 3/4	11 1/4	
141 3/4	140 1/2	144 3/4	143	140	143 1/2	143 3/8	139 1/2	148	143	120
130 1/2	136	139	135	135 7/8	136	125	132 1/2	129 1/4	130	
141 1/8	127	123 1/4	124	113 3/8	113 3/4	107 1/4	98 1/4	109	101 1/8	121
118	115	110 1/2	90 1/2	93 3/4	98 1/2	88	84	82	86 1/8	
...	105	106	106	101	106 1/4	107 1/4	107 3/8	112	109	122
...	102	102 1/2	99 3/4	96 3/4	100 1/4	101	102	101	101	
141 1/8	127	122 1/4	117 1/8	130 3/4	139	136 1/2	143	155 1/2	156 5/8	123
118	115	110 1/2	106	109 1/4	125	111 1/2	124	137	138	
...	...	...	...	107	108 1/2	108 3/4	106 1/2	107 1/2	106	124
...	...	...	...	103 1/4	104	94	99 1/2	102	96	
71 7/8	65 3/4	90	95 3/8	86 7/8	87 3/8	80 1/4	59	67 1/2	56 3/4	125
56 1/2	52 5/8	57 7/8	67	67 7/8	66 7/8	41 1/2	43	39 1/2	38 7/8	
35 3/8	18 7/8	14 9/16	21 3/16	21 1/8	21	16 3/8	17 5/16	19 5/8	15 3/8	126
17 1/4	10 1/8	9 3/4	12 1/2	11 7/8	13 5/8	7 7/8	11 3/8	9 1/8	8 7/8	
...	...	...	...	82	84 3/4	85 1/2	85 5/8	93 5/8	89 3/4	127
...	...	...	...	77 1/4	81	73	79 1/2	80	77	
118 7/8	114 1/8	113 1/4	113 3/4	123 5/8	122 3/4	114 1/2	105 3/4	107	101 7/8	128
105 1/4	105 3/4	107 7/8	98	101	111	96 3/4	98	94 1/2	90 1/4	
20 7/8	18 1/8	23 11/16	23 1/4	24	23 1/4	20 1/16	18 1/2	19 3/4	17 1/8	129
15	14 1/8	15 1/8	13	14 7/8	18	11 1/4	14 3/8	11 7/8	11 1/4	
...	...	99	102 1/4	101 1/4	109 3/4	110 3/4	113 3/4	114	111 1/2	130
...	...	95	94	94	102 1/4	105 1/2	108 1/2	108 1/2	105	
56 7/8	60 1/8	64	68 5/8	59 3/8	57 1/2	40 7/8	27 1/4	19 3/4	22 1/2	131
36	43 1/4	48 7/8	47 5/8	47 1/8	38 3/8	16 3/4	17	6 3/4	11 1/4	
...	...	...	100 1/2	99 1/2	97 3/4	94 1/4	77 1/2	71	68 3/4	132
...	...	...	96	93 3/4	92 1/2	76 1/2	57	46	55	

prices only.

APPENDIX F.

NAME OF STOCKS.	1881. H. & L.	1882. H. & L.	1883. H. & L.	1884. H. & L.	1885. H. & L.	1886. H. & L.
133 Northern Pacific Pref.	... / ...	... / ...	... / ...	... / ...	70^1 / 60	$68\tfrac{5}{8}$ / $60\tfrac{3}{8}$
134 Do. 1st Mort., 1921	... / ...	... / ...	... / ...	... / ...	$116\tfrac{1}{2}$ / $102\tfrac{3}{4}$	$123\tfrac{1}{2}$ / 113
135 Oregon & California 5% 1st Mort.	... / ...	98 / 80	101 / $91\tfrac{1}{2}$	$93\tfrac{1}{2}$ / 65	$97\tfrac{1}{2}$ / 59	$108\tfrac{1}{2}$ / 94
136 Pennsylvania	$72\tfrac{3}{8}$ / $67\tfrac{1}{4}$	$66\tfrac{7}{8}$ / 55	$66\tfrac{3}{8}$ / $57\tfrac{3}{4}$	$62\tfrac{1}{8}$ / 51	$57\tfrac{7}{8}$ / $46\tfrac{3}{4}$	$62\tfrac{5}{8}$ / $52\tfrac{1}{4}$
137 Philadelphia & Reading	$37\tfrac{1}{2}$ / $26\tfrac{1}{2}$	$35\tfrac{3}{8}$ / $25\tfrac{1}{4}$	$30\tfrac{3}{8}$ / $24\tfrac{3}{8}$	$30\tfrac{1}{2}$ / $8\tfrac{1}{2}$	$13\tfrac{7}{8}$ / $6\tfrac{3}{8}$	$26\tfrac{7}{8}$ / $9\tfrac{1}{4}$
138 St. Paul Minn. & Man. 4½%	... / ...	... / ...	... / ...	... / ...	... / ...	... / ...
139 Southern Railway Ord.	... / ...	... / ...	... / ...	.. / ..	... / ...	... / ...
140 Do. Pref.	... / ...	... / ...	... / ...	... / ...	... / ...	... / ...
141 Union Pacific	... / ...	$123\tfrac{1}{4}$ / $117\tfrac{3}{4}$	$101\tfrac{3}{4}$ / $77\tfrac{1}{2}$	84 / $30\tfrac{3}{4}$	$64\tfrac{5}{8}$ / $42\tfrac{1}{2}$	$69\tfrac{1}{4}$ / $46\tfrac{3}{4}$
142 Wabash	$61\tfrac{3}{8}$ / $35\tfrac{1}{8}$	$40\tfrac{5}{8}$ / 25	$36\tfrac{3}{8}$ / 17	20 / $4\tfrac{3}{8}$	$15\tfrac{3}{8}$ / $1\tfrac{3}{4}$	$25\tfrac{7}{8}$ / 9
143 Do. Pref.	$99\tfrac{1}{2}$ / $68\tfrac{1}{4}$	$72\tfrac{7}{8}$ / 48	$58\tfrac{1}{2}$ / $30\tfrac{7}{8}$	$32\tfrac{1}{4}$ / $10\tfrac{1}{4}$	$25\tfrac{3}{4}$ / $4\tfrac{3}{4}$	$43\tfrac{3}{8}$ / $16\tfrac{1}{4}$
144 Do. General Mort.	$107\tfrac{1}{2}$ / 91	$93\tfrac{3}{4}$ / $75\tfrac{1}{2}$	86 / 73	$70\tfrac{5}{8}$ / $35\tfrac{1}{2}$	$57\tfrac{1}{2}$ / 25	$71\tfrac{1}{2}$ / $48\tfrac{3}{4}$
Banks—						
145 Bank of England	299 / 279	$291\tfrac{1}{2}$ / $282\tfrac{1}{4}$	302 / $288\tfrac{1}{2}$	$313\tfrac{1}{4}$ / 295	$308\tfrac{1}{2}$ / $287\tfrac{1}{2}$	$299\tfrac{1}{2}$ / 291
146 Brit. of South America	... / ...	... / ...	... / ...	... / ...	... / ...	$15\tfrac{1}{4}$ / $12\tfrac{7}{8}$
147 Capital & Counties, £10 pd.	... / ...	... / ...	... / ...	... / ...	... / ...	... / ..
148 Chartd. of Ind., Aust. & China	$25\tfrac{1}{4}$ / $21\tfrac{3}{4}$	$25\tfrac{1}{4}$ / $21\tfrac{1}{2}$	$24\tfrac{5}{8}$ / $21\tfrac{1}{4}$	$24\tfrac{3}{4}$ / 20	$22\tfrac{3}{4}$ / $19\tfrac{1}{2}$	$23\tfrac{3}{4}$ / 21
149 City, Ltd.	$20\tfrac{3}{8}$ / $17\tfrac{3}{4}$	$22\tfrac{3}{8}$ / $18\tfrac{3}{4}$	$22\tfrac{1}{4}$ / 20	$21\tfrac{1}{4}$ / $18\tfrac{1}{2}$	$19\tfrac{5}{8}$ / $17\tfrac{1}{2}$	$20\tfrac{5}{16}$ / $17\tfrac{7}{8}$
150 Lloyds Ltd., £8 pd.	... / ...	... / ...	... / ...	... / ...	$24\tfrac{7}{8}$ / $21\tfrac{1}{4}$	23 / 20
151 London & County, Ltd., £20 pd.	$77\tfrac{1}{2}$ / $69\tfrac{1}{2}$	$81\tfrac{3}{4}$ / $72\tfrac{1}{4}$	$83\tfrac{1}{2}$ / $77\tfrac{1}{4}$	85 / $79\tfrac{1}{2}$	$83\tfrac{1}{2}$ / 75	$83\tfrac{7}{8}$ / $78\tfrac{1}{2}$
152 London & Midland, £12½ pd.	... / ...	... / ...	... / ...	... / ...	... / ...	... / ...

[1] Approximate

HIGHEST AND LOWEST PRICES.

1887. H. & L.	1888. H. & L.	1889. H. & L.	1890. H. & L.	1891. H. & L.	1892. H. & L.	1893. H. & L.	1894. H. & L.	1895. H. & L.	1896. H. & L.	
$65\frac{1}{4}$	$65\frac{1}{2}$	$79\frac{3}{8}$	$88\frac{1}{8}$	$81\frac{1}{2}$	$74\frac{3}{4}$	$51\frac{1}{4}$	24	$27\frac{3}{8}$	29	} 133
$43\frac{5}{8}$	$43\frac{3}{8}$	60	$56\frac{3}{4}$	$61\frac{5}{8}$	$46\frac{7}{8}$	$15\frac{1}{2}$	$12\frac{3}{4}$	$10\frac{3}{4}$	15	
$121\frac{3}{4}$	122	123	122	121	$121\frac{3}{4}$	$121\frac{3}{4}$	119	121	121	} 134
$117\frac{1}{4}$	$116\frac{1}{4}$	117	$115\frac{1}{8}$	$115\frac{1}{4}$	$118\frac{1}{8}$	100	109	$114\frac{1}{4}$	111	
$104\frac{7}{8}$	$101\frac{1}{2}$	$105\frac{1}{2}$	106	100	103	$101\frac{3}{8}$	$84\frac{3}{4}$	94	86	} 135
$104\frac{1}{8}$	$95\frac{1}{2}$	97	97	96	$96\frac{3}{4}$	80	$73\frac{1}{2}$	71	$70\frac{3}{4}$	
$61\frac{5}{8}$	58	$57\frac{1}{2}$	$58\frac{1}{2}$	$59\frac{1}{4}$	$59\frac{1}{4}$	$56\frac{3}{4}$	54	$58\frac{3}{4}$	$56\frac{5}{8}$	} 136
$54\frac{1}{2}$	53	52	49	$50\frac{3}{4}$	54	$47\frac{3}{4}$	49	$48\frac{1}{2}$	50	
$36\frac{1}{8}$	$34\frac{3}{4}$	$25\frac{3}{4}$	25	$22\frac{3}{4}$	$32\frac{1}{2}$	$27\frac{3}{8}$	$12\frac{1}{16}$	$11\frac{5}{16}$	17	} 137
$28\frac{3}{4}$	$27\frac{5}{16}$	$19\frac{3}{8}$	$14\frac{3}{8}$	$13\frac{7}{16}$	20	6	$6\frac{7}{8}$	$2\frac{1}{8}$	$5\frac{5}{8}$	
...	...	...	105	$104\frac{3}{8}$	$106\frac{1}{2}$	$106\frac{1}{2}$	$105\frac{1}{4}$	110	108	} 138
...	...	...	102	$99\frac{1}{4}$	101	$99\frac{1}{4}$	100	$102\frac{1}{2}$	101	
...	..	...	...	...	..	..	...	$15\frac{3}{4}$	$12\frac{1}{2}$	} 139
...	...	...	...	...	...	...	...	$7\frac{3}{8}$	$6\frac{1}{2}$	
...	...	...	...	...	...	...	...	$44\frac{1}{8}$	$34\frac{1}{4}$	} 140
...	...	...	...	...	...	...	...	$24\frac{1}{2}$	$16\frac{3}{8}$	
$65\frac{3}{8}$	$68\frac{1}{4}$	$73\frac{1}{8}$	$70\frac{3}{4}$	$53\frac{3}{4}$	$51\frac{3}{4}$	$43\frac{3}{4}$	$23\frac{1}{2}$	$18\frac{1}{2}$	$12\frac{3}{4}$	} 141
46	$50\frac{1}{4}$	58	$41\frac{1}{2}$	33	$36\frac{1}{4}$	$16\frac{3}{8}$	7	$3\frac{5}{8}$	$3\frac{1}{8}$	
$22\frac{5}{8}$	$16\frac{1}{2}$	$18\frac{1}{2}$	$18\frac{1}{4}$	17	$15\frac{3}{4}$	$12\frac{3}{8}$	8	$10\frac{5}{8}$	$8\frac{5}{8}$	} 142
13	$11\frac{1}{2}$	$12\frac{1}{4}$	9	9	$10\frac{3}{8}$	$6\frac{3}{8}$	6	$5\frac{7}{16}$	$4\frac{1}{4}$	
$38\frac{7}{8}$	30	35	$37\frac{1}{2}$	35	$34\frac{1}{2}$	$26\frac{13}{16}$	$19\frac{1}{4}$	27	$20\frac{3}{16}$	} 143
24	$20\frac{3}{8}$	25	$15\frac{5}{8}$	$17\frac{1}{2}$	23	$11\frac{1}{2}$	13	$12\frac{1}{2}$	12	
65	56	$55\frac{1}{2}$	$59\frac{3}{4}$	$53\frac{1}{2}$	52	$41\frac{1}{4}$	$29\frac{1}{2}$	$36\frac{1}{2}$	29	} 144
44	38	35	29	$28\frac{1}{2}$	34	19	$19\frac{3}{4}$	19	$17\frac{3}{4}$	
310	332	346	341	343	344	343	338	336	345	} 145
293	303	320	327	323	325	325	322	$322\frac{1}{2}$	322	
16	$14\frac{5}{8}$	16	$14\frac{1}{4}$	$17\frac{1}{2}$	$13\frac{7}{8}$	$13\frac{3}{4}$	$13\frac{7}{8}$	$15\frac{3}{4}$	15	} 146
$11\frac{1}{4}$	$11\frac{1}{4}$	$12\frac{3}{4}$	$11\frac{1}{2}$	10	$10\frac{7}{16}$	$10\frac{3}{4}$	$10\frac{1}{4}$	$13\frac{1}{4}$	$11\frac{1}{4}$	
...	...	...	42	$41\frac{1}{2}$	$38\frac{3}{4}$	34	$34\frac{1}{4}$	$37\frac{7}{8}$	$40\frac{1}{2}$	} 147
...	...	..	$39\frac{1}{2}$	38	$33\frac{1}{2}$	$30\frac{1}{2}$	32	$33\frac{1}{2}$	36	
$24\frac{1}{2}$	$26\frac{3}{4}$	$29\frac{1}{2}$	$30\frac{5}{8}$	$29\frac{3}{8}$	$24\frac{1}{2}$	$23\frac{3}{4}$	$24\frac{5}{8}$	$28\frac{1}{2}$	$29\frac{7}{8}$	} 148
22	$23\frac{1}{4}$	24	25	22	$19\frac{1}{4}$	18	$19\frac{1}{4}$	$22\frac{7}{16}$	$25\frac{3}{4}$	
21	$21\frac{5}{8}$	$23\frac{1}{4}$	$24\frac{7}{8}$	$24\frac{3}{4}$	$23\frac{1}{4}$	$22\frac{5}{8}$	$20\frac{3}{4}$	$18\frac{3}{4}$	$18\frac{3}{8}$	} 149
$18\frac{5}{8}$	$19\frac{1}{2}$	$20\frac{1}{2}$	22	$20\frac{3}{4}$	20	$17\frac{1}{2}$	$16\frac{1}{2}$	17	$17\frac{1}{4}$	
$22\frac{3}{4}$	$24\frac{3}{4}$	$28\frac{1}{4}$	$29\frac{3}{4}$	$29\frac{1}{2}$	$29\frac{1}{2}$	$28\frac{1}{4}$	$26\frac{5}{8}$	$26\frac{3}{4}$	$26\frac{1}{4}$	} 150
$20\frac{3}{4}$	$21\frac{1}{4}$	$24\frac{1}{2}$	$26\frac{1}{2}$	$27\frac{1}{4}$	$26\frac{1}{2}$	$24\frac{1}{8}$	23	$23\frac{1}{4}$	$24\frac{1}{4}$	
$86\frac{1}{2}$	88	$95\frac{3}{4}$	$95\frac{1}{2}$	$96\frac{1}{2}$	95	94	$94\frac{7}{8}$	$95\frac{1}{2}$	$100\frac{1}{4}$	} 151
$80\frac{1}{2}$	83	$86\frac{1}{4}$	88	90	$88\frac{1}{2}$	84	$87\frac{1}{4}$	$89\frac{1}{2}$	$93\frac{1}{4}$	
...	...	...	...	..	$38\frac{3}{4}$	37	$38\frac{1}{4}$	$40\frac{1}{2}$	46	} 152
...	...	...	...	...	$35\frac{1}{2}$	$34\frac{3}{4}$	$35\frac{1}{4}$	$37\frac{1}{4}$	$39\frac{1}{2}$	

prices only.

NAME OF STOCKS.	1881. H. & L.	1882. H. & L.	1883. H. & L.	1884. H. & L.	1885. H. & L.	1886. H. & L.
153 London & Westm'ster,	$74\frac{1}{8}$	$74\frac{1}{4}$	$71\frac{3}{8}$	71	$69\frac{3}{4}$	$66\frac{1}{4}$
Ltd., £20 pd. ...	$65\frac{1}{4}$	66	$65\frac{1}{2}$	$66\frac{3}{4}$	63	61
154 London Joint Stock,	$48\frac{3}{8}$	57	$48\frac{3}{8}$	46	41	$39\frac{1}{2}$
Ltd., £15 pd. ...	$43\frac{1}{4}$	44	44	39	$36\frac{1}{8}$	36
155 Metrop'lit'n of England	...	...	...	...	...	...
and Wales, £5 pd.	...	...	...	...	...	...
156 Nat. Prov. of England,	$47\frac{3}{8}$	$48\frac{1}{2}$	50	$50\frac{1}{2}$	51	$51\frac{1}{4}$
Ltd., £12 pd. ...	$43\frac{3}{4}$	$43\frac{1}{4}$	$45\frac{3}{4}$	45	47	$47\frac{1}{2}$
157 Nat. Prov. of England,	41	$42\frac{1}{2}$	$44\frac{1}{2}$	$43\frac{7}{8}$	44	44
Ltd., £$10\frac{1}{2}$ pd. ...	38	$38\frac{1}{4}$	40	$40\frac{1}{4}$	40	41
158 Parr's & Alliance,	...	...	...	...	...	...
£20 pd.	...	...	...	...	...	...
159 Union of Australia,	$66\frac{3}{4}$	67	76	$77\frac{3}{4}$	75	$74\frac{5}{8}$
Ltd., £25 pd. ...	$58\frac{1}{4}$	$58\frac{1}{8}$	$66\frac{1}{2}$	69	$67\frac{1}{2}$	67
160 Union of London,	$44\frac{1}{4}$	$50\frac{1}{4}$	$46\frac{3}{8}$	44	$59\frac{3}{4}$	$38\frac{1}{8}$
Ltd., £$15\frac{1}{2}$ pd. ...	40	$42\frac{1}{8}$	$42\frac{1}{2}$	38	$35\frac{3}{8}$	34
Breweries—						
161 Allsopp & Sons, Ltd.	...	...	...	...	...	...
	...	...	...	...	...	...
162 Do. 6% Pref. ...	...	...	...	...	...	...
	...	...	...	...	...	...
163 Bass, Ratcliff & Co.	...	...	...	...	...	...
Pref.	...	...	...	...	...	...
164 Guinness, Son & Co.,	...	...	...	...	...	...
Ltd.	...	...	...	...	...	...
165 Guinness, Son & Co.,	...	...	.	...	...	...
Ltd., 6% Pref. ...	...	...	...	...	...	..
166 Parker's, Burslem ...	...	...	...	...	...	...
	...	...	...	...	...	...
Commercial, Industrial, &c.						
167 British Gas Light ...	...	...	...	...	...	...
	...	...	...	...	...	...
168 City of Lond. Electric	...	...	...	...	...	...
	...	...	...	...	...	...
169 Coats, J. & P.	...	...	...	...	...	...
	...	...	...	...	..	...
170 Gas Light & Coke	200	$183\frac{1}{2}$	207	227	$241\frac{1}{2}$	253
"A" Ord.	182	167	$183\frac{1}{2}$	199	219	233
171 Gordon Hotels ...	...	...	...	...	...	...
	...	...	...	...	...	.

HIGHEST AND LOWEST PRICES.

1887. H. & L.	1888. H. & L.	1889. H. & L.	1890. H. & L.	1891. H. & L.	1892. H. & L.	1893. H. & L.	1894. H. & L.	1895. H. & L.	1896. H. & L.	
$67\frac{1}{2}$	70	$74\frac{1}{2}$	$75\frac{3}{8}$	$75\frac{1}{2}$	72	64	58	$55\frac{3}{4}$	$55\frac{1}{2}$	} 153
$61\frac{5}{8}$	64	67	$69\frac{1}{2}$	$67\frac{3}{4}$	60	52	$51\frac{1}{2}$	$49\frac{1}{2}$	$49\frac{1}{2}$	
$39\frac{1}{4}$	$40\frac{3}{4}$	$42\frac{1}{2}$	$42\frac{3}{4}$	$40\frac{3}{4}$	$38\frac{1}{4}$	$39\frac{3}{4}$	$34\frac{1}{8}$	$34\frac{1}{4}$	34	} 154
$35\frac{1}{4}$	37	$38\frac{5}{8}$	36	$35\frac{1}{2}$	$32\frac{3}{4}$	$30\frac{1}{2}$	30	$30\frac{1}{8}$	$30\frac{5}{8}$	
...	...	...	...	...	$17\frac{1}{4}$	$17\frac{7}{8}$	$16\frac{1}{4}$	$16\frac{1}{8}$	$14\frac{1}{2}$	} 155
...	...	...	...	...	16	$15\frac{1}{4}$	15	$12\frac{3}{4}$	$12\frac{1}{8}$	
$52\frac{7}{8}$	53	$57\frac{1}{2}$	64	$54\frac{1}{2}$	54	54	$51\frac{1}{8}$	$52\frac{1}{4}$	$55\frac{5}{8}$	} 156
$48\frac{3}{4}$	49	$50\frac{1}{4}$	$51\frac{1}{2}$	$49\frac{3}{4}$	$50\frac{1}{8}$	47	$46\frac{1}{2}$	$47\frac{3}{4}$	$49\frac{1}{2}$	
45	45	50	$54\frac{3}{4}$	$46\frac{1}{2}$	47	$46\frac{1}{2}$	44	$44\frac{1}{4}$	$47\frac{1}{4}$	} 157
42	$42\frac{1}{2}$	$43\frac{1}{4}$	44	$41\frac{1}{4}$	42	40	$40\frac{1}{2}$	$41\frac{1}{2}$	$42\frac{1}{2}$	
...	...	...	...	...	75	$79\frac{3}{4}$	$78\frac{1}{2}$	81	$93\frac{1}{2}$	} 158
...	...	...	...	...	$72\frac{3}{4}$	71	73	$76\frac{1}{4}$	$78\frac{1}{2}$	
$71\frac{1}{2}$	65	$68\frac{3}{4}$	$72\frac{1}{4}$	$69\frac{1}{2}$	$64\frac{1}{4}$	$58\frac{1}{2}$	$46\frac{3}{4}$	38	$30\frac{1}{4}$	} 159
$57\frac{1}{2}$	58	61	$63\frac{1}{2}$	$61\frac{1}{2}$	$52\frac{1}{2}$	33	$31\frac{1}{4}$	30	$24\frac{3}{4}$	
$39\frac{5}{8}$	$41\frac{1}{4}$	$43\frac{3}{4}$	$44\frac{1}{4}$	43	$40\frac{1}{4}$	$37\frac{1}{2}$	$34\frac{1}{4}$	$33\frac{1}{2}$	$35\frac{1}{4}$	} 160
35	$37\frac{1}{4}$	39	39	$38\frac{3}{4}$	$34\frac{1}{2}$	$30\frac{1}{4}$	$30\frac{1}{2}$	$30\frac{5}{8}$	30	
$153\frac{3}{4}$	$127\frac{1}{2}$	$93\frac{1}{8}$	$86\frac{1}{4}$	47	$27\frac{3}{4}$	55	$135\frac{1}{4}$	$150\frac{1}{4}$	187	} 161
$116\frac{1}{4}$	$77\frac{1}{2}$	$78\frac{1}{2}$	40	$20\frac{3}{4}$	$12\frac{1}{2}$	$17\frac{1}{4}$	$53\frac{1}{4}$	$127\frac{1}{4}$	135	
$131\frac{1}{4}$	135	127	116	95	$75\frac{1}{4}$	$114\frac{3}{4}$	$142\frac{3}{4}$	$150\frac{1}{2}$	173	} 162
$122\frac{1}{2}$	$107\frac{1}{2}$	$111\frac{7}{8}$	$91\frac{3}{4}$	63	$44\frac{3}{4}$	56	112	$137\frac{1}{2}$	$143\frac{1}{2}$	
...	...	...	118	$122\frac{1}{2}$	$127\frac{3}{4}$	$130\frac{7}{8}$	139	$152\frac{1}{2}$	160	} 163
...	...	...	114	115	121	121	$125\frac{1}{2}$	$135\frac{1}{4}$	$143\frac{1}{2}$	
300	$330\frac{5}{8}$	$247\frac{1}{2}$	$357\frac{1}{2}$	333	340	$345\frac{1}{2}$	364	$481\frac{1}{8}$	694	} 164
$251\frac{7}{8}$	$274\frac{3}{4}$	300	$298\frac{1}{8}$	$298\frac{1}{2}$	$312\frac{1}{2}$	$311\frac{1}{4}$	341	370	465	
$142\frac{1}{2}$	$156\frac{1}{2}$	$159\frac{3}{4}$	$159\frac{1}{2}$	$160\frac{1}{2}$	165	$166\frac{1}{2}$	175	194	203	} 165
$132\frac{1}{2}$	$141\frac{1}{4}$	151	150	$151\frac{1}{4}$	$155\frac{3}{4}$	151	162	177	$188\frac{1}{2}$	
...	...	...	14	$14\frac{1}{8}$	$14\frac{1}{4}$	$14\frac{1}{8}$	$15\frac{13}{16}$	$20\frac{13}{16}$	$27\frac{3}{8}$	} 166
...	...	...	12	$11\frac{1}{2}$	$12\frac{1}{8}$	$11\frac{1}{2}$	$12\frac{5}{16}$	$15\frac{1}{8}$	$19\frac{1}{2}$	
...	...	...	$46\frac{1}{4}$	$46\frac{1}{2}$	45	$44\frac{1}{2}$	$49\frac{3}{4}$	56	$58\frac{1}{2}$	} 167
...	...	...	43	42	$40\frac{1}{2}$	$41\frac{1}{4}$	43	$48\frac{1}{2}$	$54\frac{3}{4}$	
...	...	...	...	$10\frac{1}{16}$	$11\frac{1}{4}$	$13\frac{3}{8}$	$14\frac{1}{4}$	$15\frac{1}{4}$	$18\frac{1}{8}$	} 168
...	...	...	...	$8\frac{3}{4}$	$9\frac{1}{8}$	10	$10\frac{5}{8}$	$12\frac{3}{4}$	$12\frac{15}{16}$	
...	...	...	$12\frac{1}{2}$	$16\frac{5}{16}$	$16\frac{13}{16}$	16	$22\frac{5}{8}$	$33\frac{3}{4}$	69	} 169
...	...	...	12	12	$13\frac{3}{16}$	$13\frac{1}{2}$	$15\frac{1}{2}$	$22\frac{1}{2}$	$28\frac{9}{16}$	
$259\frac{1}{2}$	263	$269\frac{1}{2}$	254	252	$226\frac{1}{2}$	237	255	$300\frac{1}{2}$	324	} 170
228	233	239	$232\frac{1}{2}$	206	202	$217\frac{1}{2}$	$226\frac{1}{2}$	$253\frac{1}{2}$	287	
...	...	...	$13\frac{5}{8}$	$14\frac{5}{8}$	16	$16\frac{1}{2}$	$17\frac{1}{2}$	$20\frac{9}{16}$	$24\frac{5}{8}$	} 171
...	...	...	$11\frac{1}{4}$	$12\frac{3}{8}$	$14\frac{5}{16}$	$14\frac{11}{16}$	$14\frac{1}{8}$	$15\frac{5}{8}$	$19\frac{1}{4}$	

APPENDIX F.

NAME OF STOCKS.	1881. H. & L.	1882. H. & L.	1883. H. & L.	1884. H. & L.	1885. H. & L.	1886. H. & L.
172 Metro. Electric Supply	... ...	... ...	... ...	... ...	... ...	... ...
173 Pawson & Leaf, Ltd.	$6\frac{3}{4}$ $5\frac{1}{2}$	$5\frac{13}{16}$ $4\frac{3}{4}$	6 5	6 $4\frac{15}{16}$	6 $5\frac{1}{4}$	$6\frac{3}{4}$ $5\frac{1}{4}$
174 Pears, A. & F., 6% Cum. Pref.	... ...	... ...	... ...	... ...	... ...	... ...
175 Price's Patent Candles	... ...	... ...	... ...	... ...	$16\frac{1}{8}$ $11\frac{7}{8}$	$18\frac{3}{4}$ $15\frac{5}{16}$
176 Spiers & Pond ...	... ...	... ...	... ...	... ...	... ...	... ...
Telegraphs & Trusts.—						
177 Anglo-American, Ltd.	62 $47\frac{5}{8}$	$57\frac{1}{2}$ 47	$52\frac{3}{8}$ 42	$44\frac{1}{4}$ $30\frac{3}{8}$	$35\frac{1}{8}$ 26	$41\frac{5}{8}$ $30\frac{1}{4}$
178 Cuba, Ltd.	... ...	... ...	... ...	$11\frac{1}{8}$ $9\frac{5}{8}$	$12\frac{13}{16}$ $10\frac{3}{8}$	$11\frac{3}{4}$ $10\frac{1}{4}$
179 Direct U.S. Cable, Ld.	$11\frac{7}{8}$ $9\frac{13}{16}$	13 10	$13\frac{3}{8}$ $10\frac{1}{2}$	$11\frac{1}{4}$ $9\frac{9}{16}$	10 $8\frac{9}{16}$	$10\frac{1}{8}$ 8
180 Eastern Extension, Ltd.	$11\frac{3}{8}$ $9\frac{13}{16}$	$12\frac{3}{16}$ $10\frac{5}{8}$	$12\frac{5}{8}$ $11\frac{1}{2}$	$12\frac{9}{16}$ 11	$13\frac{1}{4}$ $11\frac{1}{4}$	$13\frac{3}{8}$ $10\frac{1}{2}$
181 Globe Telegraph & Trust	$6\frac{13}{16}$ $5\frac{1}{8}$	$6\frac{5}{8}$ $5\frac{13}{16}$	$7\frac{3}{8}$ $6\frac{1}{8}$	$7\frac{5}{8}$ $6\frac{3}{8}$	$7\frac{13}{16}$ $6\frac{1}{16}$	$7\frac{1}{4}$ 5
182 National Telephone, Ltd.	... ...	... ...	... ...	... ...	$13\frac{3}{8}$ $9\frac{7}{8}$	$14\frac{3}{4}$ $11\frac{5}{16}$
183 Railway Investment Pref.	... ...	... ...	... ...	... ...	... ...	96 $92\frac{1}{4}$
184 Do. Def.	... ...	... ...	... ...	... ...	... ...	$31\frac{5}{8}$ 23
185 Do. Shareholders Trust, Ltd.	... ...	... ...	... ...	... ...	... ...	9 $6\frac{7}{8}$
186 Submarine Cables Trust	297 263	288 250	262 190	208 152	105 98	$110\frac{1}{2}$ 95

HIGHEST AND LOWEST PRICES.

1887.	1888.	1889.	1890.	1891.	1892.	1893.	1894.	1895.	1896.	
H. & L.	H. & L.	H. & L.	H. & L.	H. & L.	H. & L.	H. & L.	H. & L.	H. & L.	H. & L.	
...	...	...	...	$10\frac{1}{2}$	10	$8\frac{1}{4}$	$10\frac{3}{8}$	$12\frac{3}{8}$	$14\frac{13}{16}$	} 172
...	...	...	...	$9\frac{3}{8}$	$16\frac{1}{2}$	$5\frac{7}{16}$	$7\frac{1}{4}$	$9\frac{15}{16}$	$10\frac{1}{2}$	
$6\frac{7}{8}$	$6\frac{5}{8}$	7	$7\frac{1}{8}$	$7\frac{3}{8}$	$6\frac{7}{8}$	$6\frac{1}{4}$	5	$5\frac{3}{4}$	$6\frac{7}{8}$	} 173
6	$5\frac{7}{8}$	$6\frac{1}{8}$	$6\frac{1}{2}$	$5\frac{7}{8}$	$5\frac{1}{4}$	$4\frac{1}{2}$	$3\frac{5}{16}$	$4\frac{1}{4}$	5	
...	...	...	...	...	...	$11\frac{7}{16}$	$10\frac{1}{2}$	$12\frac{3}{8}$	$14\frac{3}{4}$	} 174
...	...	...	...	...	..	$9\frac{3}{8}$	$9\frac{7}{16}$	$9\frac{1}{4}$	$12\frac{3}{8}$	
$18\frac{3}{4}$	22	$25\frac{1}{2}$	27	31	$28\frac{1}{2}$	$26\frac{1}{2}$	$27\frac{5}{8}$	$35\frac{1}{2}$	$41\frac{1}{2}$	} 175
$16\frac{1}{4}$	$17\frac{1}{4}$	$21\frac{3}{4}$	$23\frac{3}{8}$	$25\frac{5}{8}$	23	$22\frac{1}{2}$	$24\frac{1}{2}$	27	$33\frac{1}{2}$	
...	...	...	$16\frac{1}{2}$	$17\frac{5}{8}$	$16\frac{1}{4}$	$17\frac{3}{8}$	$17\frac{3}{8}$	$19\frac{7}{8}$	$27\frac{3}{4}$	} 176
...	...	...	14	$13\frac{3}{16}$	$13\frac{3}{4}$	$15\frac{1}{16}$	$15\frac{1}{4}$	$17\frac{1}{16}$	$19\frac{1}{16}$	
$40\frac{1}{4}$	$50\frac{3}{8}$	54	$53\frac{1}{2}$	51	$51\frac{7}{8}$	$55\frac{1}{4}$	$44\frac{1}{2}$	50	54	} 177
31	$35\frac{1}{2}$	48	$48\frac{1}{2}$	$42\frac{3}{4}$	$46\frac{1}{2}$	$43\frac{3}{4}$	$35\frac{1}{2}$	$38\frac{1}{2}$	41	
$12\frac{5}{8}$	$14\frac{3}{4}$	$15\frac{7}{16}$	$14\frac{3}{4}$	$11\frac{1}{4}$	$12\frac{1}{4}$	$12\frac{1}{2}$	$13\frac{1}{2}$	14	$13\frac{7}{16}$	} 178
$11\frac{1}{4}$	$12\frac{3}{8}$	14	11	10	$10\frac{1}{4}$	11	12	13	12	
$9\frac{1}{16}$	11	$11\frac{1}{8}$	$10\frac{5}{8}$	$11\frac{7}{16}$	$12\frac{1}{16}$	$12\frac{1}{4}$	$11\frac{1}{8}$	$9\frac{3}{8}$	$10\frac{1}{8}$	} 179
$7\frac{3}{8}$	$8\frac{1}{4}$	$9\frac{1}{16}$	$9\frac{1}{16}$	$10\frac{1}{8}$	$10\frac{1}{8}$	$10\frac{15}{16}$	$8\frac{1}{8}$	$8\frac{1}{4}$	$8\frac{1}{16}$	
$12\frac{1}{2}$	$13\frac{1}{2}$	14	$14\frac{1}{4}$	$15\frac{3}{8}$	$15\frac{5}{8}$	$16\frac{1}{2}$	$16\frac{5}{16}$	$18\frac{3}{8}$	$18\frac{1}{2}$	} 180
$10\frac{1}{2}$	$11\frac{15}{16}$	$12\frac{1}{2}$	$12\frac{1}{16}$	$14\frac{3}{8}$	$14\frac{5}{8}$	$14\frac{1}{16}$	$15\frac{3}{16}$	$16\frac{3}{16}$	17	
$5\frac{1}{8}$	$7\frac{9}{16}$	9	$9\frac{5}{8}$	$10\frac{7}{16}$	$10\frac{5}{8}$	$10\frac{5}{8}$	$9\frac{1}{16}$	$10\frac{7}{8}$	$11\frac{3}{4}$	} 181
$4\frac{5}{8}$	$5\frac{3}{8}$	$6\frac{13}{16}$	$8\frac{1}{2}$	$8\frac{3}{4}$	$9\frac{3}{4}$	$8\frac{3}{8}$	$8\frac{1}{16}$	$8\frac{7}{8}$	$9\frac{3}{4}$	
$13\frac{1}{16}$	$15\frac{5}{8}$	$6\frac{3}{4}$	$6\frac{1}{8}$	$5\frac{5}{8}$	$5\frac{1}{16}$	$5\frac{1}{2}$	$5\frac{3}{8}$	$6\frac{3}{8}$	$8\frac{3}{8}$	} 182
$11\frac{1}{8}$	$11\frac{3}{4}$	$5\frac{5}{8}$	4	$4\frac{1}{16}$	$4\frac{1}{16}$	$4\frac{3}{8}$	$4\frac{1}{2}$	$5\frac{1}{16}$	$5\frac{3}{8}$	
$98\frac{1}{4}$	$104\frac{1}{4}$	$106\frac{1}{4}$	$104\frac{3}{4}$	$103\frac{3}{4}$	106	104	$106\frac{3}{4}$	113	120	} 183
$93\frac{1}{4}$	98	$101\frac{1}{4}$	$99\frac{1}{2}$	98	100	96	96	106	112	
$30\frac{1}{2}$	31	32	$30\frac{1}{4}$	$23\frac{3}{4}$	$23\frac{1}{2}$	18	$20\frac{1}{4}$	$19\frac{3}{4}$	$29\frac{1}{4}$	} 184
23	23	$28\frac{3}{4}$	$23\frac{7}{16}$	$19\frac{3}{4}$	16	$13\frac{3}{4}$	$12\frac{1}{2}$	$15\frac{1}{2}$	$16\frac{1}{4}$	
9	$8\frac{1}{8}$	8	$8\frac{5}{8}$	$7\frac{1}{4}$	$6\frac{7}{8}$	$6\frac{7}{8}$	$4\frac{1}{2}$	6	6	} 185
$7\frac{5}{8}$	$6\frac{11}{16}$	$6\frac{5}{8}$	7	6	$5\frac{3}{4}$	$3\frac{3}{4}$	3	4	$4\frac{3}{16}$	
100	110	116	117	$122\frac{1}{2}$	$120\frac{1}{2}$	124	$115\frac{1}{2}$	131	144	} 186
91	93	105	109	$112\frac{1}{4}$	$115\frac{1}{2}$	116	$103\frac{3}{8}$	118	128	

APPENDIX G.

HIGHEST AND LOWEST PRICES OF PRINCIPAL MINES, 1891—1896.

NAMES.	1891. H. & L.	1892. H. & L.	1893. H. & L.	1894. H. & L.	1895. H. & L.	1896. H. & L.
African—						
Cape Copper	$4\frac{3}{4}$ $1\frac{13}{16}$	2 $1\frac{5}{16}$	$1\frac{7}{8}$ 1	$1\frac{3}{4}$ $1\frac{5}{16}$	$2\frac{3}{16}$ $1\frac{9}{16}$	$2\frac{7}{8}$ $1\frac{1}{8}$
Champ d'Or	...	...	...	$3\frac{3}{4}$ $0\frac{7}{8}$	$5\frac{1}{16}$ 2	$2\frac{3}{4}$ $0\frac{3}{4}$
Chimes, New	...	$3\frac{3}{4}$ $2\frac{1}{2}$	$2\frac{7}{8}$ $1\frac{1}{8}$	$3\frac{1}{4}$ $1\frac{1}{16}$	$4\frac{5}{16}$ $1\frac{1}{4}$	$2\frac{1}{2}$ $0\frac{7}{8}$
Consol. Bultfontein.	...	...	27/3 24/3	27/9 25/-	32/-	28/3	$1\frac{7}{8}$ 29/-
Consol. Deep Levels	...	...	...	$4\frac{7}{14}$ $1\frac{11}{10}$	$7\frac{1}{4}$ $3\frac{3}{4}$	$6\frac{1}{4}$ $3\frac{1}{2}$
Crown Reef	...	...	...	$10\frac{1}{16}$ $9\frac{1}{16}$	$12\frac{7}{8}$ $8\frac{1}{4}$	$12\frac{3}{8}$ 9
De Beers	$17\frac{1}{2}$ $10\frac{7}{8}$	$18\frac{1}{4}$ $13\frac{3}{16}$	$21\frac{9}{16}$ $13\frac{3}{4}$	$19\frac{3}{4}$ $14\frac{5}{16}$	$32\frac{1}{4}$ $18\frac{1}{4}$	$31\frac{9}{16}$ 20
Do. 5% 1st Mort. Deb.	...	...	...	$107\frac{7}{8}$ $101\frac{3}{4}$	$111\frac{1}{2}$ 105	111 $103\frac{1}{2}$
Durban Roodepoort.	...	$4\frac{7}{8}$ $2\frac{1}{2}$	$5\frac{3}{16}$ $3\frac{3}{8}$	$7\frac{1}{4}$ $4\frac{11}{16}$	$8\frac{1}{16}$ $6\frac{3}{8}$	$7\frac{7}{8}$ $5\frac{1}{4}$
East Rand	...	...	...	47/6 12/3	$12\frac{5}{8}$ $2\frac{7}{8}$	$8\frac{5}{8}$ $3\frac{3}{8}$
Gelden. Est. & G. ...	...	$4\frac{3}{16}$ $2\frac{7}{16}$	$4\frac{7}{8}$ $3\frac{13}{16}$	$6\frac{7}{8}$ 4	$7\frac{1}{4}$ $3\frac{3}{4}$	$4\frac{3}{4}$ $2\frac{1}{4}$
Gelden. Main Reef .	...	...	...	$1\frac{1}{32}$ 8/-	$1\frac{1}{16}$ $0\frac{7}{8}$	$1\frac{7}{8}$ $0\frac{1}{4}$
Glencairn	...	33/- 9/-	37/6 24/-	$4\frac{1}{8}$ $1\frac{1}{4}$	$4\frac{7}{8}$ $3\frac{1}{16}$	$4\frac{1}{4}$ $1\frac{5}{16}$
Griqualand, West ...	...	$6\frac{3}{16}$ 5	7 6	$7\frac{1}{4}$ $6\frac{7}{8}$	$8\frac{1}{4}$ $7\frac{1}{4}$	$8\frac{7}{8}$ $7\frac{3}{4}$
Heriots, New	...	$3\frac{7}{16}$ $\frac{7}{8}$	$3\frac{7}{16}$ $2\frac{1}{2}$	$8\frac{1}{2}$ $3\frac{1}{4}$	$12\frac{1}{2}$ $7\frac{11}{16}$	$10\frac{1}{2}$ 7
Jagersfontein, New..	...	$14\frac{1}{4}$ $4\frac{3}{4}$	$13\frac{1}{4}$ $13\frac{1}{2}$	$17\frac{1}{2}$ $11\frac{7}{16}$	12 $7\frac{13}{16}$	$12\frac{1}{2}$ $7\frac{7}{16}$
Jubilee	...	...	...	$7\frac{7}{8}$ $4\frac{1}{4}$	$12\frac{7}{8}$ $7\frac{7}{8}$	10 $6\frac{1}{4}$
Jumpers	...	...	...	$6\frac{3}{4}$ 3	$8\frac{1}{2}$ $4\frac{1}{2}$	$7\frac{7}{8}$ $3\frac{3}{4}$
Klerksdorp G. & D.	...	...	...	...	$1\frac{9}{16}$ $0\frac{1}{4}$	18/- 7/-
Langlaagte Estate ...	...	$3\frac{7}{8}$ $2\frac{5}{8}$	$4\frac{1}{16}$ $2\frac{7}{8}$	5 $3\frac{9}{16}$	$7\frac{1}{4}$ $4\frac{1}{16}$	$6\frac{9}{16}$ $3\frac{7}{8}$
May Consol. (New)	...	...	...	45/6 8/-	$4\frac{5}{16}$ $2\frac{1}{4}$	$3\frac{7}{8}$ 2
Meyer & Charlton...	...	...	...	$6\frac{1}{4}$ $4\frac{1}{8}$	$8\frac{1}{4}$ $4\frac{7}{8}$	$6\frac{7}{8}$ $4\frac{7}{8}$
Modderfontein ...	...	12/- 4/-	13/3 5/-	£10 5/9	$17\frac{3}{4}$ $6\frac{1}{2}$	$11\frac{1}{4}$ $2\frac{7}{8}$
Primrose, New ...	...	$4\frac{3}{4}$ 2	$5\frac{5}{16}$ $3\frac{7}{8}$	$6\frac{1}{4}$ $3\frac{7}{8}$	$8\frac{5}{16}$ $5\frac{7}{8}$	$6\frac{1}{4}$ $3\frac{3}{4}$
Randfontein Est. ...	...	13/6 9/6	13/9 7/-	10/6 9/9	$4\frac{3}{8}$ $0\frac{7}{8}$	$4\frac{7}{8}$ $1\frac{1}{8}$
Rand Mines	...	...	...	$22\frac{1}{4}$ $7\frac{1}{4}$	$45\frac{1}{2}$ $18\frac{1}{4}$	$33\frac{7}{8}$ 18
Robinson Gold ...	...	$3\frac{7}{8}$ $2\frac{7}{8}$	$4\frac{13}{16}$ $3\frac{7}{16}$	$7\frac{5}{16}$ $4\frac{7}{8}$	$11\frac{1}{2}$ 7	$10\frac{7}{8}$ $7\frac{3}{4}$
Roodepoort U. M. Reef	...	...	...	$4\frac{5}{16}$ $0\frac{21}{32}$	$8\frac{1}{4}$ $4\frac{1}{8}$	$6\frac{1}{4}$ 3
Sheba	...	24/3 19/9	15/3 15/-	$1\frac{13}{32}$ $\frac{25}{32}$	$2\frac{5}{8}$ $1\frac{1}{4}$	$2\frac{1}{16}$ $1\frac{1}{4}$
Simmer & Jack, Prop.	...	$4\frac{3}{4}$ 3	5 $3\frac{1}{4}$	$13\frac{3}{4}$ $3\frac{1}{8}$	$8\frac{1}{4}$ $4\frac{7}{8}$	$7\frac{1}{4}$ $3\frac{3}{4}$

HIGHEST AND LOWEST PRICES.

NAMES.	1891. H. & L.	1892. H. & L.	1893. H. & L.	1894. H. & L.	1895. H. & L.	1896. H. & L.
Spes Bona	...	...	...	...	$4\frac{5}{16}$ 1	$2\frac{7}{16}$ $0\frac{1}{4}$
Stanhope	...	...	...	$2\frac{9}{16}$ 1	$2\frac{11}{16}$ $0\frac{7}{8}$	$1\frac{7}{8}$ $0\frac{3}{8}$
Transvaal Coal T.	...	12/6 8/-	14/3 9/-	26/6 11/-	$3\frac{1}{16}$ 1	$2\frac{1}{4}$ $1\frac{3}{16}$
Wemmer	...	...	...	$6\frac{5}{8}$ $4\frac{7}{8}$	$13\frac{1}{8}$ $6\frac{1}{4}$	$11\frac{7}{8}$ $6\frac{1}{4}$
Worcester	...	$1\frac{7}{8}$ $1\frac{1}{2}$	$2\frac{7}{16}$ $1\frac{3}{8}$	$4\frac{3}{4}$ $1\frac{7}{8}$	6	$3\frac{3}{4}$	$4\frac{3}{4}$ $3\frac{3}{4}$

American—

Alaska Treadwell	...	...	...	...	$5\frac{5}{8}$	$2\frac{3}{4}$	$5\frac{3}{4}$ $4\frac{1}{4}$
Copiapo	$2\frac{3}{16}$ $1\frac{7}{8}$	$2\frac{9}{16}$ 2	$2\frac{1}{4}$ $1\frac{9}{16}$	$2\frac{1}{2}$ $1\frac{5}{8}$	$2\frac{5}{8}$	$1\frac{7}{16}$	3 $1\frac{1}{8}$
De Lama	...	...	...	...	29/6	18/6	21/6 5/6
Frontino & Bolivia	$1\frac{7}{8}$ $0\frac{3}{16}$	$1\frac{1}{8}$ $0\frac{15}{16}$	$1\frac{3}{8}$ $0\frac{15}{16}$	$1\frac{7}{10}$ 1	$1\frac{1}{4}$	$1\frac{3}{16}$	$1\frac{11}{16}$ $0\frac{5}{8}$
Holcomb Valley	...	...	...	...	3/-	7½d.	1/9 0/3
Montana	$0\frac{5}{8}$ $0\frac{3}{8}$	$0\frac{1}{2}$ $0\frac{1}{8}$	...	$0\frac{3}{8}$ $0\frac{1}{16}$	$0\frac{5}{8}$	$0\frac{5}{16}$	11/- 2/6
Springdale	...	...	...	...	3/8	1/3	1/9 0/3

Australian—

Aladdin's Lamp	...	...	...	...	$1\frac{13}{16}$	$0\frac{5}{8}$	$3\frac{1}{8}$ $1\frac{1}{8}$
Brilliant	...	...	...	...	20/-	9/6	$1\frac{7}{16}$ $0\frac{1}{16}$
Brilliant and St. George	...	...	...	...	$2\frac{1}{4}$	$1\frac{3}{8}$	$2\frac{1}{4}$ $1\frac{3}{8}$
Brilliant Block	...	...	...	...	$2\frac{1}{4}$	$1\frac{13}{16}$	2 $0\frac{11}{16}$
Brit. Broken Hill	$2\frac{3}{4}$ 2	...	$\frac{5}{8}$ $\frac{1}{2}$	$\frac{5}{16}$ $\frac{3}{16}$	$\frac{3}{4}$	$\frac{1}{2}$	$1\frac{7}{16}$ $0\frac{7}{8}$
Broken Hill Prop.	...	$7\frac{7}{8}$ $3\frac{1}{4}$	$4\frac{9}{16}$ $2\frac{1}{8}$	62/6 32/-	$2\frac{5}{8}$	$1\frac{7}{16}$	$3\frac{1}{8}$ $2\frac{1}{16}$
Day Dawn Block	...	...	...	...	13/9	8/6	16/6 8/6
Mount Lyell	...	...	...	...	...	...	$9\frac{3}{8}$ $3\frac{5}{8}$
Mount Morgan	...	...	...	...	$3\frac{3}{16}$	$2\frac{1}{4}$	4 $2\frac{1}{8}$
Scot. Australian	$1\frac{7}{8}$ 1	...	$1\frac{7}{16}$ $\frac{3}{4}$	$1\frac{5}{8}$ $\frac{5}{8}$	$\frac{1}{8}$	$\frac{1}{8}$	$0\frac{5}{8}$ $0\frac{1}{4}$
Wentworth	...	...	...	...	$2\frac{7}{8}$	$0\frac{9}{16}$	$1\frac{5}{16}$ $0\frac{5}{8}$

West Australian—

Associated G. M.	...	...	...	...	$2\frac{7}{8}$	$\frac{7}{8}$	$4\frac{3}{16}$ $1\frac{1}{4}$
Coolgardie Gold	...	...	...	...	$1\frac{5}{16}$	6/9	$1\frac{3}{4}$ 8/-
Coolgardie Ming.	...	...	...	...	5/-	9d.	2/- 0/6
Gt. Boulder M. R.	...	...	...	...	$1\frac{1}{16}$	$1\frac{1}{2}$	$2\frac{7}{16}$ $0\frac{1}{2}$
Gt. Boulder Prop.	...	...	...	...	$7\frac{1}{4}$	$0\frac{15}{16}$	$10\frac{5}{8}$ $4\frac{7}{8}$
Hannan's B. Hill	...	...	...	...	$8\frac{1}{8}$	$\frac{7}{16}$	$7\frac{3}{4}$ $2\frac{5}{8}$
Do. North	...	...	...	...	$1\frac{7}{16}$	$1\frac{3}{16}$	$1\frac{7}{8}$ $0\frac{1}{4}$
Do. Prop.	...	...	...	...	$\frac{7}{16}$p.m.	$\frac{7}{16}$p.m.	$2\frac{7}{8}$ $\frac{7}{8}$
Do. Reward	...	...	...	...	$4\frac{1}{4}$	$2\frac{7}{8}$	$5\frac{1}{4}$ $1\frac{1}{8}$
Ivanhoe	...	...	...	...	...	...	11 $4\frac{7}{8}$
Kalgurli	...	...	...	...	$4\frac{7}{8}$	$1\frac{7}{8}$	$2\frac{7}{16}$ $0\frac{5}{8}$
Lady Shenton	...	...	...	...	$2\frac{1}{8}$	$1\frac{5}{8}$	$3\frac{7}{16}$ $1\frac{1}{4}$
Lake View Consols	...	...	...	...	$2\frac{3}{8}$	$1\frac{1}{2}$	$11\frac{1}{2}$ 1

Continental—

Mason & Barry	$7\frac{1}{2}$ $4\frac{7}{8}$	$3\frac{1}{4}$ $2\frac{7}{8}$	$2\frac{15}{16}$ $1\frac{7}{8}$	$3\frac{3}{8}$ $1\frac{13}{16}$	$3\frac{5}{8}$	$1\frac{9}{16}$	$3\frac{5}{8}$ $2\frac{7}{8}$
Rio Tinto	$23\frac{13}{16}16\frac{5}{16}$	$19\frac{1}{4}$ $14\frac{7}{8}$	$16\frac{1}{16}12\frac{7}{16}$	$16\frac{3}{4}$ $12\frac{5}{8}$	$20\frac{1}{4}$	$12\frac{1}{4}$	$26\frac{1}{8}$ $14\frac{9}{16}$

APPENDIX G.

NAMES.	1891. H. & L.	1892. H. & L.	1893. H. & L.	1894. H. & L.	1895. H. & L.	1896. H. & L.
Indian—						
Champion Reef	...	46/- 26/-	65/9 35/-	4 3$\frac{7}{8}$	5$\frac{1}{4}$ 4	8$\frac{1}{16}$ 5$\frac{1}{8}$
Gold Fields, Mysore	3$\frac{5}{16}$ 1$\frac{13}{16}$	4$\frac{7}{8}$ 2$\frac{1}{2}$	5$\frac{7}{16}$ 3$\frac{5}{8}$	7$\frac{1}{4}$ 4$\frac{1}{8}$	30/6 13/6	29/- 17/6
Mysore Gold	6$\frac{5}{16}$ 4$\frac{3}{16}$	5$\frac{7}{8}$ 3$\frac{3}{4}$	4$\frac{7}{8}$ 3$\frac{3}{16}$	3$\frac{5}{16}$ 2$\frac{1}{2}$	3$\frac{1}{2}$ 2$\frac{1}{2}$	9$\frac{1}{8}$ 3$\frac{3}{16}$
Nundydroog	...	...	...	...	2$\frac{5}{16}$ 1$\frac{3}{4}$	4 1$\frac{13}{16}$
Ooregum	3$\frac{1}{4}$ 1$\frac{7}{8}$	4$\frac{5}{16}$ 3$\frac{1}{4}$	5$\frac{1}{4}$ 4$\frac{3}{16}$	5 2$\frac{1}{4}$	3$\frac{5}{8}$ 2$\frac{5}{8}$	4 2$\frac{7}{16}$
Do. Pf. 10% Min.	3$\frac{5}{16}$ 2$\frac{3}{8}$	4$\frac{5}{8}$ 3$\frac{1}{16}$	6 4$\frac{1}{8}$	5$\frac{1}{16}$ 3$\frac{1}{4}$	4$\frac{1}{4}$ 3$\frac{1}{4}$	4$\frac{7}{8}$ 3
Lands and Exploration—						
African Estates	...	...	...	...	3$\frac{3}{4}$ 1$\frac{7}{8}$	2$\frac{1}{4}$ 0$\frac{13}{16}$
Anglo-French Ex.	...	...	...	1$\frac{1}{2}$ 1$\frac{1}{4}$	7$\frac{5}{8}$ 3$\frac{1}{16}$	6$\frac{1}{4}$ 2$\frac{1}{4}$
Anglo-German	...	...	...	...	2$\frac{5}{8}$ 0$\frac{1}{2}$	1$\frac{3}{4}$ 0$\frac{1}{4}$
Balkis Eersteling	...	...	1/9 3d.	10/- 1d.	11/- 2/3	5/- 0/9
Balkis Land	...	...	3/- 1/4$\frac{1}{2}$	7/6 1/3	10/9 3/-	8/6 3/3
Bechuanaland Trading	...	...	...	1$\frac{5}{16}$ 0$\frac{3}{4}$	1$\frac{5}{8}$ 1	1$\frac{3}{8}$ 0$\frac{1}{4}$
British S. A. Char.	...	33/- 10/6	2$\frac{1}{2}$ $\frac{3}{4}$	2$\frac{5}{16}$ 1$\frac{5}{32}$	8$\frac{1}{16}$ 2$\frac{7}{16}$	5$\frac{1}{16}$ 2
Charterland Gold Fields	...	...	...	...	2 $\frac{5}{8}$	1$\frac{1}{4}$ 0$\frac{3}{8}$
Con. Gold Flds. S.A.	...	3$\frac{1}{4}$ 1$\frac{5}{16}$	1$\frac{5}{8}$ 1$\frac{1}{8}$	4$\frac{1}{2}$ 1$\frac{1}{16}$	19$\frac{3}{8}$ 7	14 7$\frac{3}{8}$
Do. 6% Pref	...	...	...	...	1$\frac{5}{16}$ 1$\frac{7}{16}$	1$\frac{5}{16}$ 1
Do. 5½% Debs.	...	...	...	...	114 105$\frac{1}{2}$	112$\frac{1}{2}$ 103
Eerste Fabrieken	...	...	...	...	4$\frac{5}{8}$ 2$\frac{1}{4}$	3$\frac{3}{4}$ 1
Gold Ests. of Aus.	...	...	...	...	3 1$\frac{1}{4}$	2$\frac{5}{8}$ 1$\frac{1}{4}$
Hampton Plains	...	...	...	...	5$\frac{1}{4}$ 1$\frac{3}{8}$	5$\frac{3}{8}$ 2$\frac{5}{8}$
Idaho Exploring	...	...	...	...	8/6 3/-	8/6 2/6
Johannesburg Est.	...	...	...	...	1$\frac{11}{16}$ $\frac{7}{16}$	1$\frac{11}{16}$ 0$\frac{7}{8}$
Johanburg. Water	...	...	...	26/- 16/-	3$\frac{1}{16}$ 23/6	2$\frac{5}{8}$ 1$\frac{3}{8}$
London & Orange	...	...	...	4$\frac{5}{8}$ 3$\frac{3}{8}$	6 2$\frac{1}{2}$	4$\frac{1}{2}$ 2$\frac{1}{4}$
Lon. & S. A. Explor.	15$\frac{7}{8}$ 11$\frac{5}{16}$	12$\frac{3}{4}$ 9	13$\frac{3}{4}$ 8$\frac{9}{16}$	12$\frac{1}{2}$ 9$\frac{1}{4}$	17$\frac{1}{2}$ 9$\frac{3}{4}$	15$\frac{1}{4}$ 13
W. Aust. Develop.	...	...	...	...	1$\frac{1}{4}$ $\frac{7}{8}$	1$\frac{1}{4}$ 0$\frac{5}{8}$
W. Aust. Gold Fields	...	...	...	...	8$\frac{5}{8}$ 3$\frac{5}{8}$	11$\frac{1}{8}$ 4
Miscellaneous—						
Hauraki	...	...	...	...	16/6 2/6	22/- 8/-
Johang. C. In.	...	...	...	2$\frac{5}{16}$ 1$\frac{1}{2}$	6$\frac{1}{4}$ 2$\frac{7}{16}$	4$\frac{1}{16}$ 2$\frac{1}{16}$
Robinson Banks	...	...	...	...	11$\frac{1}{4}$ 4$\frac{3}{4}$	7$\frac{1}{2}$ 4
S. African Gold T.	...	...	...	...	12$\frac{5}{8}$ 3$\frac{3}{4}$	9$\frac{3}{4}$ 5$\frac{3}{4}$
Waihi	...	...	...	...	8 5$\frac{5}{8}$	7$\frac{1}{4}$ 5$\frac{1}{4}$
Waitekauri	...	...	...	...	5$\frac{1}{4}$ 2$\frac{1}{4}$	6$\frac{1}{8}$ 3$\frac{1}{4}$

APPENDIX H.

Dividends on Leading Stocks, 1890—96.

DIVIDENDS ON LEADING STOCKS, PAID

NAMES.	1890.		1891.		1892.	
Home Rails—	1st.	2nd.	1st.	2nd.	1st.	2nd.
Barry	10	10	11	9	10	9
Brighton Ord.	4¼	9¾	3¼	9¼	3¾	9¼
,, Def.	8 for year		7 for year		7 for year	
Caledonian	5	3¾	4	4½	4	4¼
,, Def.	...	¾	1	1½	1	1¼
Chatham and Dover... ...	4⅛	4⅛	3½	4½	3⅗	4⅛
District 5 per cent. Pref....	1½	1	2½	2½	3¼	2¾
Furness	4	3½	2½	3	nil	3
Great Eastern	2	4	1½	3¾	0¾	3⅛
,, Northern "A" ...	1	6	0½	5	nil	4⅛
,, ,, Def. ...	3½	6	½	5	nil	4⅛
,, Western	5¼	7¾	5	7½	4¾	7
Lancs. and Yorks.	4	4½	3½	4¼	3¾	4
Metropolitan Cons.	3	3	3¼	3¼	3¾	3¼
,, Surplus Lands	2½	2½	2½	2¼	2¾	2½
Midland	5½	7	5¾	7	5¼	6¾
North British	3	1½	1	3	2½	3
,, Def.	1¾	nil	nil	0¾	nil	0¾
North Eastern	6¾	7¾	6	7	3	6⅝
,, Staffordshire	5	5	4¾	5¼	4¼	5
,, Western	6¾	7¾	6¼	7¾	5¾	7¼
Sheffield Ord.	¾	4¾	¼	4	¼	3
,, Pref. Ord.... ...	5½ for year		4¼ for year		3¼ for year	
South Eastern	3¾	6¼	2¼	6	1¾	6¼
,, ,, Def.	3½ for year		2¼ for year		2 for year	
,, Western	4¾	7¼	4¼	7¾	4¼	7¾
Taff Vale	3	3	2¼	2¼	3¼	3¼
Tilbury and Southend ..	2½	4½	2	5½	2½	5¼
Indian, Colonial—						
Bombay, Bar., and C. ...	£6 14/- for year		£7 15/- for year		£7 10/- for year	
Canadian Pacific	5	5	5	5	5	5

DIX H.

DURING THE LAST SEVEN YEARS.

1893.		1894.		1895.		1896.	
1st.	2nd.	1st.	2nd.	1st.	2nd.	1st.	2nd.
10	9	10	10	10	10	10	10
4¼	7¼	4¼	7¾	3⅗	8¼	4¾	8
5¾ for year		6 for year		6 for year		6¾ for year	
4	4¾	4	3¼	4½	5½	5	...
1	1¾	1	1¼	1½	2½	2	...
2⅝	4½	2¼	4½	2⅘	4½	4½	4½
2¾	1½	3¾	1½	3	2½	3½	2¼
1	1½	1	2	nil	1	1	2
0⅜	1¼	1	2¼	0⅝	4	1½	4¾
nil	nil	nil	2	nil	2½	nil	2¼
nil	nil	nil	2	nil	2½	nil	2¼
4	5⅛	4½	6	3¼	7	4¾	7¼
3¼	3	2½	4¼	3¾	5¼	5	5⅞
3¼	2½	2¾	2¾	2⅞	3	3¼	3⅜
2¾	2½	2¾	2½	2⅝	2⅝	2⅝	2⅝
4¾	3	4¾	5¾	4	6¼	5	7
3	3	3	1½	3	3	3	...
0¼	1	0¼	nil	nil	1¼	1	...
4¾	7	5	6¾	4½	6¾	5½	7¼
4	5	4	4½	3½	4½	4	5
5¼	5½	5¾	6¾	5¼	1¾	6¼	8
nil	nil	nil	1½	nil	¾	1	1½
nil for year		1½ for year		1¾ for year		2	2½
2¼	5¼	2½	5¾	2¼	6	3	6⅜
1½ for year		2 for year		2¼ for year		3⅜ for year	
4¾	7¼	4¾	7½	4½	7¾	5	8½
3¼	2½	3¼	3¼	3	3¼	3¼	3¼
2½	5	2½	5½	2½	5¾	2¾	6
£8 17/6 for year		£7 12/6 for year		£8 2/6 for year		£9 10/- for year	
5	5	5	nil	nil	1½	2	2

NAMES.	1890. 1st.	1890. 2nd.	1891. 1st.	1891. 2nd.	1892. 1st.	1892.
Delhi, Umballa, & Kalka	4	4	3	2·18/-	£2 12/-	£2
Grand Trunk Guar.	4	4	1	5½	2¼	
Great Indian Peninsula ...	£7 10/8	5	£8 13/-	5	7¼	
Hudson's Bay	2½ for year		2½ for year		$4\frac{8}{15}$ for year	
Madras	5	5	5	5	5	
South Mahratta, Limited...	4	4	4	4	4	
Suez Canal...	85·714 francs		91·206 francs		92·36 francs	
Foreign Rails—						
Buenos Ayres & Rosario ...	7	7	nil	nil	nil	
Cent. Argentine, Limited	5	5	nil	nil	nil	
,, Uruguay...	8	5	5	2	2	
Great Western of Brazil ...	10/-	12/-	12/-	10/-	10/-	
Mexican 1st Pref.	8	8	8	7½	4¼	
American Rails—						
Balt. Ohio Cap. Stock ..	nil	nil	20	5	5	
Central Pacific	2	2	2	2	2	
Cen. Rlrd. N. Jersey Cp. Sk.	6 % per ann.		6 % per ann.		7 % per ann.	
Chic. Mil. and St. Paul ...	nil	nil	nil	nil	4	
Do. Pref.	7	7	7	7	7	
Cleveland & Pittsburg Cap. Stock	7 7	7 7	7 7	7 7	7 7	7
Denver Pref.	3	5	nil	nil	nil	
Illinois Central	6	6	4	5	5	
Lake Shore	4	8	5	7	6	
Louisville and Nashville	6	6	5	5	4	
New York Central	4 4	4 6	4 4	6 5	5 5	5
Norfolk and W. Pref. ...	3	3	3	3	2	
Northern Pacific Pref. ...	4 4	4 4	4 4	4 4	4	
Pennsylvania	6	5	6	6	6	
Banks—						
Bank of England	10½	11½	10½	10	10	
Bank of Ireland...	11½	11½	11½	11½	11¼	
Brit. of South America ...	10 for year		10 for year		10 for year	
Capital and Counties ..	18	18	18	16	16	
Char. of India, A. & C. ...	14	18	14	14	14	
City, Limited	11	11	11	11	10	
Lloyds Limited, £8 Pd. ...	17½ for year		17½ for year		16¼ for year	
Lond. & County, £20 Pd.	22 for year		22 for year		20 for year	
London & Mid., £12½ Pd.	16 for year		15 for year		15 for year	
Lond. & Westr., £20 Pd.	17 for year		14½ for year		12 for year	
Lond. Joint Stk., £15 Pd.	12½ for year		11¾ for year		10 for year	
Met. of England, £5 Pd.	17½ for year		18 for year		18 for year	
Nat. Prov. of England ...	20	20	20	20	20	

1893.		1894.		1895.		1896.	
1st.	2nd.	1st.	2nd.	1st.	2nd.	1st.	2nd.
£2 16/-	£2 18/-	£3 2/-	$2\frac{1}{8}$	4	$3\frac{3}{10}$	£3 9/-	...
2	$3\frac{1}{4}$	nil	nil	nil	nil	nil	..
£6 15/4	5	£6 12/-	5	£5 16/8	5	$6\frac{1}{4}$	...
$3\frac{1}{15}$ for year		$4\frac{8}{15}$ for year		$4\frac{8}{15}$ for year		13/- for year	
5	5	5	5	£5 1/-	£5	5	...
4	4	$4\frac{1}{2}$	$4\frac{1}{2}$	$4\frac{1}{2}$	$4\frac{1}{2}$	$4\frac{1}{2}$	...
90·40 francs		89·868 francs		73·17 francs		55·458 francs.	
nil	nil	2	1	2	2	2	...
1 for year		$1\frac{1}{2}$	$1\frac{1}{2}$	2	$1\frac{1}{2}$	3	...
2	3	6	5	6	5	4	...
10/-	14/-	10/-	14/-	10/-	10	10	...
2	$1\frac{1}{4}$	$0\frac{3}{4}$	$0\frac{1}{2}$	$1\frac{3}{4}$	$0\frac{1}{2}$	$0\frac{3}{4}$	...
5	5	4	nil	nil	nil	nil	nil
2	nil	nil	nil	1	1	1	1
7% per ann.		7% per ann.		6% per ann.		5% per ann.	
4	4	4	2	2	2	2	...
7	7	7	7	7	7	7	...
7 7	7 7	7 7	7 7	7 7	7 7	7 7	7 7
nil	nil	nil	nil	nil	2	2	2
5	5	5	5	5	5	5	5
6	6	6	6	6	6	6	...
4	nil	nil	nil	nil	nil	nil	...
5 5	5 5	5 5	5 5	4 4	4 4	4 4	4 4
nil	nil	nil	nil	nil		nil	...
nil	nil	nil	nil	nil		nil	...
5	5	5	5	5	5	5	5
10	9	8	$8\frac{1}{2}$	8	$8\frac{1}{2}$	$8\frac{1}{2}$	...
$11\frac{1}{2}$	$11\frac{1}{2}$	$11\frac{1}{2}$	$10\frac{1}{2}$	$10\frac{1}{2}$	$10\frac{1}{2}$	$10\frac{1}{2}$	...
10 for year		10 for year		12	8	12	8
16	16	16	16	16	16	16	16
14	14	14	18	14	18	14	...
10	10	9	8	8	8	8	9
15 for year		15 for year		$16\frac{9}{18}$ for year		14	...
21 for year		20 for year		20 for year		20 for year	
15 for year		15 for year		15 for year		15 & bon. of 1 f.	
12 for year		10 for year		10 for year		12 for year	
10 for year		$9\frac{1}{2}$ for year		9 for year		10 for year	
18 for year		15 for year		$12\frac{1}{2}$ for year		$12\frac{1}{2}$ for year	
18	18	18	16	18	16	18	...

APPENDIX H.

NAMES.	1890.		1891.		1892.	
	1st.	2nd.	1st.	2nd.	1st.	2nd
Parr's	19	19	19	19	19	19
U. of Austral., £25 Pd. ...	14 for year		14 for year		12 for year	
U. of London, £15¼ Pd.	12½		11¼		10	
Breweries—						
Allsopp & Sons	3¼	nil	nil	nil	nil	nil
Guinness, Son & Co. ...	18	12	18	12	18	12
Parker's, Burslem	14/-	10/-	14/-	10/-	14/-	10/-
Commercial, Industrial, &c.						
Aerated Bread, Limited ...	28 for year [1]		28 for year [2]		30 for year [3]	
Armstrong (Sir W. G.) ...	17½	5	17½	5	14	5
British Gas Light	22/6	22/6	22/6	22/6	22/6	22/6
Bryant & May	7/6	10/-	7/6	10/-	7/6	10/-
City of London Electric ..	...	...	...	...	nil	nil
Coats, J. & P.	...	5	8 for year		8 for year	
Crossley (John) & Sons ...	7½ for year		7½ for year		10 for year	
Gas Light & Coke	13	13	13	12	12	12
Gordon Hotels	...	8/-	12/-	8/-	12/-	8/-
Met. Electric Supply ..	...	...	4/- for year		4/- for year	
Pawsons & Leafs	3/9	3/9	3/9	3/9	3/9	3/9
Pears Ordinary	...	...	...	...	...	8
Price's Patent Candle ...	10/-	17/6	15/-	15/-	12/6	12/6
South Met. Gas	13¼	15¼	15½	15½	15½	15¼
Spiers & Pond	10 for year		8 for year		10 for year	
Telegraphs and Trusts—						
Anglo-American, Limited	12/6 15/-	15/- 15/-	12/- 12/-	12/6 16/-	12/6 12/6	12/6 17/6
Cuba, Limited	8/-	8/-	8/-	8/-	8/-	8/-
Direct U.S. Cable	3/6 3/6	3/6 3/6	3/6 3/6	3/6 3/6	3/6 3/6	3/6 3 6
Eastern Extension, Ltd. ...	7 for year		7 for year		7 for year	
Globe Telegraph Trust ...	2/- 4/3	1/9 1/9	2/6 4/6	2/- 1/6	2/6 3/9	1/9 1/3
National Telephone, Ltd.	6	5	7	5	7	5
Railway Investment, Def.	7/-	14/-	6/-	13/-	nil	6/6
Railway Share Trust, Ltd.	4/-	4/-	4/-	4/-	4/-	4/-
Submarine Cables Trust ...	60/-	60/-	60/-	60/-	60/-	60/-

[1] And right to allotment of 1 new share at par for 30 old.

1893.		1894.		1895.		1896.		
1st.	2nd.	1st.	2nd.	1st.	2nd.	1st.	2nd.	
19	19	19	19	19	19	19	19	70
10 for year		7 for year		5½ for year		5	5	71
10		8¾		9	9	9	...	72
nil	nil	2	6	6	6	6	...	73
18	12	18	12	20	12	20	...	74
14/-	10/-	10/-	10/-	10/-	10/-	14	...	75
31 1/16 for year [4]		34 1/16 for year [4]		35 for year [1]		35 for year [1]		76
15	5	16½	5	18½	5	17½	...	77
22/6	22/6	22/6	22/6	22/6	22/6	22/6	...	78
7/6	8/9	7/6	8/9	7/6	10/-	7/6	...	79
nil	nil	nil	5	nil	10/-	nil	...	80
8 for year		8 for year		12 for year		20 for year		81
10 for year		10 for year		10 for year		7/6	...	82
12	12	12	12	12⅘	12⅗	12¾	...	83
12/-	8/-	12/-	8/-	12/-	8/-	12/-	...	84
5/- for year		6/- for year		3/-	5/-	4/-	...	85
3/9	3/-	3/-	3/9	3/-	3/-	3/-	...	86
12	8	8	8	12	8	12	...	87
10/-	15/-	10/-	17/6	15/-	17/6	16/-	...	88
15½	15½	15½	15½	15½	15½	15½	...	89
10 for year		10 for year		4/- 4/- 4/- 4/-		11/- 4/-	...	90
12/6 12/6 12/6	13/6	9/- 10/- 9/-	14/-	10/- 11/- 10/-	18/-	12/- 12/- 12/-		91
8/-	8/-	8/-	8/-	8/-	8/-	8/-	...	92
3/6 3/6 3/6	3/6	2/- 2/- 2/-	2/-	2/- 2/- 2/-	2/-	2/6 2/6 2/6		93
7 for year		7 for year		5/-	2/6	7/- for year		94
2/3 4/- 1/6	1/3	2/6 3/9 1/3	1/6	2/3 3/3 1/3	1/6	2/6 3/9 1/6		95
5	5	5	5	5	6	5	...	96
nil	nil	nil	3/11	nil	7/10	nil	...	97
nil	nil	4/- for year		6/4 for year		4 for year		98
60/-	60/-	60/-	60/-	60/-	60/- [5]	60/-	47/6 [6]	99

[2] Do. for 40 old. [3] Do. for 45 old. [4] Do. for 50 old.

[5] May, 1887, £20 shares divided; £2 10s. capital returned December, 1889, and £2 10s. March, 1890.

[6] On account October, 1896, coupon.

APPENDIX I.

DIVIDENDS ON PRINCIPAL MINES, 1890-1896.

NAMES.	1890.	1891.	1892.	1893.	1894.	1895.	1896.
African—							
Cape Copper	7/-	3/6	1/3	2/6	2/6	3/9	5/-
Champ d'Or	...	2/-	...	...	5/2	4/-	3/2
Chimes, New	...	...	40%	...	15%	55%	1/-
Consol. Bultfontein	7½%	7½%	7½%	7½%.	7½%	7½%	1/6
Consol. Deep L. ...	...	...	...	...	4/-	4/-	10/-
Crown Reef	15%	50%	55%	50%	50%	75%	32/-
De Beers	20/- p.s.	20/- p.s.	12/6 p.s.	25/- p.s.	25/- p.s.	25/- p.s.	40/-
Do. 5% 1st Mort. Deb.	...	...	...	...	5%	5%	5%
Durban Roodepoort	4/- p.s.	4/- p.s.	6/- p.s.	11/- p.s.	12/- p.s.	60%	9/-
Ferreira	...	50%	125%	85%	150%	130%	275%
Gelden Est. & Gold	...	15%	10%	25%	30%	30%	2,6
Gelden M. Reef ...	...	...	...	...	...	4/-	2/-
Glencairn	...	...	...	...	12½%	15%	2/6
Griqualand, West ...	3¼%	4%	4%	4%	8/-	8/-	8/-
Heriots, New	...	...	...	10%	40%	125%	85%
Jagersfontein, New	nil	nil	7½%	20%	20%	20%	6/-
Jubilee	55%	35%	60%	120%	120%	90%	10/-
Jumpers	...	...	...	10%	45%	50%	30%
Langlaagte Est. ...	15%	10%	20%	30%	45%	50%	8/-
May Consol., New	..	...	...	...	...	4/-	2/-
Meyer & Charlton ...	15%	50%	45%	60%	55%	50%	5/-
Primrose, New ...	...	15%	27½%	40%	40%	50%	5/-
Robinson Gold ...	...	4%	12%	8%	10%	14%	13/-
Roodepoort U. M. Reef	...	...	...	...	20%	50%	7/-
Sheba	...	...	1/- p.s.	1/6 p.s.	- p.s.	...	3/-
Simmer & Jack Pr.	...	20%	40%	40%	20%	20%	...
Stanhope	...	10%	25%	50%	100%	40%	5%
Transvaal Coal T. ...	...	2¼%	5%	6¼%	7½%	10%	1/-
Wemmer...	...	2/-	2/-	...	...	20/-	30/-
Worcester	30%	10%	17½%	15%	50%	50%	13/-
American—							
Alaska Treadwell ...	...	4/-	9/-	7/6	9/-	8/-	7/-
Copiapo	4/6	4/6	4/-	4/-	2/5	4/-	3/6
De Lama	...	1/6	4/-	4/6	6/-	4/6	3/-
Frontino & Bolivia	1/2	3/3	3/9	3/9	3/3	2/6	3/3
Montana	1/-	3d.	...	...	...	1/3	6d.
Springdale	...	...	...	2d.	4d.	..	...
Australian—							
Aladdin's Lamp ...	...	...	4/-	1/-	4/-	11/-	8/-
Brilliant	18/-	30/-	3/-	1/9	3/5	4/10	3/10

NAMES.	1890.	1891.	1892.	1893.	1894.	1895.	1896.
Brilliant Block ...	...	...	...	6d.	7/3	6/-	...
Brilliant St. George	...	...	...	...	3/10	7/6	5/9
Broken Hill Prop....	22/-	24/-	12/-	15/-	12/6	12/-	9/-
Day Dawn Block ...	...	1/-	2/6	6d.	...	6d.	2/-
Mount Morgan ...	14/-	7/10	6/-	6/-	6/-	6/-	6/-
Scot. Australian ...	10%	10%	7¾%	5½%	3¼%	1¼%	...
Wentworth	...	...	..	...	...	4/-	1/-
West Australian—							
Coolgardie Gold ...	...	...	...	...	...	4/	7/3
Gt. Boulder Prop....	...	...	...	...	...	6/-	18/-
Ivanhoe	...	...	...	...	...	...	5/-
Continental—							
Mason & Barry ...	6/-	2/-	2/-	2/-	2/6	2/6	2/6
Rio Tinto	16½%	10%	7%	7%	4%	11%	30/-
Indian—							
Champion Reef ...	...	...	...	...	7/-	11/-	18/6
Gold Fields, Mysore	...	...	1/-	...	...	...	...
Mysore Gold	15/-	13/-	10/-	10/-	5/-	7/-	17/6
Nundydroog	19 1/16%	25%	28¾%	2/6	3/-	4/6	6/-
Ooregum...	1/-	3/6	/6	10/6	7/6	7/6	6/6
Do. Pref. 10% min.	3/-	5/6	9/6	12/6	9/6	9/6	8/6
Lands and Explorations—							
African Estates ...	...	...	...	...	...	10%[1]	...
Anglo-French Ex....	...	...	...	...	10%	5/6	10/-
Anglo-German ...	...	...	...	...	...	5/-	2/6
Bechuanaland Trading ...	...	...	18½% & 6% bns.	5%	10½%	15%	2/-
Cons. Gold Fields, S.A.	...	...	...	10%	15%	125%	25/-
Do. 6% Pref.	...	...	...	...	3%	6%	0/7·2
Do. 5½% Debs.	...	...	...	...	2¾%	5½%	£2¾
Eerste Fabricken ...	...	...	16%	16%	16%	20%	3/2·4
Gold Estates of Aus.	...	...	...	...	...	6/- on f.p. shs. 3/- „ pt. pd. „	3/-
Idaho Exploring ...	...	...	...	...	2d.	...	6d.
Johannesburg Est....	10%	...	10½%	10%	10%	15%	3/-
Do. Water...	...	5%	5%	6%	6¼%	7½%	7½%
London & Orange...	160%	10%	...	10%	5/-	5/-	2/6
London & S. A. Explor.	16/6	12/6	15/6	17/-	11/-	14/-	12/-
W. Aust. Develop.	...	..	...	...	...	10/-	...
Miscellaneous—							
Hauraki	...	...	...	...	...	4/-	4/-
Johang. C. Invest.	...	...	...	...	20%	6%	5/-
S. African Gold Trust	...	...	2/-	3/-	8/	11/-	22/6
Waihi	...	...	...	...	...	9/-	8/-
Waitekauri	...	...	...	...	...	...	1/-

[1] Plus 175% paid on £16,000, the original capital.

APPEN

TABLE FOR COM

PRICE OF STOCK.	YIELDS PER CENT. ON THE PURCHASE PRICE WHEN			
£ per cent.	£1 %	£1½ %	£2 %	£2½ %
100	1 0 0	1 10 0	2 0 0	2 10 0
101	0 19 9	1 9 8	1 19 7	2 9 6
102	0 19 7	1 9 4	1 19 2	2 9 0
103	0 19 5	1 9 1	1 18 10	2 8 7
104	0 19 2	1 8 10	1 18 5	2 8 0
105	0 19 0	1 8 7	1 18 1	2 7 7
106	0 18 10	1 8 3	1 17 8	2 7 2
107	0 18 7	1 8 0	1 17 4	2 6 8
108	0 18 6	1 7 9	1 17 0	2 6 3
109	0 18 4	1 7 6	1 16 8	2 5 10
110	0 18 2	1 7 3	1 16 4	2 5 5
111	0 18 0	1 7 0	1 16 0	2 5 0
112	0 17 10	1 6 9	1 15 8	2 4 7
113	0 17 8	1 6 6	1 15 4	2 4 2
114	0 17 6	1 6 3	1 15 1	2 3 10
115	0 17 5	1 6 1	1 14 9	2 3 6
116	0 17 2	1 5 10	1 14 5	2 3 1
117	0 17 1	1 5 7	1 14 2	2 2 8
118	0 16 11	1 5 5	1 13 10	2 2 4
119	0 16 9	1 5 2	1 13 7	2 2 0
120	0 16 8	1 5 0	1 13 4	2 1 8

DIX K.

PUTING DIVIDENDS.

THE DIVIDENDS ARE AT THE FOLLOWING RATES.					PRICE OF STOCK.
£3 %	£3½ %	£4 %	£4½ %	£5 %	£ per cent.
3 0 0	3 10 0	4 0 0	4 10 0	5 0 0	100
2 19 4	3 9 3	3 19 2	4 9 1	4 19 0	101
2 18 9	3 8 7	3 18 5	4 8 2	4 18 0	102
2 18 3	3 7 11	3 17 8	4 7 5	4 17 1	103
2 17 8	3 7 3	3 16 11	4 6 6	4 16 1	104
2 17 1	3 6 8	3 16 2	4 5 8	4 15 2	105
2 16 7	3 6 0	3 15 5	4 4 10	4 14 4	106
2 16 0	3 5 5	3 14 9	4 4 1	4 13 5	107
2 15 6	3 4 9	3 14 0	4 3 4	4 12 6	108
2 15 0	3 4 2	3 13 4	4 2 6	4 11 8	109
2 14 6	3 3 7	3 12 8	4 1 9	4 10 10	110
2 14 0	3 3 0	3 12 0	4 1 0	4 10 1	111
2 13 6	3 2 6	3 11 5	4 0 0	4 9 3	112
2 13 1	3 1 11	3 10 9	3 19 6	4 8 5	113
2 12 8	3 1 4	3 10 2	3 18 11	4 7 8	114
2 12 2	3 0 10	3 9 6	3 18 3	4 6 11	115
2 11 8	3 0 4	3 8 11	3 17 7	4 6 2	116
2 11 3	2 19 9	3 8 4	3 16 11	4 5 5	117
2 10 10	2 19 3	3 7 9	3 16 3	4 4 8	118
2 10 5	2 18 9	3 7 2	3 15 7	4 4 0	119
2 10 0	2 18 4	3 6 8	3 15 0	4 3 4	120

STOCK EXCHANGE INVESTMENTS.

PRESS NOTICES OF THE FIRST EDITION.

"The subjects ably dealt with include the growth of capital, the history of joint-stock enterprise, and Stock Exchange methods; with sound advice as to the choice of investments."—*Daily News.*

"Contains a number of curious and entertaining facts connected with commerce, and a concise sketch of the development of finance in this country."—*Morning Post.*

"Many valuable features which make the book a useful addition to the investor's Library."—*Financial News.*

"Deals in a clear and instructive manner with theories, and embodies facts and figures from the latest authorities."—*Financial Post.*

"A pleasant and useful compendium of financial knowledge, seldom presented in so compact and clear a form."—*Pall Mall Gazette.*

"Interesting and instructive to all concerned."—*Westminster Gazette.*

"We must candidly own that it is a very readable and well got-up exposition and history of Stock Exchange affairs."—*Statist.*

"A comprehensive work. Every topic of interest to the investor is dealt with in an expert manner."—*Star.*

"A well turned-out book."—*Speaker.*

"Thoroughly comprehensive and lucid, and presented in a compact and systematic manner."—*Public Opinion.*

"A striking feature in the wholesale trade is the inquiry for Aubrey's 'Stock Exchange Investments,' which is selling freely."—*The Bookman.*

"A well-timed volume. The style is clear and concise."—*City Press.*

"A storehouse of financial and economic knowledge. It cannot fail to be of the greatest value."—*Black and White.*

"Essentially a philosophical work, intended for the instruction of the general public. It is pleasantly written and admirably got up. At the same time it is thoroughly practical and accurate."—*Sketch.*

"Of considerable use to all who have dealings on the Stock Exchange."—*Money.*

PRESS NOTICES—Continued.

"Those who are fortunate enough to have capital to invest will find this book a most complete guide."—*Rock.*

"Largely composed of valuable historical and statistical information on different classes and methods of investments."—*Publishers' Circular.*

"Demonstrates how the wealth of the country is accumulating, and the necessity for safe and profitable channels for its use."—*Whitehall Review.*

"Suggests certain safe rules, based upon wide experience and observation."—*Weekly Times and Echo.*

"The chapter on Booms and Panics is most enlightening and interesting."—*Lloyd's Weekly Newspaper.*

"There ought to be a brisk demand for a book which gives much sound guidance to investors."—*The People.*

"Practical counsels and cautions on the choice of stocks, on unreasonable expectations, and on hidden pitfalls."—*Mining World.*

"This is a book which commends itself to us. It is a very useful and valuable work."—*Mining Journal.*

"A great deal of useful information is crammed into this book, which will be found very interesting."—*South Africa.*

"Contains much information of interest and service to investors and speculators. The counsels are perfectly true."—*South American Journals.*

"Combines modern economic history, technical explanation, criticism, and advice. It ought to be acceptable to a wide circle."—*Manchester Guardian.*

"Covers the entire field."—*Manchester City News.*

"An eminently practical guide. The 'Safe Rules' are particularly worthy of attention."—*Manchester Courier.*

"Cannot fail to be of the greatest service."—*Liverpool Post.*

"In this admirable treatise every aspect of the subject is dealt with most skilfully and concisely."—*Liverpool Courier.*

"Persons with money to invest should keep the book on their library table."—*Liverpool Mercury.*

"Much useful information and many cautions to the unwary."—*Leeds Mercury.*

"A most useful book, thoroughly up-to-date."—*Leeds Daily News.*

"A plain, straightforward, and readily comprehensible work on a most intricate and difficult subject. A clear, succinct, and trustworthy guide to investors."—*Sheffield Independent.*

"A concise and pleasantly-written guide. The information is carefully condensed and lucidly arranged."—*Birmingham Daily Gazette.*

PRESS NOTICES—Continued.

" It traverses the whole subject."—*Birmingham Daily Post.*

" A compendium of financial and economic knowledge."—*Nottingham Daily Guardian.*

" Various questions connected with finance are put forward in an intelligible, systematic way, and in a form that is easy reading."—*Midland Counties Herald.*

" A book that ought to be closely studied. It contains a great amount of information as to what to do and avoid, and a mass of figures and facts of general importance. The book is an ideal one on the large subject with which it deals."—*Leicester Daily Post.*

" We have examined the work with some care, and are able to pronounce it a very valuable contribution to the subject."—*Staffordshire Sentinel.*

" Deals with the subject of investments with a thoroughness and a lucidity which leave nothing to be desired."—*Northern Daily Telegraph.*

" A good and really useful work. Every form of investment is dealt with thoroughly.—*Huddersfield Examiner.*

" Covers the ground very fully. Sensible advice as to the choice of investments. A careful and copious manual of useful information."—*North British Daily Mail.*

" Well informed, and written clearly and sensibly."—*Edinburgh News.*

" A readable and instructive book ; well informed, and intelligently written. Any one who wishes to have a knowledge of the machinery of finance should read this volume."—*Scotsman.*

" A useful book in a variety of ways."—*Glasgow Herald.*

" Contains a digest of such information as every investor wants to obtain. It should prove welcome to all business men."—*Inverness Courier.*

" An exceedingly handy reference book."—*Dundee Courier.*

" Presents an array of facts, and not a few inferences and maxims, with judicious counsels."—*Aberdeen Free Press.*

" A plain, clear, and authentic elucidation.—*Dundee Advertiser.*

" It is not a mere manual for investors. It goes into the subject thoroughly, critically as well as historically and descriptively, and will be found of immense value to all persons having dealings on the Stock Exchange."—*Newcastle Daily Journal.*

" Gives in clear and concise language a history of our commercial greatness, and the story reads like a chapter from a fairy tale."—*Chester Chronicle.*

PRESS NOTICES—*Continued.*

" We are unacquainted with any work so readable as this. The information is conveyed in an agreeable form."—*Eastern Daily Press.*

" An ably-written work, dealing with all branches of Stock Exchange business."—*Cambridge Chronicle.*

" A manual of really reliable information; certainly one of the best that has appeared. We have no hesitation in recommending this clever and useful work."—*Norfolk Daily Standard.*

" The very valuable tables are only a small part of the work."—*Western Daily Mercury (Plymouth).*

" An enormous mass of facts and figures. Investors ought to feel thankful for the valuable information and advice.—*Western Morning News (Plymouth).*

" A good deal of history is given in the volume. There is an interesting chapter on the eight millions wasted yearly in the employment of Stockbrokers."—*Western Mail (Cardiff).*

" Deals thoroughly with the matter, and in a most interesting manner." —*Western Daily Press (Bristol).*

" An exhaustive and practical treatise, brightly written."—*Bristol Times.*

" The author has contrived to condense into a handy volume a great amount of valuable and interesting information. The book is certain to be welcomed by investors.—*South Wales Daily News.*

" The work is really more than its title denotes, as the reader is furnished with a concise history, giving many details as startling as they are interesting. Every kind of investment is touched upon with a masterly hand."—*Monmouthshire Beacon.*

" Have you money to put out, and are you unacquainted with the ways of the Money Market? If so, your first investment should be 5s. in this new work."—*Hampshire Telegraph.*

" This handsome volume is the result of the able execution of a happily-conceived design. It goes into the subject very thoroughly, and covers a wide field most ably, with care and sound judgment."—*Northern Whig (Belfast).*

" The book has a unique value."—*Cork Examiner.*

" In every way an excellent publication. Independent of its financial features, it is decidedly interesting."—*Belfast News-Letter.*

Commendatory Notices have also appeared in the following Newspapers, among many others :—*Morning, The Sun, Academy, Literary World, United Service Gazette, Stock Exchange Journal, Colliery Guardian, Shareholder, South Eastern Gazette, Yorkshire Post, Warrington Guardian, Eastern Morning News (Hull), South London Observer, Huddersfield Daily Chronicle, Derby Advertiser, Western Times, Halifax Courier, Sunderland Daily Echo, Stamford Mercury, Bristol Mercury, Leicester Advertiser, Bath Chronicle, Louth Times, Boston Guardian, &c., &c.*

UNIVERSAL STOCK EXCHANGE, Ltd.
Established in 1885.

The OLDEST ESTABLISHED and LARGEST INDEPENDENT STOCK DEALERS. Originators of the Three-Monthly Settlement System, and a Uniform Rate of Interest.

All classes of Stock Exchange Securities bought and sold against Cash or for Forward Delivery, free of Commission. Accounts opened with responsible customers on the Fortnightly or Three-monthly System to suit their convenience. Particulars sent on application.

Directors.

MAJOR C. H. STRUTT, *Chairman.*
G. B. NORTHCOTE, Esq.
Col. CHAS. DASHWOOD.
H. M. MACKUSICK, *Managing Director.*

Bankers:
THE METROPOLITAN BANK (of England and Wales), 60, Gracechurch Street, E.C., and Branches.
Messrs. CHAS. HOPKINSON & SONS, 3, Regent Street, S.W.

Solicitors:
Messrs. LAST & SONS, 19, Pall Mall East, S.W.

Auditors and Accountants:
Messrs. W. H. PANNELL & Co., Chartered Accountants, 13 & 14, Basinghall Street, E.C.

Secretary and Offices:
E. WEBLIN, Cockspur Street, Pall Mall, London, S.W.
Telegraphic Address: "CLIENTELE, LONDON."

RESERVE FUND.

Every customer has the advantage of being able to ascertain the standing and the financial strength of the Universal Stock Exchange. Its capital is £300,000, of which £270,099 have been issued and paid up. The following assets have been set aside by the Directors as a RESERVE FUND:

DESCRIPTION.	VALUE.
	£
Waterloo House, as per Valuation by Messrs. Hampton	32,700
£2,100 2¾ per cent. Consols	2,315
£1,600 North-Eastern Consols	2,844
$8,000 Nashville, Florence and Sheffield 1st Mortgage 5 per Cent., 1937	1,344
$8,000 Norfolk and Western Improvement and Extension 6 per Cent. Bonds, 1934 ...	1,864
£3,900 Halifax and Bermudas Cable 4½ per Cent. Debentures	3,900
£1,000 Atlantic and North-Western 5 per Cent. 1st Mortgage Guaranteed	1,190
£1,500 Atlantic 1st Leased Lines Rental Trust 4 per Cent.	1,485
$10,000 Alleghany Valley 7 per Cent. 1st Mortgage Bond	2,520
	£50,162

PRICE ONE SHILLING.

A Special List for Investors

OF

Perfectly Sound Securities,

Paying from 2 to 6 per cent.

The following are specimens :—

4. LEEDS CORPORATION 4 PER CENT. CONSOLIDATED DEBENTURE STOCK.—Redeemable 1927 by means of a Sinking Fund, which is being invested under Government supervision. Dividends payable 1st January and 1st July. Amount of Stock, £2,302,050.

Highest price, 1896, $130\frac{1}{2}$ } Mean price, 127.
Lowest price, 1896, $123\frac{1}{2}$ } Yield to Investors about £$2\frac{5}{8}$ p.c.

16. DOMINION OF CANADA LOAN FOR £5,000,000 $3\frac{1}{2}$ PER CENT. STERLING BONDS OR INSCRIPTIONS.—Redeemable 1904 to 1934. Dividends payable 1st June and 1st December. Amount of Bonds, £470,700; Inscribed Stock, £4,529,300.

Bonds ... { Highest price, 1896, $111\frac{3}{8}$ } Mean price, $106\frac{15}{16}$
{ Lowest price, 1896, $102\frac{1}{2}$ } Yield to Investor about £$2\frac{7}{8}$ p.c.

Inscribed Stock { Highest price, 1896, $111\frac{7}{8}$ } Mean price, $106\frac{7}{16}$
{ Lowest price, 1896, 101 } Yield to Investor about £$2\frac{7}{8}$ p.c.

38. GREAT EASTERN RAILWAY CONSOLIDATED 4 PER CENT. PREFERENCE STOCK.—Dividends payable February and August. Amount of Stock, £5,038,800.

Highest price, 1896, 156 } Mean price, $149\frac{1}{2}$
Lowest price, 1896, 143 } Yield to Investor about £$2\frac{5}{8}$ p.c.

142. J. & P. COATS, LIMITED, 4½ PER CENT. DEBENTURE STOCK.—Issued as perpetual, but Company reserves right of paying off whole or part of issue any time after January 1st, 1901, at 110 per cent. Dividends payable 1st January and 1st July. Amount of Stock, £2,000,000.

Highest price, 1896, 118½ } Mean price, 115½
Lowest price, 1896, 112½ } Yield to Investor about £3 p.c.

81. EAST LONDON WATERWORKS COMPANY 4½ PER CENT. DEBENTURE STOCK.—Dividends payable 1st January and 1st July. Amount of Stock, £654,740.

Highest price, 1896, 167¾ } Mean price, 163¼
Lowest price, 1896, 158¾ } Yield to Investor about £2¾ p.c.

93. NEW SOUTH WALES GOVERNMENT 4 PER CENT. INSCRIBED STOCK.—Redeemable at par at Bank of England, 1st July, 1933.—Dividend payable 1st January and 1st July at above Bank. Amount of Stock, £9,686,300.

Highest price, 1896, 123¼ } Mean price, 118⅛
Lowest price, 1896, 113 } Yield to Investor about £3⅛ p.c.

114. BOMBAY - BARODA RAILWAY CONSOLIDATED STOCK.—(Transfer form required, fee 2s. 6d. per deed.) This Railway was incorporated in 1855 under an Agreement with the Indian Government, who guarantee a minimum dividend of 5 per cent. for 99 years, *i.e.*, until 1954. Dividends payable January and July. Any surplus revenue is equally divided between the Government and the Stockholders. Amount of Stock, £7,550,300.

Highest price, 1896, 253½ } Average price, 236¼
Lowest price, 1896, 219 } Yield to Investor about £3¼ p.c.

LONDON:

PUBLISHED BY THE UNIVERSAL STOCK EXCHANGE, LTD.

PUBLISHED ON FRIDAYS.

Post Free 5/- a Year.

THE
UNIVERSAL STOCK EXCHANGE MARKET REPORT.

THE above has a large and an influential circulation. No expense or trouble is spared to ensure early and accurate information on the important Financial subjects treated every week by an able staff of writers.

During the past year articles have appeared on the following subjects, among many others :—Banks, Railways, Mining, New Companies, Sound Investments, American Railways and Finance, Australia and other Colonies, India, Argentine, Brazil, Mexico, South Africa, Breweries, Cycles, Electrical and Gas Undertakings, Light Railways, Fluctuations in Prices, &c., and on matters relating to Stocks, Shares, and Investments generally.

Special features are made of the American Letter, wired from New York every Thursday; of the Closing Quotations of Mines, showing the rise and fall; and of the highest and lowest Prices of a Selected List of the Best Investments day by day during the week, compared with three preceding years, with the approximate yield. "Answers to Inquiries" deal with questions of interest to Investors, and supply desired and reliable information.

www.ingramcontent.com/pod-product-compliance
Lightning Source LLC
Chambersburg PA
CBHW022059230426
43672CB00008B/1223